C-3822   CAREER EXAMINATION SERIES

This is your
PASSBOOK for...

Pharmacy Technician

Test Preparation Study Guide
Questions & Answers

COPYRIGHT NOTICE

This book is SOLELY intended for, is sold ONLY to, and its use is RESTRICTED to individual, bona fide applicants or candidates who qualify by virtue of having seriously filed applications for appropriate license, certificate, professional and/or promotional advancement, higher school matriculation, scholarship, or other legitimate requirements of education and/or governmental authorities.

This book is NOT intended for use, class instruction, tutoring, training, duplication, copying, reprinting, excerption, or adaptation, etc., by:

1) Other publishers
2) Proprietors and/or Instructors of "Coaching" and/or Preparatory Courses
3) Personnel and/or Training Divisions of commercial, industrial, and governmental organizations
4) Schools, colleges, or universities and/or their departments and staffs, including teachers and other personnel
5) Testing Agencies or Bureaus
6) Study groups which seek by the purchase of a single volume to copy and/or duplicate and/or adapt this material for use by the group as a whole without having purchased individual volumes for each of the members of the group
7) Et al.

Such persons would be in violation of appropriate Federal and State statutes.

PROVISION OF LICENSING AGREEMENTS – Recognized educational, commercial, industrial, and governmental institutions and organizations, and others legitimately engaged in educational pursuits, including training, testing, and measurement activities, may address request for a licensing agreement to the copyright owners, who will determine whether, and under what conditions, including fees and charges, the materials in this book may be used them. In other words, a licensing facility exists for the legitimate use of the material in this book on other than an individual basis. However, it is asseverated and affirmed here that the material in this book CANNOT be used without the receipt of the express permission of such a licensing agreement from the Publishers. Inquiries re licensing should be addressed to the company, attention rights and permissions department.

All rights reserved, including the right of reproduction in whole or in part, in any form or by any means, electronic or mechanical, including photocopying, recording, or by any information storage and retrieval system, without permission in writing from the Publisher.

Copyright © 2024 by
National Learning Corporation

212 Michael Drive, Syosset, NY 11791
(516) 921-8888 • www.passbooks.com
E-mail: info@passbooks.com

PASSBOOK® SERIES

THE *PASSBOOK® SERIES* has been created to prepare applicants and candidates for the ultimate academic battlefield – the examination room.

At some time in our lives, each and every one of us may be required to take an examination – for validation, matriculation, admission, qualification, registration, certification, or licensure.

Based on the assumption that every applicant or candidate has met the basic formal educational standards, has taken the required number of courses, and read the necessary texts, the *PASSBOOK® SERIES* furnishes the one special preparation which may assure passing with confidence, instead of failing with insecurity. Examination questions – together with answers – are furnished as the basic vehicle for study so that the mysteries of the examination and its compounding difficulties may be eliminated or diminished by a sure method.

This book is meant to help you pass your examination provided that you qualify and are serious in your objective.

The entire field is reviewed through the huge store of content information which is succinctly presented through a provocative and challenging approach – the question-and-answer method.

A climate of success is established by furnishing the correct answers at the end of each test.

You soon learn to recognize types of questions, forms of questions, and patterns of questioning. You may even begin to anticipate expected outcomes.

You perceive that many questions are repeated or adapted so that you can gain acute insights, which may enable you to score many sure points.

You learn how to confront new questions, or types of questions, and to attack them confidently and work out the correct answers.

You note objectives and emphases, and recognize pitfalls and dangers, so that you may make positive educational adjustments.

Moreover, you are kept fully informed in relation to new concepts, methods, practices, and directions in the field.

You discover that you are actually taking the examination all the time: you are preparing for the examination by "taking" an examination, not by reading extraneous and/or supererogatory textbooks.

In short, this PASSBOOK®, used directedly, should be an important factor in helping you to pass your test.

PHARMACY TECHNICIAN

DUTIES
As a Pharmacy Technician, you would work under the direct and immediate supervision of a Pharmacist, assisting in dispensing medication and performing a series of non-professional activities. These activities might include, but would not be limited to, maintaining an inventory of pharmaceutical supplies; assisting in the preparation of pharmaceutical orders; receiving pharmaceutical supplies; making necessary entries in appropriate records; assisting in the prepackaging of prescriptions, the repackaging and delivery of drugs; and the maintenance of a clean, safe and professional environment within the pharmacy.

SCOPE OF THE EXAMINATION
The written test is designed to test for knowledge, skills and/or abilities in such areas as:
1. **Keeping simple inventory records** - These questions test for the ability to follow instructions in order to keep records of different materials received and distributed from a central location. You will be given written directions for a set of records and forms on which records are kept. Questions will be based on the following two formats:
   - You will be given several incomplete inventory records for different materials. On the basis of this information, you will be asked to complete the records and answer questions based on the completed records.
   - You will be given information in the form of a list of materials. You will be asked to complete several blank records from the information given in the material listing and to answer questions based on the completed records. You may be asked to compute total costs from quantities and unit prices. Ability to add, subtract, multiple and divide will be required. Specific knowledge of record-keeping systems and techniques will not be required.
2. **Name and number checking** - These questions test your ability to distinguish between sets of words, letters, and/or numbers that are almost exactly alike. Material is usually presented in two or three columns, and you will have to determine how the entry in the first column compares with the entry in the second column and possibly in the third. You will be instructed to mark your answers according to a designated code provided in the directions.
3. **Pharmaceutical terminology, principles and practices** - These questions test for knowledge required to perform non-professional duties in a pharmacy. Questions may cover such topics as classes, types, and forms of drugs; handling and storage of drugs; abbreviations used in prescription writing; dosage units and metric conversions.

HOW TO TAKE A TEST

I. YOU MUST PASS AN EXAMINATION

A. *WHAT EVERY CANDIDATE SHOULD KNOW*

Examination applicants often ask us for help in preparing for the written test. What can I study in advance? What kinds of questions will be asked? How will the test be given? How will the papers be graded?

As an applicant for a civil service examination, you may be wondering about some of these things. Our purpose here is to suggest effective methods of advance study and to describe civil service examinations.

Your chances for success on this examination can be increased if you know how to prepare. Those "pre-examination jitters" can be reduced if you know what to expect. You can even experience an adventure in good citizenship if you know why civil service exams are given.

B. *WHY ARE CIVIL SERVICE EXAMINATIONS GIVEN?*

Civil service examinations are important to you in two ways. As a citizen, you want public jobs filled by employees who know how to do their work. As a job seeker, you want a fair chance to compete for that job on an equal footing with other candidates. The best-known means of accomplishing this two-fold goal is the competitive examination.

Exams are widely publicized throughout the nation. They may be administered for jobs in federal, state, city, municipal, town or village governments or agencies.

Any citizen may apply, with some limitations, such as the age or residence of applicants. Your experience and education may be reviewed to see whether you meet the requirements for the particular examination. When these requirements exist, they are reasonable and applied consistently to all applicants. Thus, a competitive examination may cause you some uneasiness now, but it is your privilege and safeguard.

C. *HOW ARE CIVIL SERVICE EXAMS DEVELOPED?*

Examinations are carefully written by trained technicians who are specialists in the field known as "psychological measurement," in consultation with recognized authorities in the field of work that the test will cover. These experts recommend the subject matter areas or skills to be tested; only those knowledges or skills important to your success on the job are included. The most reliable books and source materials available are used as references. Together, the experts and technicians judge the difficulty level of the questions.

Test technicians know how to phrase questions so that the problem is clearly stated. Their ethics do not permit "trick" or "catch" questions. Questions may have been tried out on sample groups, or subjected to statistical analysis, to determine their usefulness.

Written tests are often used in combination with performance tests, ratings of training and experience, and oral interviews. All of these measures combine to form the best-known means of finding the right person for the right job.

II. HOW TO PASS THE WRITTEN TEST

A. NATURE OF THE EXAMINATION

To prepare intelligently for civil service examinations, you should know how they differ from school examinations you have taken. In school you were assigned certain definite pages to read or subjects to cover. The examination questions were quite detailed and usually emphasized memory. Civil service exams, on the other hand, try to discover your present ability to perform the duties of a position, plus your potentiality to learn these duties. In other words, a civil service exam attempts to predict how successful you will be. Questions cover such a broad area that they cannot be as minute and detailed as school exam questions.

In the public service similar kinds of work, or positions, are grouped together in one "class." This process is known as *position-classification*. All the positions in a class are paid according to the salary range for that class. One class title covers all of these positions, and they are all tested by the same examination.

B. FOUR BASIC STEPS

1) Study the announcement

How, then, can you know what subjects to study? Our best answer is: "Learn as much as possible about the class of positions for which you've applied." The exam will test the knowledge, skills and abilities needed to do the work.

Your most valuable source of information about the position you want is the official exam announcement. This announcement lists the training and experience qualifications. Check these standards and apply only if you come reasonably close to meeting them.

The brief description of the position in the examination announcement offers some clues to the subjects which will be tested. Think about the job itself. Review the duties in your mind. Can you perform them, or are there some in which you are rusty? Fill in the blank spots in your preparation.

Many jurisdictions preview the written test in the exam announcement by including a section called "Knowledge and Abilities Required," "Scope of the Examination," or some similar heading. Here you will find out specifically what fields will be tested.

2) Review your own background

Once you learn in general what the position is all about, and what you need to know to do the work, ask yourself which subjects you already know fairly well and which need improvement. You may wonder whether to concentrate on improving your strong areas or on building some background in your fields of weakness. When the announcement has specified "some knowledge" or "considerable knowledge," or has used adjectives like "beginning principles of…" or "advanced … methods," you can get a clue as to the number and difficulty of questions to be asked in any given field. More questions, and hence broader coverage, would be included for those subjects which are more important in the work. Now weigh your strengths and weaknesses against the job requirements and prepare accordingly.

3) Determine the level of the position

Another way to tell how intensively you should prepare is to understand the level of the job for which you are applying. Is it the entering level? In other words, is this the position in which beginners in a field of work are hired? Or is it an intermediate or advanced level? Sometimes this is indicated by such words as "Junior" or "Senior" in the class title. Other jurisdictions use Roman numerals to designate the level – Clerk I, Clerk II, for example. The word "Supervisor" sometimes appears in the title. If the level is not indicated by the title, check the description of duties. Will you be working under very close supervision, or will you have responsibility for independent decisions in this work?

4) Choose appropriate study materials

Now that you know the subjects to be examined and the relative amount of each subject to be covered, you can choose suitable study materials. For beginning level jobs, or even advanced ones, if you have a pronounced weakness in some aspect of your training, read a modern, standard textbook in that field. Be sure it is up to date and has general coverage. Such books are normally available at your library, and the librarian will be glad to help you locate one. For entry-level positions, questions of appropriate difficulty are chosen – neither highly advanced questions, nor those too simple. Such questions require careful thought but not advanced training.

If the position for which you are applying is technical or advanced, you will read more advanced, specialized material. If you are already familiar with the basic principles of your field, elementary textbooks would waste your time. Concentrate on advanced textbooks and technical periodicals. Think through the concepts and review difficult problems in your field.

These are all general sources. You can get more ideas on your own initiative, following these leads. For example, training manuals and publications of the government agency which employs workers in your field can be useful, particularly for technical and professional positions. A letter or visit to the government department involved may result in more specific study suggestions, and certainly will provide you with a more definite idea of the exact nature of the position you are seeking.

III. KINDS OF TESTS

Tests are used for purposes other than measuring knowledge and ability to perform specified duties. For some positions, it is equally important to test ability to make adjustments to new situations or to profit from training. In others, basic mental abilities not dependent on information are essential. Questions which test these things may not appear as pertinent to the duties of the position as those which test for knowledge and information. Yet they are often highly important parts of a fair examination. For very general questions, it is almost impossible to help you direct your study efforts. What we can do is to point out some of the more common of these general abilities needed in public service positions and describe some typical questions.

1) General information

Broad, general information has been found useful for predicting job success in some kinds of work. This is tested in a variety of ways, from vocabulary lists to questions about current events. Basic background in some field of work, such as sociology or economics, may be sampled in a group of questions. Often these are principles which have become familiar to most persons through exposure rather than through formal training. It is difficult to advise you how to study for these questions; being alert to the world around you is our best suggestion.

2) Verbal ability

An example of an ability needed in many positions is verbal or language ability. Verbal ability is, in brief, the ability to use and understand words. Vocabulary and grammar tests are typical measures of this ability. Reading comprehension or paragraph interpretation questions are common in many kinds of civil service tests. You are given a paragraph of written material and asked to find its central meaning.

3) Numerical ability

Number skills can be tested by the familiar arithmetic problem, by checking paired lists of numbers to see which are alike and which are different, or by interpreting charts and graphs. In the latter test, a graph may be printed in the test booklet which you are asked to use as the basis for answering questions.

4) Observation

A popular test for law-enforcement positions is the observation test. A picture is shown to you for several minutes, then taken away. Questions about the picture test your ability to observe both details and larger elements.

5) Following directions

In many positions in the public service, the employee must be able to carry out written instructions dependably and accurately. You may be given a chart with several columns, each column listing a variety of information. The questions require you to carry out directions involving the information given in the chart.

6) Skills and aptitudes

Performance tests effectively measure some manual skills and aptitudes. When the skill is one in which you are trained, such as typing or shorthand, you can practice. These tests are often very much like those given in business school or high school courses. For many of the other skills and aptitudes, however, no short-time preparation can be made. Skills and abilities natural to you or that you have developed throughout your lifetime are being tested.

Many of the general questions just described provide all the data needed to answer the questions and ask you to use your reasoning ability to find the answers. Your best preparation for these tests, as well as for tests of facts and ideas, is to be at your physical and mental best. You, no doubt, have your own methods of getting into an exam-taking mood and keeping "in shape." The next section lists some ideas on this subject.

IV. KINDS OF QUESTIONS

Only rarely is the "essay" question, which you answer in narrative form, used in civil service tests. Civil service tests are usually of the short-answer type. Full instructions for answering these questions will be given to you at the examination. But in case this is your first experience with short-answer questions and separate answer sheets, here is what you need to know:

1) Multiple-choice Questions

Most popular of the short-answer questions is the "multiple choice" or "best answer" question. It can be used, for example, to test for factual knowledge, ability to solve problems or judgment in meeting situations found at work.

A multiple-choice question is normally one of three types—
- It can begin with an incomplete statement followed by several possible endings. You are to find the one ending which *best* completes the statement, although some of the others may not be entirely wrong.
- It can also be a complete statement in the form of a question which is answered by choosing one of the statements listed.

- It can be in the form of a problem – again you select the best answer.

Here is an example of a multiple-choice question with a discussion which should give you some clues as to the method for choosing the right answer:

When an employee has a complaint about his assignment, the action which will *best* help him overcome his difficulty is to
- A. discuss his difficulty with his coworkers
- B. take the problem to the head of the organization
- C. take the problem to the person who gave him the assignment
- D. say nothing to anyone about his complaint

In answering this question, you should study each of the choices to find which is best. Consider choice "A" – Certainly an employee may discuss his complaint with fellow employees, but no change or improvement can result, and the complaint remains unresolved. Choice "B" is a poor choice since the head of the organization probably does not know what assignment you have been given, and taking your problem to him is known as "going over the head" of the supervisor. The supervisor, or person who made the assignment, is the person who can clarify it or correct any injustice. Choice "C" is, therefore, correct. To say nothing, as in choice "D," is unwise. Supervisors have and interest in knowing the problems employees are facing, and the employee is seeking a solution to his problem.

2) True/False Questions

The "true/false" or "right/wrong" form of question is sometimes used. Here a complete statement is given. Your job is to decide whether the statement is right or wrong.

SAMPLE: A roaming cell-phone call to a nearby city costs less than a non-roaming call to a distant city.

This statement is wrong, or false, since roaming calls are more expensive.

This is not a complete list of all possible question forms, although most of the others are variations of these common types. You will always get complete directions for answering questions. Be sure you understand *how* to mark your answers – ask questions until you do.

V. RECORDING YOUR ANSWERS

Computer terminals are used more and more today for many different kinds of exams.

For an examination with very few applicants, you may be told to record your answers in the test booklet itself. Separate answer sheets are much more common. If this separate answer sheet is to be scored by machine – and this is often the case – it is highly important that you mark your answers correctly in order to get credit.

An electronic scoring machine is often used in civil service offices because of the speed with which papers can be scored. Machine-scored answer sheets must be marked with a pencil, which will be given to you. This pencil has a high graphite content which responds to the electronic scoring machine. As a matter of fact, stray dots may register as answers, so do not let your pencil rest on the answer sheet while you are pondering the correct answer. Also, if your pencil lead breaks or is otherwise defective, ask for another.

Since the answer sheet will be dropped in a slot in the scoring machine, be careful not to bend the corners or get the paper crumpled.

The answer sheet normally has five vertical columns of numbers, with 30 numbers to a column. These numbers correspond to the question numbers in your test booklet. After each number, going across the page are four or five pairs of dotted lines. These short dotted lines have small letters or numbers above them. The first two pairs may also have a "T" or "F" above the letters. This indicates that the first two pairs only are to be used if the questions are of the true-false type. If the questions are multiple choice, disregard the "T" and "F" and pay attention only to the small letters or numbers.

Answer your questions in the manner of the sample that follows:

32. The largest city in the United States is
    A. Washington, D.C.
    B. New York City
    C. Chicago
    D. Detroit
    E. San Francisco

1) Choose the answer you think is best. (New York City is the largest, so "B" is correct.)
2) Find the row of dotted lines numbered the same as the question you are answering. (Find row number 32)
3) Find the pair of dotted lines corresponding to the answer. (Find the pair of lines under the mark "B.")
4) Make a solid black mark between the dotted lines.

VI. BEFORE THE TEST

Common sense will help you find procedures to follow to get ready for an examination. Too many of us, however, overlook these sensible measures. Indeed, nervousness and fatigue have been found to be the most serious reasons why applicants fail to do their best on civil service tests. Here is a list of reminders:

- Begin your preparation early – Don't wait until the last minute to go scurrying around for books and materials or to find out what the position is all about.
- Prepare continuously – An hour a night for a week is better than an all-night cram session. This has been definitely established. What is more, a night a week for a month will return better dividends than crowding your study into a shorter period of time.
- Locate the place of the exam – You have been sent a notice telling you when and where to report for the examination. If the location is in a different town or otherwise unfamiliar to you, it would be well to inquire the best route and learn something about the building.
- Relax the night before the test – Allow your mind to rest. Do not study at all that night. Plan some mild recreation or diversion; then go to bed early and get a good night's sleep.
- Get up early enough to make a leisurely trip to the place for the test – This way unforeseen events, traffic snarls, unfamiliar buildings, etc. will not upset you.
- Dress comfortably – A written test is not a fashion show. You will be known by number and not by name, so wear something comfortable.

- Leave excess paraphernalia at home – Shopping bags and odd bundles will get in your way. You need bring only the items mentioned in the official notice you received; usually everything you need is provided. Do not bring reference books to the exam. They will only confuse those last minutes and be taken away from you when in the test room.
- Arrive somewhat ahead of time – If because of transportation schedules you must get there very early, bring a newspaper or magazine to take your mind off yourself while waiting.
- Locate the examination room – When you have found the proper room, you will be directed to the seat or part of the room where you will sit. Sometimes you are given a sheet of instructions to read while you are waiting. Do not fill out any forms until you are told to do so; just read them and be prepared.
- Relax and prepare to listen to the instructions
- If you have any physical problem that may keep you from doing your best, be sure to tell the test administrator. If you are sick or in poor health, you really cannot do your best on the exam. You can come back and take the test some other time.

VII. AT THE TEST

The day of the test is here and you have the test booklet in your hand. The temptation to get going is very strong. Caution! There is more to success than knowing the right answers. You must know how to identify your papers and understand variations in the type of short-answer question used in this particular examination. Follow these suggestions for maximum results from your efforts:

1) Cooperate with the monitor

The test administrator has a duty to create a situation in which you can be as much at ease as possible. He will give instructions, tell you when to begin, check to see that you are marking your answer sheet correctly, and so on. He is not there to guard you, although he will see that your competitors do not take unfair advantage. He wants to help you do your best.

2) Listen to all instructions

Don't jump the gun! Wait until you understand all directions. In most civil service tests you get more time than you need to answer the questions. So don't be in a hurry. Read each word of instructions until you clearly understand the meaning. Study the examples, listen to all announcements and follow directions. Ask questions if you do not understand what to do.

3) Identify your papers

Civil service exams are usually identified by number only. You will be assigned a number; you must not put your name on your test papers. Be sure to copy your number correctly. Since more than one exam may be given, copy your exact examination title.

4) Plan your time

Unless you are told that a test is a "speed" or "rate of work" test, speed itself is usually not important. Time enough to answer all the questions will be provided, but this does not mean that you have all day. An overall time limit has been set. Divide the total time (in minutes) by the number of questions to determine the approximate time you have for each question.

5) Do not linger over difficult questions

If you come across a difficult question, mark it with a paper clip (useful to have along) and come back to it when you have been through the booklet. One caution if you do this – be sure to skip a number on your answer sheet as well. Check often to be sure that you have not lost your place and that you are marking in the row numbered the same as the question you are answering.

6) Read the questions

Be sure you know what the question asks! Many capable people are unsuccessful because they failed to *read* the questions correctly.

7) Answer all questions

Unless you have been instructed that a penalty will be deducted for incorrect answers, it is better to guess than to omit a question.

8) Speed tests

It is often better NOT to guess on speed tests. It has been found that on timed tests people are tempted to spend the last few seconds before time is called in marking answers at random – without even reading them – in the hope of picking up a few extra points. To discourage this practice, the instructions may warn you that your score will be "corrected" for guessing. That is, a penalty will be applied. The incorrect answers will be deducted from the correct ones, or some other penalty formula will be used.

9) Review your answers

If you finish before time is called, go back to the questions you guessed or omitted to give them further thought. Review other answers if you have time.

10) Return your test materials

If you are ready to leave before others have finished or time is called, take ALL your materials to the monitor and leave quietly. Never take any test material with you. The monitor can discover whose papers are not complete, and taking a test booklet may be grounds for disqualification.

VIII. EXAMINATION TECHNIQUES

1) Read the general instructions carefully. These are usually printed on the first page of the exam booklet. As a rule, these instructions refer to the timing of the examination; the fact that you should not start work until the signal and must stop work at a signal, etc. If there are any *special* instructions, such as a choice of questions to be answered, make sure that you note this instruction carefully.

2) When you are ready to start work on the examination, that is as soon as the signal has been given, read the instructions to each question booklet, underline any key words or phrases, such as *least, best, outline, describe* and the like. In this way you will tend to answer as requested rather than discover on reviewing your paper that you *listed without describing*, that you selected the *worst* choice rather than the *best* choice, etc.

3) If the examination is of the objective or multiple-choice type – that is, each question will also give a series of possible answers: A, B, C or D, and you are called upon to select the best answer and write the letter next to that answer on your answer paper – it is advisable to start answering each question in turn. There may be anywhere from 50 to 100 such questions in the three or four hours allotted and you can see how much time would be taken if you read through all the questions before beginning to answer any. Furthermore, if you come across a question or group of questions which you know would be difficult to answer, it would undoubtedly affect your handling of all the other questions.

4) If the examination is of the essay type and contains but a few questions, it is a moot point as to whether you should read all the questions before starting to answer any one. Of course, if you are given a choice – say five out of seven and the like – then it is essential to read all the questions so you can eliminate the two that are most difficult. If, however, you are asked to answer all the questions, there may be danger in trying to answer the easiest one first because you may find that you will spend too much time on it. The best technique is to answer the first question, then proceed to the second, etc.

5) Time your answers. Before the exam begins, write down the time it started, then add the time allowed for the examination and write down the time it must be completed, then divide the time available somewhat as follows:
    - If 3-1/2 hours are allowed, that would be 210 minutes. If you have 80 objective-type questions, that would be an average of 2-1/2 minutes per question. Allow yourself no more than 2 minutes per question, or a total of 160 minutes, which will permit about 50 minutes to review.
    - If for the time allotment of 210 minutes there are 7 essay questions to answer, that would average about 30 minutes a question. Give yourself only 25 minutes per question so that you have about 35 minutes to review.

6) The most important instruction is to *read each question* and make sure you know what is wanted. The second most important instruction is to *time yourself properly* so that you answer every question. The third most important instruction is to *answer every question*. Guess if you have to but include something for each question. Remember that you will receive no credit for a blank and will probably receive some credit if you write something in answer to an essay question. If you guess a letter – say "B" for a multiple-choice question – you may have guessed right. If you leave a blank as an answer to a multiple-choice question, the examiners may respect your feelings but it will not add a point to your score. Some exams may penalize you for wrong answers, so in such cases *only*, you may not want to guess unless you have some basis for your answer.

7) Suggestions
    a. Objective-type questions
        1. Examine the question booklet for proper sequence of pages and questions
        2. Read all instructions carefully
        3. Skip any question which seems too difficult; return to it after all other questions have been answered
        4. Apportion your time properly; do not spend too much time on any single question or group of questions

5. Note and underline key words – *all, most, fewest, least, best, worst, same, opposite*, etc.
6. Pay particular attention to negatives
7. Note unusual option, e.g., unduly long, short, complex, different or similar in content to the body of the question
8. Observe the use of "hedging" words – *probably, may, most likely*, etc.
9. Make sure that your answer is put next to the same number as the question
10. Do not second-guess unless you have good reason to believe the second answer is definitely more correct
11. Cross out original answer if you decide another answer is more accurate; do not erase until you are ready to hand your paper in
12. Answer all questions; guess unless instructed otherwise
13. Leave time for review

b. Essay questions
1. Read each question carefully
2. Determine exactly what is wanted. Underline key words or phrases.
3. Decide on outline or paragraph answer
4. Include many different points and elements unless asked to develop any one or two points or elements
5. Show impartiality by giving pros and cons unless directed to select one side only
6. Make and write down any assumptions you find necessary to answer the questions
7. Watch your English, grammar, punctuation and choice of words
8. Time your answers; don't crowd material

8) Answering the essay question

Most essay questions can be answered by framing the specific response around several key words or ideas. Here are a few such key words or ideas:

M's: manpower, materials, methods, money, management
P's: purpose, program, policy, plan, procedure, practice, problems, pitfalls, personnel, public relations

a. Six basic steps in handling problems:
1. Preliminary plan and background development
2. Collect information, data and facts
3. Analyze and interpret information, data and facts
4. Analyze and develop solutions as well as make recommendations
5. Prepare report and sell recommendations
6. Install recommendations and follow up effectiveness

b. Pitfalls to avoid
1. *Taking things for granted* – A statement of the situation does not necessarily imply that each of the elements is necessarily true; for example, a complaint may be invalid and biased so that all that can be taken for granted is that a complaint has been registered

2. *Considering only one side of a situation* – Wherever possible, indicate several alternatives and then point out the reasons you selected the best one
3. *Failing to indicate follow up* – Whenever your answer indicates action on your part, make certain that you will take proper follow-up action to see how successful your recommendations, procedures or actions turn out to be
4. *Taking too long in answering any single question* – Remember to time your answers properly

IX. AFTER THE TEST

Scoring procedures differ in detail among civil service jurisdictions although the general principles are the same. Whether the papers are hand-scored or graded by machine we have described, they are nearly always graded by number. That is, the person who marks the paper knows only the number – never the name – of the applicant. Not until all the papers have been graded will they be matched with names. If other tests, such as training and experience or oral interview ratings have been given, scores will be combined. Different parts of the examination usually have different weights. For example, the written test might count 60 percent of the final grade, and a rating of training and experience 40 percent. In many jurisdictions, veterans will have a certain number of points added to their grades.

After the final grade has been determined, the names are placed in grade order and an eligible list is established. There are various methods for resolving ties between those who get the same final grade – probably the most common is to place first the name of the person whose application was received first. Job offers are made from the eligible list in the order the names appear on it. You will be notified of your grade and your rank as soon as all these computations have been made. This will be done as rapidly as possible.

People who are found to meet the requirements in the announcement are called "eligibles." Their names are put on a list of eligible candidates. An eligible's chances of getting a job depend on how high he stands on this list and how fast agencies are filling jobs from the list.

When a job is to be filled from a list of eligibles, the agency asks for the names of people on the list of eligibles for that job. When the civil service commission receives this request, it sends to the agency the names of the three people highest on this list. Or, if the job to be filled has specialized requirements, the office sends the agency the names of the top three persons who meet these requirements from the general list.

The appointing officer makes a choice from among the three people whose names were sent to him. If the selected person accepts the appointment, the names of the others are put back on the list to be considered for future openings.

That is the rule in hiring from all kinds of eligible lists, whether they are for typist, carpenter, chemist, or something else. For every vacancy, the appointing officer has his choice of any one of the top three eligibles on the list. This explains why the person whose name is on top of the list sometimes does not get an appointment when some of the persons lower on the list do. If the appointing officer chooses the second or third eligible, the No. 1 eligible does not get a job at once, but stays on the list until he is appointed or the list is terminated.

X. HOW TO PASS THE INTERVIEW TEST

The examination for which you applied requires an oral interview test. You have already taken the written test and you are now being called for the interview test – the final part of the formal examination.

You may think that it is not possible to prepare for an interview test and that there are no procedures to follow during an interview. Our purpose is to point out some things you can do in advance that will help you and some good rules to follow and pitfalls to avoid while you are being interviewed.

What is an interview supposed to test?

The written examination is designed to test the technical knowledge and competence of the candidate; the oral is designed to evaluate intangible qualities, not readily measured otherwise, and to establish a list showing the relative fitness of each candidate – as measured against his competitors – for the position sought. Scoring is not on the basis of "right" and "wrong," but on a sliding scale of values ranging from "not passable" to "outstanding." As a matter of fact, it is possible to achieve a relatively low score without a single "incorrect" answer because of evident weakness in the qualities being measured.

Occasionally, an examination may consist entirely of an oral test – either an individual or a group oral. In such cases, information is sought concerning the technical knowledges and abilities of the candidate, since there has been no written examination for this purpose. More commonly, however, an oral test is used to supplement a written examination.

Who conducts interviews?

The composition of oral boards varies among different jurisdictions. In nearly all, a representative of the personnel department serves as chairman. One of the members of the board may be a representative of the department in which the candidate would work. In some cases, "outside experts" are used, and, frequently, a businessman or some other representative of the general public is asked to serve. Labor and management or other special groups may be represented. The aim is to secure the services of experts in the appropriate field.

However the board is composed, it is a good idea (and not at all improper or unethical) to ascertain in advance of the interview who the members are and what groups they represent. When you are introduced to them, you will have some idea of their backgrounds and interests, and at least you will not stutter and stammer over their names.

What should be done before the interview?

While knowledge about the board members is useful and takes some of the surprise element out of the interview, there is other preparation which is more substantive. It *is* possible to prepare for an oral interview – in several ways:

1) Keep a copy of your application and review it carefully before the interview

This may be the only document before the oral board, and the starting point of the interview. Know what education and experience you have listed there, and the sequence and dates of all of it. Sometimes the board will ask you to review the highlights of your experience for them; you should not have to hem and haw doing it.

2) Study the class specification and the examination announcement

Usually, the oral board has one or both of these to guide them. The qualities, characteristics or knowledges required by the position sought are stated in these documents. They offer valuable clues as to the nature of the oral interview. For example, if the job involves supervisory responsibilities, the announcement will usually indicate that knowledge of modern supervisory methods and the qualifications of the candidate as a supervisor will be tested. If so, you can expect such questions, frequently in the form of a hypothetical situation which you are expected to solve. NEVER go into an oral without knowledge of the duties and responsibilities of the job you seek.

3) Think through each qualification required

Try to visualize the kind of questions you would ask if you were a board member. How well could you answer them? Try especially to appraise your own knowledge and background in each area, *measured against the job sought*, and identify any areas in which you are weak. Be critical and realistic – do not flatter yourself.

4) Do some general reading in areas in which you feel you may be weak

For example, if the job involves supervision and your past experience has NOT, some general reading in supervisory methods and practices, particularly in the field of human relations, might be useful. Do NOT study agency procedures or detailed manuals. The oral board will be testing your understanding and capacity, not your memory.

5) Get a good night's sleep and watch your general health and mental attitude

You will want a clear head at the interview. Take care of a cold or any other minor ailment, and of course, no hangovers.

What should be done on the day of the interview?

Now comes the day of the interview itself. Give yourself plenty of time to get there. Plan to arrive somewhat ahead of the scheduled time, particularly if your appointment is in the fore part of the day. If a previous candidate fails to appear, the board might be ready for you a bit early. By early afternoon an oral board is almost invariably behind schedule if there are many candidates, and you may have to wait. Take along a book or magazine to read, or your application to review, but leave any extraneous material in the waiting room when you go in for your interview. In any event, relax and compose yourself.

The matter of dress is important. The board is forming impressions about you – from your experience, your manners, your attitude, and your appearance. Give your personal appearance careful attention. Dress your best, but not your flashiest. Choose conservative, appropriate clothing, and be sure it is immaculate. This is a business interview, and your appearance should indicate that you regard it as such. Besides, being well groomed and properly dressed will help boost your confidence.

Sooner or later, someone will call your name and escort you into the interview room. *This is it.* From here on you are on your own. It is too late for any more preparation. But remember, you asked for this opportunity to prove your fitness, and you are here because your request was granted.

What happens when you go in?

The usual sequence of events will be as follows: The clerk (who is often the board stenographer) will introduce you to the chairman of the oral board, who will introduce you to the other members of the board. Acknowledge the introductions before you sit down. Do not be surprised if you find a microphone facing you or a stenotypist sitting by. Oral interviews are usually recorded in the event of an appeal or other review.

Usually the chairman of the board will open the interview by reviewing the highlights of your education and work experience from your application – primarily for the benefit of the other members of the board, as well as to get the material into the record. Do not interrupt or comment unless there is an error or significant misinterpretation; if that is the case, do not hesitate. But do not quibble about insignificant matters. Also, he will usually ask you some question about your education, experience or your present job – partly to get you to start talking and to establish the interviewing "rapport." He may start the actual questioning, or turn it over to one of the other members. Frequently, each member undertakes the questioning on a particular area, one in which he is perhaps most competent, so you can expect each member to participate in the examination. Because time is limited, you may also expect some rather abrupt switches in the direction the questioning takes, so do not be upset by it. Normally, a board member will not pursue a single line of questioning unless he discovers a particular strength or weakness.

After each member has participated, the chairman will usually ask whether any member has any further questions, then will ask you if you have anything you wish to add. Unless you are expecting this question, it may floor you. Worse, it may start you off on an extended, extemporaneous speech. The board is not usually seeking more information. The question is principally to offer you a last opportunity to present further qualifications or to indicate that you have nothing to add. So, if you feel that a significant qualification or characteristic has been overlooked, it is proper to point it out in a sentence or so. Do not compliment the board on the thoroughness of their examination – they have been sketchy, and you know it. If you wish, merely say, "No thank you, I have nothing further to add." This is a point where you can "talk yourself out" of a good impression or fail to present an important bit of information. Remember, *you close the interview yourself*.

The chairman will then say, "That is all, Mr. _____, thank you." Do not be startled; the interview is over, and quicker than you think. Thank him, gather your belongings and take your leave. Save your sigh of relief for the other side of the door.

How to put your best foot forward

Throughout this entire process, you may feel that the board individually and collectively is trying to pierce your defenses, seek out your hidden weaknesses and embarrass and confuse you. Actually, this is not true. They are obliged to make an appraisal of your qualifications for the job you are seeking, and they want to see you in your best light. Remember, they must interview all candidates and a non-cooperative candidate may become a failure in spite of their best efforts to bring out his qualifications. Here are 15 suggestions that will help you:

1) Be natural – Keep your attitude confident, not cocky

If you are not confident that you can do the job, do not expect the board to be. Do not apologize for your weaknesses, try to bring out your strong points. The board is interested in a positive, not negative, presentation. Cockiness will antagonize any board member and make him wonder if you are covering up a weakness by a false show of strength.

2) Get comfortable, but don't lounge or sprawl

Sit erectly but not stiffly. A careless posture may lead the board to conclude that you are careless in other things, or at least that you are not impressed by the importance of the occasion. Either conclusion is natural, even if incorrect. Do not fuss with your clothing, a pencil or an ashtray. Your hands may occasionally be useful to emphasize a point; do not let them become a point of distraction.

3) Do not wisecrack or make small talk

This is a serious situation, and your attitude should show that you consider it as such. Further, the time of the board is limited – they do not want to waste it, and neither should you.

4) Do not exaggerate your experience or abilities
In the first place, from information in the application or other interviews and sources, the board may know more about you than you think. Secondly, you probably will not get away with it. An experienced board is rather adept at spotting such a situation, so do not take the chance.

5) If you know a board member, do not make a point of it, yet do not hide it
Certainly you are not fooling him, and probably not the other members of the board. Do not try to take advantage of your acquaintanceship – it will probably do you little good.

6) Do not dominate the interview
Let the board do that. They will give you the clues – do not assume that you have to do all the talking. Realize that the board has a number of questions to ask you, and do not try to take up all the interview time by showing off your extensive knowledge of the answer to the first one.

7) Be attentive
You only have 20 minutes or so, and you should keep your attention at its sharpest throughout. When a member is addressing a problem or question to you, give him your undivided attention. Address your reply principally to him, but do not exclude the other board members.

8) Do not interrupt
A board member may be stating a problem for you to analyze. He will ask you a question when the time comes. Let him state the problem, and wait for the question.

9) Make sure you understand the question
Do not try to answer until you are sure what the question is. If it is not clear, restate it in your own words or ask the board member to clarify it for you. However, do not haggle about minor elements.

10) Reply promptly but not hastily
A common entry on oral board rating sheets is "candidate responded readily," or "candidate hesitated in replies." Respond as promptly and quickly as you can, but do not jump to a hasty, ill-considered answer.

11) Do not be peremptory in your answers
A brief answer is proper – but do not fire your answer back. That is a losing game from your point of view. The board member can probably ask questions much faster than you can answer them.

12) Do not try to create the answer you think the board member wants
He is interested in what kind of mind you have and how it works – not in playing games. Furthermore, he can usually spot this practice and will actually grade you down on it.

13) Do not switch sides in your reply merely to agree with a board member
Frequently, a member will take a contrary position merely to draw you out and to see if you are willing and able to defend your point of view. Do not start a debate, yet do not surrender a good position. If a position is worth taking, it is worth defending.

14) Do not be afraid to admit an error in judgment if you are shown to be wrong

The board knows that you are forced to reply without any opportunity for careful consideration. Your answer may be demonstrably wrong. If so, admit it and get on with the interview.

15) Do not dwell at length on your present job

The opening question may relate to your present assignment. Answer the question but do not go into an extended discussion. You are being examined for a *new* job, not your present one. As a matter of fact, try to phrase ALL your answers in terms of the job for which you are being examined.

Basis of Rating

Probably you will forget most of these "do's" and "don'ts" when you walk into the oral interview room. Even remembering them all will not ensure you a passing grade. Perhaps you did not have the qualifications in the first place. But remembering them will help you to put your best foot forward, without treading on the toes of the board members.

Rumor and popular opinion to the contrary notwithstanding, an oral board wants you to make the best appearance possible. They know you are under pressure – but they also want to see how you respond to it as a guide to what your reaction would be under the pressures of the job you seek. They will be influenced by the degree of poise you display, the personal traits you show and the manner in which you respond.

ABOUT THIS BOOK

This book contains tests divided into Examination Sections. Go through each test, answering every question in the margin. We have also attached a sample answer sheet at the back of the book that can be removed and used. At the end of each test look at the answer key and check your answers. On the ones you got wrong, look at the right answer choice and learn. Do not fill in the answers first. Do not memorize the questions and answers, but understand the answer and principles involved. On your test, the questions will likely be different from the samples. Questions are changed and new ones added. If you understand these past questions you should have success with any changes that arise. Tests may consist of several types of questions. We have additional books on each subject should more study be advisable or necessary for you. Finally, the more you study, the better prepared you will be. This book is intended to be the last thing you study before you walk into the examination room. Prior study of relevant texts is also recommended. NLC publishes some of these in our Fundamental Series. Knowledge and good sense are important factors in passing your exam. Good luck also helps. So now study this Passbook, absorb the material contained within and take that knowledge into the examination. Then do your best to pass that exam.

EXAMINATION SECTION

EXAMINATION SECTION
TEST 1

DIRECTIONS: Each question or incomplete statement is followed by several suggested answers or completions. Select the one that BEST answers the question or completes the statement. *PRINT THE LETTER OF THE CORRECT ANSWER IN THE SPACE AT THE RIGHT.*

Questions 1-2.

DIRECTIONS: Questions 1 and 2 are to be answered on the basis of the information given below.

```
JOAN SMITH            40yoWO+          437B

   Protein Hydrolysate 5%
   NaCl 40mEq
   KCl 40mEq
   MgSO₄ 5mEq
   B & C

                        DR. JONES
```

1. Which of the following medications has been ordered by the physician for the patient Joan Smith?   1.____

   A. 500 mg ascorbic acid
   B. Monosodium glutamate
   C. 5M magnesium sulfate
   D. 40 Milliequivalents sodium chloride

2. The above prescription may be termed _____ therapy.   2.____

   A. hyperalimentation   B. hyperlimitation
   C. nitrogen infusion   D. hypoalimentation

3. The effect of dimenhydrinate given in a dose of 25-50 mg, 3-4 times a day, on a patient is that it   3.____

   A. exhibits a high incidence of sedation
   B. exhibits a low incidence of sedation
   C. is contra-indicated in patients taking phenoxymethyl penicillin
   D. exhibits a negative antivertilian effect

4. A physician's order for *acetominophen USP, 10 grs Q4H prn* should be interpreted as a MAXIMUM of _____ tablets daily.   4.____

   A. 4   B. 5   C. 6   D. 12

5. Assume that you are reviewing an order for 2mg Busulfan tablets from a physician. Which of the following should be dispensed?   5.____

   A. Auralgan   B. Leukeran   C. Myleran   D. Immuran

6. *Pro Time* refers to _____ time.

   A. prothrombin determination
   B. positive reactive oxygenation
   C. professional rate observation
   D. sedimentation

7. Which one of the following doses does NOT legally require a physician's prescription?

   A. Chlorpheniramine malcate 2mg/dose
   B. Nitroglycerine 0.6mg/dose
   C. Chlorpromazine 10 mg/dose
   D. Methyltestosterone 25mg/dose

8. Toxius, toxoids, and vaccines MUST conform to standards established by the

   A. W.H.O.   B. N.I.H.   C. U.S.P.   D. F.D.A.

9. The MINIMUM amount that may be weighed on a Class A prescription balance is

   A. 120mg
   B. 200mg
   C. determined by the sensitivity reciprocal
   D. 4 grains

10. Pyrogen testing, as outlined by acceptable standards, requires biological testing on

    A. goldfish   B. rabbits   C. cats   D. pigeons

11. A Laminar Flow Hood is used when sterile intravenous solution additives are

    A. labeled   B. prepared
    C. stored   D. administered

12. Which of the following gives the meaning of *HEPA* as used in *HEPA filter*?

    A. High efficiency particulate air
    B. High energy particle aeration
    C. The name of the manufacturer
    D. High energy particulate aerosol

13. Which one of the following is TRUE with regard to Phenylephrine hydrochloride, USP? It

    A. is a parasympathomimetic agent
    B. exhibits a vasodilatory activity in hypotensive states
    C. is a useful mydriatic when used opthalmically
    D. may be administered only topically

14. Which of the following drugs are placed under Controlled Substances requirements?

    A. Trancycypromine   B. Trinitoin
    C. Chlordiazepoxide   D. Chlorpheniramine

15. Which one of the following preparations should be kept at a temperature of 0 to -10C during storage?   15._____

    A. Insulin, USP
    B. Rocky mountain spotted fever vaccine
    C. ACTH gel (80 U only)
    D. Immunine serum globin (human)

16. *Tablet friability* refers to tablet   16._____

    A. dissolution rate
    B. disintegration time
    C. fragility and durability when tested
    D. size

17. Iodine solution, N.F., should MOST preferably be stored   17._____

    A. in a frozen gel   B. below 35°C
    C. at room temperature   D. above 35°C

18. Which class or classes of controlled substances require a Bureau of Narcotics and Dangerous Drugs order form?   18._____

    A. II   B. I & II
    C. I, II, & III   D. All classes

19. Fenfluramine, a new anorexigenic, falls into which control class?   19._____

    A. II   B. III   C. IV   D. V

20. Secobarbital falls into which control class?   20._____

    A. V   B. IV   C. III   D. II

21. Which one of the following is a MAJOR disadvantage in the implementation of a unit dose system?   21._____
    It

    A. requires the pharmacist to increase his involvement with the nursing staff
    B. requires additional equipment and labor costs to package those drugs not readily available in unit dose form from drug manufacturers
    C. makes the dispensing process a monotonous task due to the standardization of doses and drugs
    D. requires the pharmacist to prepare all injectable doses

22. A unit dose package can be defined as a   22._____

    A. vial of 1 gram of Keflin, to be reconstituted by the nurse sent to the nursing unit (assuming the dose is 1 gram q 4h 1V)
    B. package containing the exact dosage of drugs to be administered to a patient at a specific time
    C. package containing enough medication for the next three doses
    D. bottle containing enough medication for 24 hours

23. Which one of the following statements is an advantage of the *floor stock* system of drug distribution?
It

    A. requires the increased professional involvement of the pharmacist
    B. brings the drug to the patient the fastest
    C. has the lowest incidence of medication errors
    D. is the most efficient, from a fiscal point of view

24. Which one of the following is unaffected by unit dose dispensing?

    A. Drug inventory levels
    B. Medication errors
    C. Drug administration to patients
    D. Personnel allotment

25. Which one of the following is NOT an acceptable method of sterilization?

    A. Autoclave
    B. Laminar flow
    C. Membrane
    D. Gas

26. In pharmaceutical terms, *proof* is defined as

    A. the receipt from the distiller showing proof of purchase of the alcohol
    B. one-half the percent of ethyl alcohol by volume of 60° F
    C. twice the percent of ethyl alcohol by volume at 60° F
    D. matching records of dispensation of alcohol to actual inventory

27. A Patterson-Kelly powder blender is ALSO called a(n)

    A. Waring blender
    B. twin shell blender
    C. Hobart mixer
    D. oscillating vibrator

28. For an existing ongoing program, which one of the following is MOST desirable for the pharmacist to have in preparing an annual budget?

    A. Last year's budget and this year's estimated actual expenses
    B. This year's budget and this year's estimated actual expenses
    C. Budgets and actual expense figures for the last five years
    D. Last year's budget and actual expenses

29. Which one of the following is NOT a recommended code account for a pharmacy department budget?

    A. Miscellaneous supplies and expense
    B. Drugs and Pharmaceuticals
    C. Salaries and wages
    D. Floor stock drugs

30. Pharmacy workload reports compare workload to

    A. available professional time
    B. number of prescriptions filled
    C. pharmacists' time devoted to it
    D. pharmacy personnel budget

KEY (CORRECT ANSWERS)

1.	D		16.	C
2.	C		17.	B
3.	A		18.	A
4.	D		19.	C
5.	C		20.	C
6.	A		21.	B
7.	A		22.	B
8.	B		23.	B
9.	A		24.	C
10.	B		25.	B
11.	B		26.	C
12.	A		27.	B
13.	C		28.	B
14.	A		29.	D
15.	B		30.	A

TEST 2

DIRECTIONS: Each question or incomplete statement is followed by several suggested answers or completions. Select the one that BEST answers the question or completes the statement. *PRINT THE LETTER OF THE CORRECT ANSWER IN THE SPACE AT THE RIGHT.*

1. Which one of the following groups is LEAST vital for treatment in an *Emergency Box* situation? 1.____

   A. Sengstachen Blakemore tube and Xylocaine HCl
   B. Nalorphine, HCl and Epinephrine, HCl
   C. Triplennamine HCl tablets and bropheniramine maleate
   D. Heparin, USP, and Nalorphine, HCl

2. For sterility tests to be definitive, suture material must be incubated under standard conditions for a period of _____ day(s). 2.____

   A. 1   B. 4   C. 15   D. 30

3. Which one of the following sieve sizes has the SMALLEST openings? 3.____

   A. 1.0   B. 2.0   C. 20.0   D. 200.0

4. A low rate of inventory turnover is GENERALLY indicative of 4.____

   A. the presence of dead inventory on the shelves
   B. poor servicing of accounts by drug companies
   C. failure to take advantage of discounts
   D. small volume purchasing

5. Of the following, an example of an injectable unit dose is 5.____

   A. kapseal   B. spansule   C. tubex   D. insulin

6. When dispensing tetracycline capsules to a patient in an OPD pharmacy, the pharmacist should 6.____

   A. dispense the medication without comment
   B. tell the patient to take the capsules one hour before or 2 hours after meals and to avoid milk and antacids immediately before and after his dose of the drug
   C. tell the patient not to take the capsules with milk, antacids or food
   D. tell the patient to take the capsules immediately after meals and to avoid antacids and milk

7. When conducting nursing station inspections, one need NOT look for _____ drugs. 7.____

   A. improperly stored   B. expiration dates on
   C. unlabelled   D. unlicensed

8. Which one of the following statements regarding the formulary system generally is TRUE? 8.____
   It does not

   A. allow the pharmacist the right of product selection
   B. deprive the physician of his right to prescribe the drug of his choice

C. save the hospital any money
D. represent the current thinking of the medical staff of the hospital

9. The one of the following factors which does NOT affect the removal of an active drug from a site of action is

   A. the amount of carboxymethylcellulose present
   B. excretion of the active drug
   C. redistribution to other tissues
   D. metabolism of an active drug to an inactive metabolite

10. Of the following types of pharmaceutical products, which is LEAST often manufactured by the hospital pharmacy?

    A. Sterile irrigating solutions
    B. Allergenic extracts
    C. Galenicals
    D. Non-commercially available products

11. Even though the purchasing agent, a non-pharmacist, may actually procure medications for a hospital, a pharmacist MUST

    A. receive on-site inspection reports of the purchasing agent
    B. provide price range and a list of generics
    C. provide acceptable vendors and specific procurement requirements
    D. provide general specifications of storage requirements

12. A non-proprietary hospital is usually eligible to purchase tax-free alcohol. In order to do so, it must meet certain criteria, among which is that it

    A. add a denaturant to all stored alcohol to prevent its consumption by unauthorized personnel
    B. charge patients for any medicinal product containing tax-free alcohol
    C. store alcohol in containers smaller than one gallon proof
    D. obtain a bond of surety

13. According to the regulations established by the State Bureau of Narcotics, a *running* inventory must be maintained by the primary source of distribution (pharmacy) in all institutions for drugs in Class(es)

    A. II, III, IV, and V   B. II and III
    C. II only   D. II, III, and IV

14. Pharmacy purchase records must contain all of the following information EXCEPT

    A. last price   B. therapeutic class
    C. usage rate   D. vendor

15. Drug inventory files must contain all of the following information EXCEPT

    A. minimum order quantity   B. usage rate
    C. last price   D. vendor

16. Inventory turnover rate is determined by

    A. dividing the average of opening and closing inventories by the cost of goods sold
    B. dividing the cost of goods sold by the average of opening and closing inventories
    C. dividing the opening inventory by the closing inventory
    D. multiplying the average of opening and closing inventories by one-tenth of the cost of goods sold and dividing that result by 25

17. The ratio, *cost of drugs per patient day,* compares cost of drugs with

    A. average daily census
    B. annual admissions
    C. total of all the daily censuses for the year, excluding bassinets
    D. total of all the daily censuses for the year, including bassinets

18. In order to provide accurate drug information, MOST local hospital pharmacies have developed

    A. a 24-hour drug information service
    B. computerized techniques to disseminate drug information
    C. consumer-oriented information centers
    D. monthly newsletters covering drug information highlights

19. The PRIMARY goal of a hospital formulary is to

    A. save a hospital money
    B. strictly control prescribing in a hospital
    C. insure that patients receive the best care possible
    D. influence medical staff to use approved drugs only

20. The pharmacy and therapeutics committee is NOT designed to

    A. serve an educational function
    B. advise on professional policies involving the use of drugs in the hospital
    C. save the hospital money
    D. recommend in-service programs relating to drugs

21. When a supervising pharmacist serves on the pharmacy and therapeutics committee, which of the following types of detailed information SHOULD be supplied by him for consideration and evaluation?

    A. The agenda and minutes of the meetings
    B. Information pertaining to the economic aspects of a drug only
    C. Information pertaining to the pharmaceutic and economic aspects of a drug
    D. Information pertaining to the therapeutic, pharmaceutic, and economic aspects of a drug

22. Administrative policies for a pharmacy unit are GENERALLY developed

    A. with the approval of the pharmacy and therapeutics committee
    B. with the approval of the medical and/or nursing staffs (depending upon the particular policy)
    C. with the approval of the administrative officers of the hospital
    D. by the pharmacy unit alone

23. Which one of the following does NOT have to be in the form of a written policy and procedure in the pharmacy?

    A. Patient admissions
    B. Handling flammable materials
    C. Orienting new pharmacy employees
    D. Handling of narcotics

24. Non-licensed personnel play an IMPORTANT role in the hospital pharmacy because

    A. many of them aspire to be pharmacists, and working in the hospital pharmacy provides training
    B. they can be trained to act in the place of a pharmacist within 3 months
    C. they can perform certain functions under the supervision of a registered pharmacist and, therefore, frees other pharmacists to perform more professional duties
    D. two technicians can be hired in place of each pharmacist, thereby increasing staff complement without increasing expenditure

25. The use of an investigational new drug within a particular institution requires that the

    A. institution be certified by the FDA
    B. licensed prescriber be approved by the manufacturer or chief investigator
    C. hospital administrator, licensed prescriber, and pharmacy be certified by the FDA
    D. institution and the physician be certified by the FDA

26. One requirement of the State Bureau of Narcotics for registered hospital pharmacies is that

    A. they dispense all Schedule I, II, III, IV, and V medications with an orange label
    B. they maintain accurate procurement and distribution records and perform a physical inventory annually
    C. they maintain a *running* inventory on all Schedule II, III, and IV drugs
    D. the hospitals' nursing staffs must inventory all *floor stock* every 24 hours

27. The Internal Revenue Service requires that annual inventory on all tax-free alcohol be reported in which of the following units? _____ gallons.

    A. *Alcohol*   B. Proof   C. Wine   D. Spirit

28. The documentation and preparation of the pharmacy annual report should be based PRIMARILY on the

    A. general activities of the previous fiscal year only
    B. general activities to be developed during upcoming fiscal year only
    C. qualifications of the director of pharmacy service
    D. fiscal activities only for the previous year

29. It is suggested that in hospitals where manufacturing of any drug or dosage is being performed, the *manufacturing standards* conform to the Food, Drug and Cosmetics Act standards known as

    A. GNP   B. NDA   C. GMP   D. IND

30. A written proposal for a new project or service submitted by a supervising pharmacist should 30._____

    A. contain as many technical terms as possible
    B. substantiate any claims in professional literature and how it relates to the institution
    C. emphasize the advantages of the project or service and minimize its shortcomings
    D. contain information relative to another institution which has implemented a similar administrative proposal

KEY (CORRECT ANSWERS)

1.	C	16.	B
2.	C	17.	C
3.	D	18.	D
4.	A	19.	C
5.	C	20.	C
6.	B	21.	D
7.	D	22.	C
8.	B	23.	A
9.	A	24.	C
10.	B	25.	B
11.	C	26.	B
12.	D	27.	B
13.	C	28.	A
14.	B	29.	C
15.	C	30.	B

EXAMINATION SECTION
TEST 1

DIRECTIONS: Each question or incomplete statement is followed by several suggested answers or completions. Select the one that BEST answers the question or completes the statement. *PRINT THE LETTER OF THE CORRECT ANSWER IN THE SPACE AT THE RIGHT.*

1. One of the ingredients of Compound Sodium Cyclamate Solution is   1._____

   A. calcium cyclamate B. glycerol
   C. saccharin sodium   D. sorbitol

2. The one of the following galenicals which is NOT official at present is   2._____

   A. Anthralin Ointment   B. Arnica Tincture
   C. Belladonna Liniment   D. Taraxacum Fluidextract

3. Belladonna Ointment is prepared from   3._____

   A. Belladonna Leaf Fluidextract
   B. Belladonna Root Fluidextract
   C. Pilular Belladonna Extract
   D. Powdered Belladonna Extract

4. Of the following official galenicals, the one which is a supersaturated solution in water is   4._____

   A. Aluminum Subacetate Solution
   B. Boric Acid Solution
   C. Mannitol Injection
   D. Potassium Iodide Solution

5. Ethyl Aminobenzoate is MOST soluable in   5._____

   A. ethanol   B. glycerol   C. olive oil   D. water

6. The process of lypophilization involves   6._____

   A. alpha hemolysis   B. electrophoresis
   C. freeze drying   D. plasmoptysis

7. The pH of a solution of Tetracycline Hydrochloride for Injection is between   7._____

   A. 2 and 3   B. 4 and 5   C. 6 and 7   D. 8 and 9

8. Of the following, the compound which is MOST soluble in water at 25° C. is   8._____

   A. codeine sulfate
   B. dihydromorphinone hydrochloride
   C. ethylmorphine hydrochloride
   D. quinine sulfate

9. Thiamine hydrochloride is INCOMPATIBLE with   9._____

   A. ferrous gluconate   B. glycerol
   C. sodium citrate   D. sorbitol solution

10. The PRINCIPAL solvent used in the preparation of Medicinal Soft Soap Liniment is

   A. chloroform
   B. ethanol
   C. glycerol
   D. isopropanol

11. The solubility of codeine phosphate compared with that of codeine sulfate, at room temperature, is _____ times greater.

   A. four
   B. six
   C. eight
   D. twelve

12. Glycerin is a constituent of

   A. Chalk Mixture
   B. Compound Sarsaparilla Syrup
   C. Liquid Petrolatum Emulsion
   D. Phenobarbital Elixir

13. Of the following acids, the one LEAST soluble in water at 25° C. has the formula

   A. $HC_2H_3O_2$
   B. $HC_7H_5O_2$
   C. $H_2C_4H_4O_6$
   D. H_3BO_3

14. Romilar Syrup is INCOMPATIBLE with

   A. Elixir Three Bromides
   B. Sedulon Syrup
   C. Syrup Hydriodic Acid
   D. Thephorin Syrup

15. Wild Cherry Syrup U.S.P. is made from the bark of

   A. Cassia acutifolia
   B. Prunus cerasus
   C. Prunus serotina
   D. Rhamnus purshiana

16. Myciguent is an ointment containing as the PRINCIPAL ingredient

   A. Griseofulvin
   B. Neomycin
   C. Novabiocin
   D. Nystatin

17. Monoethanolamine is a pharmaceutical NECESSITY in

   A. Nitrofurazone Ointment
   B. Nitromersal Solution
   C. Thiomersal Ointment
   D. Thiomersal Solution

18. The ointment base used in the preparation of Phenol Ointment N.F. is

   A. Hydrophilic Ointment
   B. White Ointment
   C. White Petrolatum
   D. Yellow Petrolatum

19. Thephorin Syrup is INCOMPATIBLE with

   A. ammonium chloride
   B. ephedrine sulfate
   C. ethylmorphine hydrochloride
   D. potassium guaiacolsulfonate

20. A eutectic mixture will be obtained when camphor is triturated with an EQUAL weight of

   A. mannitol
   B. saccharin
   C. saligenin
   D. thymol

21. The ointment base used in the preparation of the official Ichthammol Ointment consists of Wool Fat and _____.

    A. Hydrophylic Ointment
    B. Liquid Petrolatum
    C. White Ointment
    D. Yellow Petrolatum

22. The percentage range of isopropanol present in the official Isopropyl Alcohol Rubbing Compound is _____ percent.

    A. 55 - 60   B. 68 - 72   C. 82 - 88   D. 92 - 99

23. In the preparation of Yellow Mercuric Oxide Ointment, the Yellow Mercuric Oxide is rubbed with Liquid Petrolatum until the mixture is smooth. This process is called

    A. alligation
    B. comminution
    C. levigation
    D. maceration

24. The OFFICIAL synonym for Noscapine Hydrochloride is

    A. Naepaine Hydrochloride
    B. Naphazoline Hydrochloride
    C. Narcotine Hydrochloride
    D. Nylidrin Hydrochloride

25. A substance NO LONGER permitted legally as a denaturant of ethyl alcohol is

    A. acetone
    B. boric acid
    C. camphor
    D. isopropyl alcohol

KEY (CORRECT ANSWERS)

1.	C	11.	D
2.	C	12.	D
3.	C	13.	B
4.	C	14.	C
5.	A	15.	C
6.	C	16.	B
7.	A	17.	D
8.	B	18.	B
9.	C	19.	D
10.	B	20.	D

21. D
22. B
23. C
24. C
25. B

TEST 2

DIRECTIONS: Each question or incomplete statement is followed by several suggested answers or completions. Select the one that BEST answers the question or completes the statement. *PRINT THE LETTER OF THE CORRECT ANSWER IN THE SPACE AT THE RIGHT.*

1. A substance used as a preservative for galenicals is

   A. benzalkonium chloride
   B. methyl parahydroxybenzoate
   C. parachlorophenol
   D. phenylmercuric nitrate

   1.____

2. The ACTIVE component of Liquor Carbonis Detergens is

   A. Coal Tar
   B. Juniper Tar
   C. Pine Tar
   D. Rectified Tar Oil

   2.____

3. Methadon hydrochloride is INCOMPATIBLE with

   A. Aromatic Elixir
   B. Orange Syrup
   C. Peppermint Water
   D. Wild Cherry Syrup

   3.____

4. Persic Oil is an ingredient used in the preparation of

   A. Calamine Lotion
   B. Chrysarobin Ointment
   C. Lime Liniment
   D. Rose Water Ointment

   4.____

5. Cherry Syrup is INCOMPATIBLE with

   A. ascorbic acid
   B. codeine phosphate
   C. potassium citrate
   D. thiamine hydrochloride

   5.____

6. Sulfur Ointment is NOT prepared by the fusion method because the

   A. ointment base becomes rancid
   B. sulfur is precipitated
   C. sulfur reacts with the ointment base
   D. sulfur is volatilized

   6.____

7. Of the following, the one which is a component used in the preparation of Chalk Mixture is

   A. Bentonite Magma
   B. Bismuth Magma
   C. Methylcellulose
   D. Sodium Alginate

   7.____

8. The formula CH_3CHNH_2COOH represents the compound

   A. alanine
   B. fumaric acid
   C. glutamic acid
   D. tryptophane

   8.____

9. A compound permitted for use as an antibacterial agent in opthalmic solutions has the formula

   A. $C_6H_5C_2H_4OH$
   B. $C_6H_8(OH)_6$
   C. C_6H_5CHO
   D. $C_6H_4(OH)COOH$

   9.____

10. A proteolytic enzyme obtained from the pancreas gland of the ox is   10.____
    A. lipase   B. pepsin   C. rennin   D. trypsin

11. Ethylcellulose is characterized as an   11.____
    A. alcohol   B. ester   C. ether   D. inner oxide

12. An alkaloid which is a DERIVATIVE of ecgonine is   12.____
    A. atropine   B. brucine
    C. cocaine   D. lobeline

13. An antibacterial substance produced by the growth of Bacillus brevis is   13.____
    A. Nystatin   B. Polymyxin
    C. Tetracycline   D. Tyrothricin

14. A solution of formaldehyde in concentrated sulfuric acid is used as a reagent to test for   14.____
    the presence of
    A. atropine   B. marijuana   C. morphine   D. phenobarbital

15. Of the following compounds, the one which has the HIGHEST vapor pressure at room   15.____
    temperature is
    A. amphetamine   B. atropine
    C. ephedrine   D. epinephrine

16. Of the following alkaloids, the one which is a liquid at 25° C. is   16.____
    A. emetine   B. lobeline
    C. papaverine   D. scopolamine

17. Of the following, the one employed as a gaseous fumigant has the formula   17.____
    A. CH_3Br B. $(C_2H_5)_2O$ C. CH_3COOH D. C_6H_5CHO

18. When a prescription calls for $C_6H_4OOCH_3COOH$, the substance required is   18.____
    A. acetaminophenol   B. acetylsalicylic acid
    C. benzoic acid   D. phenyl salicylate

19. Chloropropamide is a DERIVATIVE of   19.____
    A. ethylenediamine   B. oxazolidine
    C. pyrrolidine   D. sulfonylurea

20. Nordefrin hydrochloride is ISOMETRIC with _____ hydrochloride.   20.____
    A. ephedrine   B. epinephrine
    C. norephedrine   D. phenylephrine

21. Peritrate is a DERIVATIVE of   21.____
    A. pentaerythritol   B. phenobarbital
    C. sorbitol   D. tartaric acid

22. A NATURAL source of an official steroid glycoside is

    A. Brassica nigra
    B. Digitalis purpurea
    C. Fagopyrum esculentum
    D. Prunus serotina

23. Peanut Oil is obtained from the seed kernels of

    A. Arachis hypogaea
    B. Aralis racemosa
    C. Gossypium hirsutum
    D. Zea mays

24. A balsam obtained from the trunk of Liquidambar orientalis is an ingredient of Compound _____.

    A. Colocynth and Jalap Pills
    B. Resorcinol Ointment
    C. Tincture of Benzoin
    D. White Pine Syrup

25. An OFFICIAL natural source of Santonin is

    A. Aralia racemosa
    B. Artemisia cina
    C. Candida utilis
    D. Smilaz regelii

KEY (CORRECT ANSWERS)

1.	B	11.	C
2.	A	12.	C
3.	D	13.	D
4.	D	14.	C
5.	C	15.	A
6.	B	16.	B
7.	A	17.	A
8.	A	18.	B
9.	A	19.	D
10.	D	20.	B

21. A
22. B
23. A
24. C
25. B

TEST 3

DIRECTIONS: Each question or incomplete statement is followed by several suggested answers or completions. Select the one that BEST answers the question or completes the Statement. *PRINT THE LETTER OF THE CORRECT ANSWER IN THE SPACE AT THE RIGHT.*

1. The botanical source of Mexican Scammony Resin is

    A. Exogonium purga
    B. Ipomaea orizabensis
    C. Pistacia lentiscus
    D. Phamnus purshiana

    1._____

2. The seed of Anamirta cocculus is the source of the active *principle*

    A. pavatrine
    B. phenylalanine
    C. picrotoxin
    D. pilocarpine

    2._____

3. The following prescription is to be compounded:
    Rx

    | Atropine Sulfate | 0.300 gram |
    | Sodium Chloride | q.s. |
    | Distilled water to make | 30.0 ml. |

    Prepare an isotonic solution.
    The sodium chloride equivalent for atropine sulfate is 0.12. The weight of sodium chloride required is _____ milligrams.

    A. 36   B. 117   C. 234   D. 306

    3._____

4. Blood plasma contains 5.0 milliequivalents of combined potassium per liter. Assuming that all the potassium is present as KCl, the corresponding weight of potassium chloride is, MOST NEARLY, _____ grams.
    (The formula weight for potassium chloride is 74.6 the atomic weight for potassium is 39.1.)

    A. 3.73   B. 0.373   C. 0.0373   D. 0.00373

    4._____

5. The volume of a sodium hydroxide solution having a specific gravity of 1.530 and containing 49.0% of NaOH (by weight) required to prepare 2500 milliliters of a 0.2000 Normal solution of NaOH is, MOST NEARLY, _____ ml.
    (Molecular weight of NaOH = 40.0)

    A. 10.6   B. 13.3   C. 26.6   D. 37.5

    5._____

6. A pesticide formula contains 25 grams of ethohexadiol (specific gravity 0.940) in 100 ml. of solution. The volume of ethohexadiol required to prepare one gallon of this preparation is, MOST NEARLY, _____ ml.

    A. 889   B. 946   C. 1006   D. 1064

    6._____

7. The hydrogen ion concentration of a solution with a pOH equal to 10 is _____ molar.

    A. 1×10^{-4} B. 8×10^{-6} C. 4×10^{-10} D. 2×10^{-12}

    7._____

8. The weight of H_2SO_4 (formula weight = 98.06) required to prepare 2500 ml. of a solution with a pH of 3 is, MOST NEARLY, _____ milligrams.

   A. 61.3   B. 122.6   C. 245.2   D. 490.4

9. The weight in milligrams of a ten per cent (by weight) triturate of atropine sulfate required to prepare 100 capsules, each to contain 1/200 grain of atropine sulfate, is

   A. 648   B. 405   C. 324   D. 162

10. The molar concentration of a 1:5000 solution of potassium permanganate is _____. (The molecular weight of potassium permanganate is 158.)

    A. 0.0630   B. 0.00126   C. 0.00025   D. 0.00002

11. An effective surface anaesthetic useful in ophthalmology is

    A. Benoxinate Hydrochloride
    B. Hydroxydione Sodium Succinate
    C. Pramoxine Hydrochloride
    D. Thiamyal Sodium

12. Plasmolysis is caused by a solution which is

    A. hypertonic   B. hypotonic
    C. isohydric   D. mutagenic

13. A compound possessing the properties of an ozytocic is

    A. Ephedrine sulfate   B. Homatropine hydrobromide
    C. Lanatoside C.   D. Sparteine sulfate

14. Mannitol is used as a

    A. diagnostic agent for kidney function
    B. pharmaceutical necessity in ointments
    C. preservative for sucrose solutions
    D. solvent for volatile oils

15. Gout is ESSENTIALLY a disease caused by

    A. deposit of uric acid derivatives
    B. increase in renin excretion
    C. reduction of exchangeable phosphorus
    D. streptococcus endotoxin

16. Ascorbic acid is CLOSELY related to

    A. benzoic acid   B. cyclic amines
    C. monosaccharide sugars   D. phosphopyruvic acid

17. The microorganism Streptomyces fradiae is the source of the antibiotic

    A. Chloroamphenicol   B. Neomycin
    C. Streptomycin   D. Tetracycline

18. The PRIMARY therapeutic use of Salicylanilide is as a(n)

    A. analgesic
    B. anthelmintic
    C. antifungal
    D. keratolytic

19. A compound classified as a cholinergic blocking agent is

    A. diphenhydramine hydrochloride
    B. methylergonovine tartrate
    C. papaverine hydrochloride
    D. propantheline bromide

20. The NATURAL habitat of enteric organisms is the

    A. axillae
    B. digestive tract
    C. epidermis
    D. oral cavity

21. Moniliasis is a disease caused by infection with

    A. Candida albicans
    B. Cryptococcus neoformans
    C. Pseudomonas aeruginosa
    D. Treponema pallidum

22. Sodium Radiochromate Injection is used

    A. as a biological tracer to tag erythrocytes
    B. as a means of detecting brain tumors
    C. as a neoplastic suppressant
    D. in measuring absorption of vitamin B_{12}

23. Sodium Radioiodide solution is used as a diagnostic aid in

    A. determining thyroid function
    B. determining kidney function
    C. estimating total body water
    D. evaluating liver function

24. A drug used in the treatment of motion sickness is

    A. apomorphine hydrochloride
    B. bentyl hydrochloride
    C. hexamethonium chloride
    D. meclizine hydrochloride

25. The use of reserpine in daily doses above 250 mg. is CONTRAINDICATED in cases of

    A. hyperglycemia
    B. hypertension
    C. migraine
    D. peptic ulcer

KEY (CORRECT ANSWERS)

1.	B	11.	A
2.	C	12.	A
3.	C	13.	D
4.	B	14.	A
5.	C	15.	A
6.	C	16.	C
7.	A	17.	B
8.	B	18.	C
9.	C	19.	D
10.	B	20.	B

21. A
22. A
23. A
24. D
25. D

TEST 4

DIRECTIONS: Each question or incomplete statement is followed by several suggested answers or completions. Select the one that BEST answers the question or completes the statement. *PRINT THE LETTER OF THE CORRECT ANSWER IN THE SPACE AT THE RIGHT.*

1. Of the following, the one used as an antitussive is

    A. carbetapentane citrate
    B. hydroxychloroquine sulfate
    C. hydroxyzine hydrochloride
    D. metabutethamine hydrochloride

2. The USUAL adult dose for Levorphanol Tartrate is _____ milligrams.

    A. 0.5   B. 3   C. 10   D. 30

3. Of the following insecticides, the one LEAST toxic to humans is

    A. allethrin   B. dieldrin
    C. lindane   D. parathion

4. The USUAL adult dose of ethylmorphine hydrochloride is _____ gram.

    A. 0.001   B. 0.005   C. 0.020   D. 0.050

5. Of the following, the one which is used in the treatment of hyperglycemia is

    A. Ethoxzolamide   B. Isocarboxazid
    C. Mepazine   D. Tolbutamide

6. Smallpox Vaccine consists of

    A. dead bacteria   B. live bacteria
    C. dead virus   D. live virus

7. Warfarin Sodium is used as a(n)

    A. anticoagulant   B. hemostatic
    C. insect repellant D. scabicide

8. The microorganism Clostridium perfringens is responsible for the disease known as

    A. botulism   B. gas gangrene
    C. lockjaw   D. whooping cough

9. A vaccine prepared from a saline suspension of a pure culture of the bacteria responsible for an individual's own infection is called

    A. autogenous   B. heterologous
    C. opsonic   D. pyrogenic

10. Isofluorphate is used in the treatment of

    A. dental caries   B. glaucoma
    C. hypertension   D. otitis media

1.____
2.____
3.____
4.____
5.____
6.____
7.____
8.____
9.____
10.____

11. The name *Spansule* identifies a product manufactured by   11.____

    A. Eli Lilly & Company
    B. Parke Davis & Company
    C. Smith, Kline & French Laboratories
    D. Wallace Laboratories

12. A drug subject to the law governing the dispensing of narcotic preparations is _____   12.____
    hydrochloride.

    A. eucatropine   B. bentyl
    C. marezine   D. meperidine

13. Perphenazine is the GENERIC name for   13.____

    A. Compazine   B. Librium
    C. Stelazine   D. Trilafon

14. The one of the following which is NOT a trade name for Tetracycline U.S.P. is   14.____

    A. Achromycin   B. Panmycin
    C. Pen-Vee   D. Steclin

15. Sulfamethoxypyridazine is the GENERIC name for the product marketed under the name   15.____

    A. Compazine   B. Exna
    C. Kynex   D. Sandrel

16. A PROPRIETARY tablet containing hydroxyzine pamoate is manufactured by   16.____

    A. Pfizer Laboratories
    B. Roche Laboratories
    C. Smith, Kline & French Laboratories
    D. Wallace Laboratories

17. The name *Kapseal* identifies a product manufactured by   17.____

    A. Burroughs, Wellcome & Co.
    B. Eli Lilly & Company
    C. Merck, Sharp & Dohme
    D. Parke Davis & Company

18. The following prescription is to be compounded: 18.____

    R_x

Ethyl aminobenzoate	3.60 gm
Resorcinol	7.00 gm
Bismuth Subgallate	14.00 gm
White Petrolatum	70.00 gm

    The MOST expensive component of this prescription, as written, is

    A. Bismuth Subgallate   B. Ethyl aminobenzoate
    C. Resorcinol   D. White Petrolatum

19. Of the following, the one which is the LOWER limit of the temperature range required for the storage of bacterial vaccines is

    A. -10° C   B. 2° C   C. 12° C   D. 18° C

20. The expiration date for Smallpox Vaccine is NOT MORE THAN _____ months after the date of issue.

    A. eighteen   B. six
    C. three   D. twelve

21. Triethanolamine must be preserved in tight, light-resistant containers in order to minimize

    A. absorption of carbon dioxide
    B. conversion to ammonium acetate
    C. reduction to carbamide
    D. volatilization of ammonia

22. In considering storage temperature, a cold place is officially defined in the U.S.P. as one having a temperature NOT EXCEEDING

    A. 15° C   B. 20° C   C. 32° C   D. 49° C

23. Lime Water is directed to be stored at a temperature not exceeding 25° C in order to prevent

    A. deposition of calcium carbonate
    B. formation of calcium bicarbonate
    C. formation of calcium silicate
    D. precipitation of calcium hydroxide

24. The PREFERRED glass container for the storage of Injections is Type _____.

    A. I   B. II   C. III   D. IV

25. Ephedrine MUST be stored in a cold place because it

    A. decomposes rapidly at 40° C
    B. has a low melting point
    C. is deliquescent at room temperature
    D. volatilizes at 30° C

KEY (CORRECT ANSWERS)

1. A
2. B
3. A
4. B
5. D

6. D
7. A
8. B
9. A
10. B

11. C
12. D
13. D
14. C
15. C

16. A
17. D
18. A
19. B
20. C

21. A
22. A
23. D
24. A
25. B

CLERICAL ABILITIES
EXAMINATION SECTION
TEST 1

DIRECTIONS: Each question or incomplete statement is followed by several suggested answers or completions. Select the one that BEST answers the question or completes the statement. *PRINT THE LETTER OF THE CORRECT ANSWER IN THE SPACE AT THE RIGHT.*

Questions 1-4.

DIRECTIONS: Questions 1 through 4 are to be answered on the basis of the information given below.

The most commonly used filing system and the one that is easiest to learn is alphabetical filing. This involves putting records in an A to Z order, according to the letters of the alphabet. The name of a person is filed by using the following order: first, the surname or last name; second, the first name; third, the middle name or middle initial. For example, *Henry C. Young* is filed under *Y* and thereafter under *Young, Henry C.* The name of a company is filed in the same way. For example, *Long Cabinet Co.* is filed under *L* while *John T. Long Cabinet Co.* is filed under *L* and thereafter under *Long, John T. Cabinet Co.*

1. The one of the following which lists the names of persons in the CORRECT alphabetical order is:
   A. Mary Carrie, Helen Carrol, James Carson, John Carter
   B. James Carson, Mary Carrie, John Carter, Helen Carrol
   C. Helen Carrol, James Carson, John Carter, Mary Carrie
   D. John Carter, Helen Carrol, Mary Carrie, James Carson

2. The one of the following which lists the names of persons in the CORRECT alphabetical order is:
   A. Jones, John C.; Jones, John A.; Jones, John P.; Jones, John K.
   B. Jones, John P.; Jones, John K.; Jones, John C.; Jones, John A.
   C. Jones, John A.; Jones, John C.; Jones, John K.; Jones, John P.
   D. Jones, John K.; Jones, John C.; Jones, John A.; Jones, John P.

3. The one of the following which lists the names of the companies in the CORRECT alphabetical order is:
   A. Blane Co., Blake Co., Block Co., Blear Co.
   B. Blake Co., Blane Co., Blear Co., Block Co.
   C. Block Co., Blear Co., Blane Co., Blake Co.
   D. Blear Co., Blake Co., Blane Co., Block Co.

4. You are to return to the file an index card on *Barry C. Wayne Materials and Supplies Co.*
   Of the following, the CORRECT alphabetical group that you should return the index card to is
   A. A to G   B. H to M   C. N to S   D. T to Z

Questions 5-10.

DIRECTIONS: In each of Questions 5 through 10, the names of four people are given. For each question, choose as your answer the one of the four names given which should be filed FIRST according to the usual system of alphabetical filing of names, as described in the following paragraph.

In filing names, you must start with the last name. Names are filed in order of the first letter of the last name, then the second letter, etc. Therefore, BAILY would be filed before BROWN, which would be filed before COLT. A name with fewer letters of the same type comes first, i.e., Smith before Smithe. If the last names are the same, the names are filed alphabetically by the first name. If the first name is an initial, a name with an initial would come before a first name that starts with the same letter as the initial. Therefore, I. BROWN would come before IRA BROWN. Finally, if both last name and first name are the same, the name would be filed alphabetically by the middle name, once again an initial coming before a middle name which starts with the same letter as the initial. If there is no middle name at all, the name would come before those with middle initials or names.

SAMPLE QUESTION:
A. Lester Daniels
B. William Dancer
C. Nathan Danzig
D. Dan Lester

The last names beginning with D are filed before the last name beginning with L. Since DANIELS, DANCER, and DANZIG all begin with the same three letters, you must look at the fourth letter of the last name to determine which name should be filed first. C comes before I or Z in the alphabet, so DANCER is filed before DANIELS or DANZIG. Therefore, the answer to the above sample question is B.

5. A. Scott Biala
   B. Mary Byala
   C. Martin Baylor
   D. Francis Bauer

6. A. Howard J. Black
   B. Howard Black
   C. J. Howard Black
   D. John H. Black

7. A. Theodora Garth Kingston
   B. Theadore Barth Kingston
   C. Thomas Kingston
   D. Thomas T. Kingston

8. A. Paulette Mary Huerta
    B. Paul M. Huerta
    C. Paulette L. Huerta
    D. Peter A. Huerta

9. A. Martha Hunt Morgan
    B. Martin Hunt Morgan
    C. Mary H. Morgan
    D. Martine H. Morgan

10. A. James T. Meerschaum
    B. James M. Mershum
    C. James F. Mearshaum
    D. James N. Meshum

Questions 11-14.

DIRECTIONS: Questions 11 through 14 are to be answered SOLELY on the basis of the following information.

You are required to file various documents in file drawers which are labeled according to the following pattern:

DOCUMENTS

MEMOS		LETTERS	
File	Subject	File	Subject
84PM1	(A-L)	84PC1	(A-L)
84PM2	(M-Z)	84PC2	(M-Z)

REPORTS		INQUIRIES	
File	Subject	File	Subject
84PR1	(A-L)	84PQ1	(A-L)
84PR2	(M-Z)	84PQ2	(M-Z)

11. A letter dealing with a burglary should be filed in the drawer labeled
    A. 84PM1   B. 84PC1   C. 84PR1   D. 84PQ2

12. A report on Statistics should be found in the drawer labeled
    A. 84PM1   B. 84PC2   C. 84PR2   D. 84PQS

13. An inquiry is received about parade permit procedures. It should be filed in the drawer labeled
    A. 84PM2   B. 84PC1   C. 84PR1   D. 84PQ2

14. A police officer has a question about a robbery report you filed. You should pull this file from the drawer labeled
    A. 84PM1   B. 84PM2   C. 84PR1   D. 84PR2

Questions 15-22.

DIRECTIONS: Each of Questions 15 through 22 consists of four or six numbered names. For each question, choose the option (A, B, C, or D) which indicates the order in which the names should be filed in accordance with the following filing instructions:
- File alphabetically according to last name, then first name, then middle initial.
- File according to each successive letter within a name.
- When comparing two names in which the letters in the longer name are identical to the corresponding letters in the shorter name, the shorter name is filed first.
- When the last names are the same, initials are always filed before names beginning with the same letter.

15. I.   Ralph Robinson
     II. Alfred Ross
     III. Luis Robles
     IV. James Roberts

   The CORRECT filing sequence for the above names should be
   A. IV, II, I, III   B. I, IV, III, II   C. III, IV, I, II   D. IV, I, III, II

16. I.   Irwin Goodwin
     II. Inez Gonzalez
     III. Irene Goodman
     IV. Ira S. Goodwin
     V.   Ruth I. Goldstein
     VI. M.B. Goodman

   The CORRECT filing sequence for the above names should be
   A. V, II, I, IV, III, VI   B. V, II, VI, III, IV, I
   C. V, II, III, VI, IV, I   D. V, II, III, VI, I, IV

17. I.   George Allan
     II. Gregory Allen
     III. Gary Allen
     IV. George Allen

   The CORRECT filing sequence for the above names should be
   A. IV, III, I, II   B. I, IV, II, III   C. III, IV, I, II   D. I, III, IV, II

5 (#1)

18. I. Simon Kauffman
    II. Leo Kaufman
    III. Robert Kaufmann
    IV. Paul Kauffmann

    The CORRECT filing sequence for the above names should be
    A. I, IV, II, III   B. II, IV, III, I   C. III, II, IV, I   D. I, II, III, IV

    18.____

19. I. Roberta Williams
    II. Robin Wilson
    III. Roberta Wilson
    IV. Robin Williams

    The CORRECT filing sequence for the above names should be
    A. III, II, IV, I   B. I, IV, III, II   C. I, II, III, IV   D. III, I, II, IV

    19.____

20. I. Lawrence Shultz
    II. Albert Schultz
    III. Theodore Schwartz
    IV. Thomas Schwarz
    V. Alvin Schultz
    VI. Leonard Shultz

    The CORRECT filing sequence for the above names should be
    A. II, V, III, IV, I, VI   B. IV, III, V, I, II, VI
    C. II, V, I, VI, III, IV   D. I, VI, II, V, III, IV

    20.____

21. I. McArdle
    II. Mayer
    III. Maletz
    IV. McNiff
    V. Meyer
    VI. MacMahon

    The CORRECT filing sequence for the above names should be
    A. I, IV, VI, III, II, V   B. II, I, IV, VI, III, V
    C. VI, III, II, I, IV, V   D. VI, III, II, V, I, IV

    21.____

22. I. Jack E. Johnson
    II. R.H. Jackson
    III. Bertha Jackson
    IV. J.T. Johnson
    V. Ann Johns
    VI. John Jacobs

    The CORRECT filing sequence for the above names should be
    A. II, III, VI, V, IV, I   B. III, II, VI, V, IV, I
    C. VI, II, III, I, V, IV   D. III, II, VI, IV, V, I

    22.____

Questions 23-30.

DIRECTIONS: The code table below shows 10 letters with matching numbers. For each question, there are three sets of letters. Each set of letters is followed by a set of numbers which may or may not match their correct letter according to the code table. For each question, check all three sets of letters and numbers and mark your answer:
    A. if no pairs are correctly matched
    B. if only one pair is correctly matched
    C. if only two pairs are correctly matched
    D. if all three pairs are correctly matched

CODE TABLE

T	M	V	D	S	P	R	G	B	H
1	2	3	4	5	6	7	8	9	0

SAMPLE QUESTION: TMVDSP – 123456
                                 RGBHTM – 789011
                                 DSPRGB – 256789

In the sample question above, the first set of numbers correctly match its set of letters. But the second and third pairs contain mistakes. In the second pair, M is correctly matched with number 1. According to the code table, letter M should be correctly matched with number 2. In the third pair, the letter D is incorrectly matched with number 2. According to the code table, letter D should be correctly matched with number 4. Since only one of the pairs is correctly matched, the answer to this sample question is B.

23.   RSBMRM – 759262   23.____
       GDSRVH – 845730
       VDBRTM - 349713

24.   TGVSDR – 183247   24.____
       SMHRDP – 520647
       TRMHSR – 172057

25.   DSPRGM – 456782   25.____
       MVDBHT – 234902
       HPMDBT - 062491

26.   BVPTRD – 936184   26.____
       GDPHMB – 807029
       GMRHMV – 827032

27.   MGVRSH – 283750   27.____
       TRDMBS – 174295
       SPRMGV – 567283

28. SGBSDM – 489542   28.____
    MGHPTM – 290612
    MPBMHT - 269301

29. TDPBHM – 146902   29.____
    VPBMRS – 369275
    GDMBHM - 842902

30. MVPTBV – 236194   30.____
    PDRTMB – 47128
    BGTMSM - 981232

KEY (CORRECT ANSWERS)

1.	A	11.	B	21.	C
2.	C	12.	C	22.	B
3.	B	13.	D	23.	B
4.	D	14.	D	24.	B
5.	D	15.	D	25.	C
6.	B	16.	C	26.	A
7.	B	17.	D	27.	D
8.	B	18.	A	28.	A
9.	A	19.	B	29.	D
10.	C	20.	A	30.	A

TEST 2

DIRECTIONS: Each question or incomplete statement is followed by several suggested answers or completions. Select the one that BEST answers the question or completes the statement. *PRINT THE LETTER OF THE CORRECT ANSWER IN THE SPACE AT THE RIGHT.*

Questions 1-10.

DIRECTIONS: Questions 1 through 10 each consists of two columns, each containing four lines of names, numbers and/or addresses. For each question, compare the lines in Column I with the lines in Column II to see if they match exactly, and mark your answer A, B, C, or D, according to the following instructions:
    A. all four lines match exactly
    B. only three lines match exactly
    C. only two lines match exactly
    D. only one line matches exactly

<u>COLUMN I</u>   <u>COLUMN II</u>

1.   I.   Earl Hodgson   Earl Hodgson   1.____
       II.   1409870   1408970
       III.   Shore Ave.   Schore Ave.
       IV.   Macon Rd.   Macon Rd.

2.   I.   9671485   9671485   2.____
       II.   470 Astor Court   470 Astor Court
       III.   Halprin, Phillip   Halperin, Phillip
       IV.   Frank D. Poliseo   Frank D. Poliseo

3.   I.   Tandem Associates   Tandom Associates   3.____
       II.   144-17 Northern Blvd.   144-17 Northern Blvd.
       III.   Alberta Forchi   Albert Forchi
       IV.   Kings Park, NY 10751   Kings Point, NY 10751

4.   I.   Bertha C. McCormack   Bertha C. McCormack   4.____
       II.   Clayton, MO   Clayton, MO
       III.   976-4242   976-4242
       IV.   New City, NY 10951   New City, NY 10951

5.   I.   George C. Morill   George C. Morrill   5.____
       II.   Columbia, SC 29201   Columbia, SD 29201
       III.   Louis Ingham   Louis Ingham
       IV.   3406 Forest Ave.   3406 Forest Ave.

6.   I.   506 S. Elliott Pl.   506 S. Elliott Pl.   6.____
       II.   Herbert Hall   Hurbert Hall
       III.   4712 Rockaway Pkwy   4712 Rockaway Pkwy
       IV.   169 E. 7 St.   169 E. 7 St.

2 (#2)

7. I.   345 Park Ave.   345 Park Pl.   7.____
    II. Colman Oven Corp.   Coleman Oven Corp.
    III. Robert Conte   Robert Conti
    IV. 6179846   6179846

8. I.   Grigori Schierber   Grigori Schierber   8.____
    II. Des Moines, Iowa   Des Moines, Iowa
    III. Gouverneur Hospital   Gouverneur Hospital
    IV. 91-35 Cresskill Pl.   91-35 Cresskill Pl.

9. I.   Jeffery Janssen   Jeffrey Janssen   9.____
    II. 8041071   8041071
    III. 40 Rockefeller Plaza   40 Rockafeller Plaza
    IV. 407 6 St.   406 7 St.

10. I.   5971996   5871996   10.____
    II. 3113 Knickerbocker Ave.   31123 Knickerbocker Ave.
    III. 8434 Boston Post Rd.   8424 Boston Post Rd.
    IV. Penn Station   Penn Station

Questions 11-14.

DIRECTIONS: Questions 11 through 14 are to be answered by looking at the four groups of names and addresses listed below (I, II, III, and IV), and then finding out the number of groups that have their corresponding numbered lies exactly the same.

	GROUP I	GROUP II
Line 1.	Richmond General Hospital	Richman General Hospital
Line 2.	Geriatric Clinic	Geriatric Clinic
Line 3.	3975 Paerdegat St.	3975 Peardegat St.
Line 4.	Loudonville, New York 11538	Londonville, New York 11538

	GROUP III	GROUP IV
Line 1.	Richmond General Hospital	Richmend General Hospital
Line 2.	Geriatric Clinic	Geriatric Clinic
Line 3.	3795 Paerdegat St.	3975 Paerdegat St.
Line 4.	Loudonville, New York 11358	Loudonville, New York 11538

1. In how many groups is line one exactly the same?   11.____
    A. Two   B. Three   C. Four   D. None

12. In how many groups is line two exactly the same?   12.____
    A. Two   B. Three   C. Four   D. None

13. In how many groups is line three exactly the same?   13.____
    A. Two   B. Three   C. Four   D. None

3 (#2)

14. In how many groups is line four exactly the same? 14.____
    A. Two B. Three C. Four D. None

Questions 15-18.

DIRECTIONS: Each of Questions 15 through 18 has two lists of names and addresses. Each list contains three sets of names and addresses. Check each of the three sets in the list on the right to see if they are the same as the corresponding set in the list on the left. Mark your answers:
    A. if none of the sets in the right list are the same as those in the left list
    B. if only one of the sets in the right list is the same as those in the left list
    C. if only two of the sets in the right list are the same as those in the left list
    D. if all three sets in the right list are the same as those in the left list

15. Mary T. Berlinger   Mary T. Berlinger   15.____
    2351 Hampton St.   2351 Hampton St.
    Monsey, N.Y. 20117   Monsey, N.Y. 20117

    Eduardo Benes   Eduardo Benes
    483 Kingston Avenue   473 Kingston Avenue
    Central Islip, N.Y. 11734   Central Islip, N.Y. 11734

    Alan Carrington Fuchs   Alan Carrington Fuchs
    17 Gnarled Hollow Road   17 Gnarled Hollow Road
    Los Angeles, CA 91635   Los Angeles, CA 91685

16. David John Jacobson   David John Jacobson   16.____
    178 34 St. Apt. 4C   178 53 St. Apt. 4C
    New York, N.Y. 00927   New York, N.Y. 00927

    Ann-Marie Calonella   Ann-Marie Calonella
    7243 South Ridge Blvd.   7243 South Ridge Blvd.
    Bakersfield, CA 96714   Bakersfield, CA 96714

    Pauline M. Thompson   Pauline M. Thomson
    872 Linden Ave.   872 Linden Ave.
    Houston, Texas 70321   Houston, Texas 70321

17. Chester LeRoy Masterton   Chester LeRoy Masterson   17.____
    152 Lacy Rd.   152 Lacy Rd.
    Kankakee, Ill. 54532   Kankakee, Ill. 54532

    William Maloney   William Maloney
    S. LaCrosse Pla.   S. LaCross Pla.
    Wausau, Wisconsin 52136   Wausau, Wisconsin 52146

    Cynthia V. Barnes   Cynthia V. Barnes
    16 Pines Rd.   16 Pines Rd.
    Greenpoint, Miss. 20376   Greenpoint,, Miss. 20376

4 (#2)

18. Marcel Jean Frontenac
8 Burton On The Water
Calender, Me. 01471

J. Scott Marsden
174 S. Tipton St.
Cleveland, Ohio

Lawrence T. Haney
171 McDonough St.
Decatur, Ga. 31304

Marcel Jean Frontenac
6 Burton On The Water
Calender, Me. 01471

J. Scott Marsden
174 Tipton St.
Cleveland, Ohio

Lawrence T. Haney
171 McDonough St.
Decatur, Ga. 31304

18._____

Questions 19-26.

DIRECTIONS: Each of Questions 19 through 26 has two lists of numbers. Each list contains three sets of numbers. Check each of the three sets in the list on the right to see if they are the same as the corresponding set in the list on the left. Mark your answers:
- A. if none of the sets in the right list are the same as those in the left list
- B. if only one of the sets in the right list is the same as those in the left list
- C. if only two of the sets in the right list are the same as those in the left list
- D. if all three sets in the right list are the same as those in the left lists

	Left	Right	
19.	7354183476 4474747744 5791430231	7354983476 4474747774 57914302311	19._____
20.	7143592185 8344517699 9178531263	7143892185 8344518699 9178531263	20._____
21.	2572114731 8806835476 8255831246	257214731 8806835476 8255831246	21._____
22.	331476853821 6976658532996 3766042113715	331476858621 6976655832996 3766042113745	22._____
23.	8806663315 74477138449 211756663666	88066633115 74477138449 211756663666	23._____

24. 990006966996   99000696996   24._____
     53022219743   53022219843
     4171171117717   4171171177717

25. 24400222433004   24400222433004   25._____
     5300030055000355 5300030055500355
     20000075532002022 20000075532002022

26. 61116664066001116 61116664066001116 26._____
     7111300117001100733 7111300117001100733
     26666446664476518 26666446664476518

Questions 27-30.

DIRECTIONS: Questions 27 through 30 are to be answered by picking the answer which is in the correct numerical order, from the lowest number to the highest number, in each question.

27. A. 44533, 44518, 44516, 44547   27._____
     B. 44516, 44518, 44533, 44547
     C. 44547, 44533, 44518, 44516
     D. 44518, 44516, 44547, 44533

28. A. 95587, 95593, 95601, 95620   28._____
     B. 95601, 95620, 95587, 95593
     C. 95593, 95587, 95601. 95620
     D. 95620, 95601, 95593, 95587

29. A. 232212, 232208, 232232, 232223 29._____
     B. 232208, 232223, 232212, 232232
     C. 232208, 232212, 232223, 232232
     D. 232223, 232232, 232208, 232208

30. A. 113419, 113521, 113462, 113462 30._____
     B. 113588, 113462, 113521, 113419
     C. 113521, 113588, 113419, 113462
     D. 113419, 113462, 113521, 113588

KEY (CORRECT ANSWERS)

1.	C	11.	A	21.	C
2.	B	12.	C	22.	A
3.	D	13.	A	23.	D
4.	A	14.	A	24.	A
5.	C	15.	C	25.	C
6.	B	16.	B	26.	C
7.	D	17.	B	27.	B
8.	A	18.	B	28.	A
9.	D	19.	B	29.	C
10.	C	20.	B	30.	D

FILING

EXAMINATION SECTION
TEST 1

DIRECTIONS: For each of the following, you are given a name above and three other names in alphabetical order below. The letters A, B, C, and D stand for spaces where you could file the name. Find the CORRECT space for the name given above so that it will be in alphabetical order with the names below it. The letter that stands for that space is the answer to the question.

1. CURRAN, THOMAS
   A CURLEY, MARY B CURR, SAMUEL C CURREN, KATIE D

   1.____

2. KAPLIN, EDWIN
   A KAPLEN, MICHAEL B KAPLIN, JULIA C KAPLON, DAVID D

   2.____

3. PENSKY, LEONA
   A PENSLER, SANDY B PENSLEY, JOEL C PENSLEY, JOSEPH D

   3.____

4. ROWEN, MARCIA
   A ROWEN, CHRISTOPHER B ROWEN, LOUIS C ROWEN, MARTIN D

   4.____

5. FOSTER, GRACE
   A FOSS, EARL B FOSSE, NICHOLE C FOSTER, KEITH D

   5.____

6. KO, FAI
   A KO, HOK B KO, HUNG-FAI C KO, HYUN JUNG D

   6.____

7. MICHALIK, ANTHONY
   A MICHALIC, GARY B MICHALIS, HELEN C MICHALK, KLAUS D

   7.____

8. MINTZ, JUDITH
   A MINTZ, JAKE B MINTZ, JAMES C MINTZ, JULIUS D

   8.____

9. POWERS, ANN
   A POUST, THERESE B POWELL, LUTHER C POWER, RACHEL D

   9.____

10. PRACTICAL STUDIO, INC.
    A PRACTICAL PUBLISHING B PRACTICE DEVELOPMENT C PRACTICE SERVICE CORP. D

    10.____

11. SHERWIN, ROBERTA
    A SHERWIN, RAUL B SHERWIN, RICHARD C SHERWIN, ROBERT D

    11.____

12. JACOBSEN, JENNIFER
    A JACOBSON, PETER B JACOBY, JACK C JACOVITZ, GAIL D

    12.____

13. BLEINHEIM, GLORIA
    A BLELOCK, JULIA B BLENCOWE, FRED C BLENMAN, ANTHONY D

    13.____

14. FIRST STERLING CORP.   14._____
    <u>A</u> FIRST STATE PRODUCTS <u>B</u> FIRST STEP INC. <u>C</u> FIRST STOP CORP. <u>D</u>

15. VICKERS, GEORGE   15._____
    <u>A</u> VICHEY, LOUIS <u>B</u> VICHI, MARIO <u>C</u> VICKI, SUSAN <u>D</u>

16. STEIN, DAVID   16._____
    <u>A</u> STEIN, CRAIG <u>B</u> STEIN, DANIEL <u>C</u> STEIN, DEBORAH <u>D</u>

17. IGLESIAS, BERNADETTE   17._____
    <u>A</u> IGER, MARTIN <u>B</u> IGLEHEART, PHYLICIA <u>C</u> IGLEWSKI, RICHARD <u>D</u>

18. IDEAL ROOFING CORP.   18._____
    <u>A</u> IDEAL REPRODUCTION <u>B</u> IDEAL RESTAURANT <u>C</u> IDEAL RUBBER PRODUCTS
    <u>D</u>

19. TODARO, JOSEPH   19._____
    <u>A</u> TODD, ANNE <u>B</u> TODE, WALLY <u>C</u> TODMAN, JUDITH <u>D</u>

20. WILKERSON, RUTH   20._____
    <u>A</u> WILKENS, FRANK <u>B</u> WILKES, BARRY <u>C</u> WILKIE, JANE <u>D</u>

21. HUGHES, MARY   21._____
    <u>A</u> HUGHES, MANUEL <u>B</u> HUGHES, MARGARET <u>C</u> HUGHES, MARTHA <u>D</u>

22. GODWIN, JAMES   22._____
    <u>A</u> GODFREY, SONDRA <u>B</u> GODMAN, GABRIEL <u>C</u> GODREAU, ROBERT <u>D</u>

23. NACHMAN, DAVID   23._____
    <u>A</u> NACHT, JAMES <u>B</u> NACK, SAUL <u>C</u> NACKENSON, LORI <u>D</u>

24. CASPER, LAURENCE   24._____
    <u>A</u> CASPER, LEONARD <u>B</u> CASPER, LESTER <u>C</u> CASPER, LINDA <u>D</u>

25. CULEN, ELLEN   25._____
    <u>A</u> CULHANE, JOHN <u>B</u> CULICHI, RADU <u>C</u> CULIN, TERRY <u>D</u>

KEY (CORRECT ANSWERS)

1. C
2. B
3. A
4. C
5. C

6. A
7. B
8. C
9. D
10. B

11. D
12. A
13. A
14. C
15. C

16. C
17. C
18. C
19. A
20. B

21. D
22. D
23. A
24. A
25. A

TEST 2

DIRECTIONS: For each of the following, you are given a name above and three other names in alphabetical order below. The letters A, B, C, and D stand for spaces where you could file the name. Find the CORRECT space for the name given above so that it will be in alphabetical order with the names below it. The letter that stands for that space is the answer to the question.

1. HARMAN, HENRY
   A HARLEY, LILLIAN B HARMER, RALPH C HARMON, CECIL D

2. MANNING, JOHNSON
   A MANNING, JAMES B MANNING, JEROME C MANNING, JOHN D

3. NOGUCHI, JANICE
   A NOEL, WALTER B NOGUET, DANIELLE C NOH, DAVID D

4. PARRON, ALFONSE
   A PARRIS, LEON B PARRISH, LINDA C PARROTT, BETTY D

5. GROSS, ELANA
   A GROSS, ELAINE B GROSS, ELIZABETH C GROSS, ELLIOT D

6. HORSTMANN, ANNA
   A HORSMAN, ALLAN B HORST, VALERIE C HORSTMAN, JAMES D

7. JONES, EMILY
   A JONES, ELMA B JONES, ELOISE C JONES, EMMA D

8. LESSING, FRED
   A LESSER, MARTHA B LESSIN, ELLIE C LESSNER, ERWIN D

9. ROSENBLUM, JULIUS
   A ROSENBLUTH, SYLVIA B ROSENBORG, ERIC C ROSENBURG, JANE D

10. YOUNG, THEODORE
    A YOUNG, TERRY B YOUNG, THELMA C YOUNG, THOMAS D

11. RENICK, KAREN
    A RENIE, JOSEPH B RENITA, JOSE C RENKO, DORIS D

12. ADLER, HELEN
    A ADLER, HAROLD B ADLER, HARRY C ADLER, HENRY D

13. BURKHARDT, ANN
    A BURKET, HARRIET B BURKHOLDER, CARL C BURKHOLZ, SCOTT D

14. DE LUCA, PAUL
    A DE LUCA, JOHN B DE LUCIA, AUDREY C DE LUCIA, ROBERT D

15. DEMBSKI, STEPHEN
    A DEMBLING, JOAN B DEMBNER, PETER C DEMBROW, HELEN D

1. ____
2. ____
3. ____
4. ____
5. ____
6. ____
7. ____
8. ____
9. ____
10. ____
11. ____
12. ____
13. ____
14. ____
15. ____

16. FLYNN, ARCHIE 16._____
 A FLYNN, AGNES B FLYNN, ANDREW C FLYNN, ANNMARIE D

17. GRAFFY, PAUL 17._____
 A GRAFMAN, ANDREW B GRAFSTEIN, BETTY C GRAFTON, MELVIN D

18. KERMIT, FRANK 18._____
 A KERMAN, LINDA B KERMISH, RHODA C KERMOYAN, MICKI D

19. METZLER, MAURICE 19._____
 A METZGER, ALFRED B METZIER, SONIA C METZINGER, PAUL D

20. PADDINGTON, TIMOTHY 20._____
 A PADDEN, MICHAEL B PADDISON, BRUCE C PADELL, EUNICE D

21. RICHARDSON, BLANCHE 21._____
 A RICHARDSON, BETTY B RICHARDSON, BEVERLY C RICHARDSON, BRENDA D

22. ISEKI, EMILE 22._____
 A ISELIN, CAROL B ISEN, RICHARD C ISENEE, CYNTHIA D

23. CONNELL, EUGENE 23._____
 A CONNELL, EDWARD B CONNELL, HELEN C CONNELL, HUGH D

24. MAC LEOD, LAURIE 24._____
 A MAC LEOD, LORNA B MC LANE, PAUL C MC LAREN, DUNCAN D

25. BOLE, KENNETH 25._____
 A BOLDEN, ROSIE B BOLDT, LINDA C BOLELLA, DENNIS D

KEY (CORRECT ANSWERS)

1.	B		11.	A
2.	D		12.	C
3.	B		13.	B
4.	C		14.	B
5.	B		15.	D
6.	D		16.	D
7.	C		17.	A
8.	C		18.	C
9.	A		19.	D
10.	C		20.	B

21. C
22. A
23. B
24. A
25. C

TEST 3

DIRECTIONS: For each of the following, you are given a name above and three other names in alphabetical order below. The letters A, B, C, and D stand for spaces where you could file the name. Find the CORRECT space for the name given above so that it will be in alphabetical order with the names below it. The letter that stands for that space is the answer to the question.

1. CARLISLE, ALAN
   A CARLINSKY, LEONA B CARLITOS, JUAN C CARLL, CHARLES D

2. COLLINS, KAREN
   A COLLINS, KATHLEEN B COLLINS, KATHRYN C COLLINS, KAY D

3. GALLOTTI, OSCAR
   A GALLONTY, FRANCIS B GALLOP, LILLIAN C GALLOU, ALEXIS D

4. MAHADY, JOHN
   A MAHADEO, PRATAB B MAHAJAN, ASHA C MAHARAJAH, MIARIAM D

5. WINGATE, REBECCA
   A WINGARD, LUCILLE B WINGAT, ROBERT C WINGER, HOLLY D

6. ZWEIGHAFT, FREDA
   A ZWEIG, BERTRAM B ZWEIGBAUM, BENJAMIN C ZWEIGENTHAL, DOROTHY D

7. MAXWELL, GEORGE
   A MAXWELL, EDWARD B MAXWELL, FRANK C MAXWELL, HARRIS D

8. O'DOHERTY, SALLY
   A ODETTE, CHARLES B ODIOTTI, MASSIE C ODNORALOV, MIKHAEL D

9. JAMES, ROGER
   A JAMIESON, KELLY B JAMNER, ELIZABETH C JAMPOLSKY, MILTON D

10. PADIN, FRANCIS
    A PADILLA, ANGELA B PADINGER, JENNY C PADLEY, RAYMOND D

11. AAARMAN, ALEC
    A AABY, JANE B AACH, ALBERT C AACHEN, HENRY D

12. BILLHARDT, PHILIP
    A BILLERA, FRANKLIN B BILLIG, LESLIE C BILLINGS, CAROL D

13. LADEROS, ELANA
    A LADENHEIM, HELENE B LADERMAN, SAM C LADHA, SANDRA D

14. PUCKERING, DENNIS
    A PUCKETT, AUDREY B PUCKNAT, JOHN C PUCKO, BENNY D

15. SCHOLZE, GEORGE
    A SCHOLNICK, LEONARD B SCHOLOSS, JACK C SCHOLZ, PAUL D

1. ____
2. ____
3. ____
4. ____
5. ____
6. ____
7. ____
8. ____
9. ____
10. ____
11. ____
12. ____
13. ____
14. ____
15. ____

16. WILSON, MERYL
   A WILSON, MERIMAN B WILSON, MERRY C WILSON, MERRYL D
   16.____

17. ZUKOWSKI, MICHAEL
   A ZWACK, ALEXA B ZYKO, KATHERINE C ZYMAN, HERBERT D
   17.____

18. MC CANNA, THOMAS
   A MC CANN, GERALD B MC CANNA, JANET C MC CANTS, MOLLIE D
   18.____

19. PHILIPP, SUSANE
   A PHILIP, PETER B PHILIPOSE, ANDREW C PHILIPPE, BEATRICE D
   19.____

20. KINGPIN, PAUL
   A KINGDON, KENNETH B KINGMAN, JEAN C KINGOLD, RICHARD D
   20.____

21. HAMILTON, DONALD
   A HAMILTON, DON B HAMILTON, DOROTHY C HAMILTON, DOUGLAS D
   21.____

22. BAEL, ELAINE
   A BAELE, GUSTAVE B BAEN, JAMES C BAENA, ARIEL D
   22.____

23. BILL, KASEY
   A BILGINER, NATHAN B BILKAY, WILLIAM C BILLES, BRADFORD D
   23.____

24. CARLEN, ELLIOT
   A CARINO, NAN B CARLE, JOHN C CARLESI, ANTHONY D
   24.____

25. LOURIE, DONALD
   A LOUIE, ROSE B LOUIS, STEVE C LOVE, MARCIA D
   25.____

KEY (CORRECT ANSWERS)

1.	B	11.	A
2.	A	12.	B
3.	C	13.	C
4.	B	14.	A
5.	C	15.	D
6.	D	16.	D
7.	C	17.	A
8.	D	18.	C
9.	A	19.	C
10.	B	20.	D

21. B
22. A
23. C
24. C
25. C

TEST 4

DIRECTIONS: For each of the following, you are given a name above and three other names in alphabetical order below. The letters A, B, C, and D stand for spaces where you could file the name. Find the CORRECT space for the name given above so that it will be in alphabetical order with the names below it. The letter that stands for that space is the answer to the question.

1. DEMOPOULOS, GUS
   A DEMOPOULOS, DIMITRI B DEMOPOULOS, HELEN C DEMOPOULOS, LAURA D
   1.____

2. DRUMWRIGHT, BRUCE
   A DRUMMOND, RANDY B DRUMMUND, WALTER C DRUMRIGHT, JULIUS D
   2.____

3. GRAHAM, LETICIA
   A GRAHAM, LEON B GRAHAM, LEROY C GRAHAM, LESLIE D
   3.____

4. KELLEHER, KEVIN
   A KELLARD, WILLIAM B KELLEDY, JAMES C KELLEHER, KRISTINE D
   4.____

5. LIANG, JAN
   A LIANG, JIE B LIANG, JIN CHANG C LIANG, JIN HE D
   5.____

6. MOLINELLI, STEVE
   A MOLINAR, RICARDO B MOLINER, LOUISA C MOLINI, OSCAR D
   6.____

7. PARRILLA, EMANUEL
   A PARRAS, TONY B PARRETTA, JOSEPHINE C PARRETTA, NANCY D
   7.____

8. SILBERFARD, MILDRED
   A SILBERBERG, SEYMOUR B SILBERBLATT, JOHN C SILBERFARB, SYLVIA D
   8.____

9. TOLANI, ROHET
   A TOLAN, DOROTHY B TOLASSI, JOANNA C TOLBERT, ALICE D
   9.____

10. VIERA, DIANE
    A VIERA, DIANA B VIERA, ELLIOT C VIERA, JAMES D
    10.____

11. KLAUER, MICHAEL
    A KLAUBER, ALFRED B KLAUBERG, SUSAN C KLAUS, MARJORIE D
    11.____

12. REEVES, MARIE
    A REEVES, MATTHEW B REEVES, MELVIN C REEVES, ORALEE D
    12.____

13. DEL VALLE, JULIA
    A DEL VALLE, EMMA B DEL VALLE, GLORIA C DEL VALLE, JOSEPH D
    13.____

14. LAIO, SHU-YU
    A LAING, VINCENT B LAIRO, SCOTT C LAIS, STEVE D
    14.____

15. MENDEZ, ROBERTO
    A MENDELSON, SOL B MENDES, MAE C MENDOZA, HUGO D
    15.____

2 (#4)

16. ALBRIGHT, LEE
    A ALBRACHT, MARIE B ALBRECHT, VICTOR C ALBRINK, JOAN D

16._____

17. CAIN, STEPHEN
    A CAIN, SAMUEL B CAIN, SHARON C CAIN, SIBOL D

17._____

18. HOPKOWITZ, THOMAS
    A HOPKINS, CYNTHIA B HOPPENFELD, DENIS C HOPPER, ELSA D

18._____

19. LUMBLY, KAREN
    A LUMBI, JENNY B LUME, JIMMIE C LUMEN, GAIL D

19._____

20. MAYER, MORTON
    A MAYER, MONROE B MAYER, MORRIS C MAYER, MYRON D

20._____

21. YOUNGER, LORRAINE
    A YOUNGHEM, THEODORE B YOUNGMAN, LEIF C YOUNGS, FRED D

21._____

22. THORSEN, HILDA
    A THORNWELL, PERCY B THORON, LLOYD C THORP, JACQUELINE D

22._____

23. MC DERMOTT, BETTY
    A MC DEARMON, WILLIAM B MC DEVITT, BERYL C MC DONAGH, DANIEL D

23._____

24. BLUMENTHAL, SIMON
    A BLUMENTHAL, SHIRLEY B BLUMENTHAL, SIDNEY C BLUMENTHAL, SOLOMON D

24._____

25. ERVINS, RICHARD
    A ERVIN, BERTHA B ERVING, THELMA C ERWIN, EUGENE D

25._____

KEY (CORRECT ANSWERS)

1.	B		11.	C
2.	D		12.	A
3.	D		13.	D
4.	C		14.	B
5.	A		15.	C
6.	B		16.	C
7.	D		17.	D
8.	D		18.	B
9.	B		19.	B
10.	B		20.	C

21. A
22. D
23. B
24. C
25. C

TEST 5

DIRECTIONS: For each of the following, you are given a name above and three other names in alphabetical order below. The letters A, B, C, and D stand for spaces where you could file the name. Find the CORRECT space for the name given above so that it will be in alphabetical order with the names below it. The letter that stands for that space is the answer to the question.

1. GUIDRY, THELMA
   A GUIDONE, GEORGE B GUIGLI, PAMELA C GUIGNON, DANIEL D

2. JAMES, ALLAN
   A JAMES, ALMA B JAMES, AMY C JAMES, ANNA D

3. LESSOFF, CONNIE
   A LESSIK, JAKE B LESSING, LEONARD C LESSNER, ADELE D

4. MONTNER, LUIS
   A MONTEFIORE, ANDREW B MONTILLA, IRIS C MONTINI, ALEXANDRA D

5. PHELPS, KENNETH
   A PHELEN, JAMES B PHELON, RANDY C PHETT, GARY D

6. STAVSKY, STANLEY
   A STAVROS, MIKE B STAWSKI, LILLIAN C STAWSKI, NAOMI D

7. GROSSMAN, WILL
   A GROSSMAN, WENDY B GROSSMANN, WAYNE C GROSSMANN, WILLA D

8. IRES, JEFFREY
   A IRENA, THOMAS B IRENE, JAY C IRES, HOWARD D

9. NIKOLAOU, CHRISTINE
   A NIKOLAIS, GERRARD B NIKOLAKAKOS, GEORGE C NIKOLATOS, HARRY D

10. TURCO, KEITH
    A TURCHIN, DEBORAH B TURCI, GINA C TURCK, KATHRYN D

11. WORLEY, DIANE
    A WORMAN, STELLA B WORMER, SARA C WORMLEY, ROBERT D

12. DRUSIN, GUY
    A DRURY, JESSICA B DRUSE, KEN C DRUSS, THERESA D

13. LYONS, JAMES
    A LYONS, ERNST B LYONS, INGRID C LYONS, KEVIN D

14. NOBLE, BERNARD
    A NOBEL, LOUISE B NOBILE, DENNIS C NOBIS, JAMES D

15. O'DELL, ERIN
    A O'DAY, PATRICIA B O'DEA, MAUREEN C O'DELL, GWYNN D

16. POUPON, LOUIS   16.____
    A POULSON, SIMON B POURE, DAMIAN C POURIDAS, CARMEN D

17. REMEY, NAOMI   17.____
    A REMES, STUART B REMEZ, ALFREDO C REMIEN, ROBERT D

18. WATSON, LAURENCE   18.____
    A WATSON, LENORA B WATSON, LEONARD C WATSON, LLOYD D

19. AMSILI, MORTON   19.____
    A AMSDEN, ESTHER B AMSEL, HYMAN C ARES, MEYER D

20. CLEMMONS, BERTHA   20.____
    A CLEMENT, GILBERT B CLEMINSON, DEAN C CLEMONS, GLADYS D

21. LAMPERT, EDNA   21.____
    A LAMPIER, JANICE B LAMPKIN, ALYCE C LAMPKOWSKI, DENNIS D

22. LIBERTO, DON   22.____
    A LIBERMAN, MATTIE B LIBERSON, MIRIAM C LIBERTY, ARTHUR D

23. REVENZON, ISABELLA   23.____
    A REVELEY, RUTH B REVELLE, GRACE C REVERE, EDITH D

24. BURKHALTER, HAZEL   24.____
    A BURKE, WINSTON B BURKETT, BENJAMIN C BURKEY, WAYNE D

25. DORSEY, HAROLD   25.____
    A DOSHER, EILEEN B DOSHIRE, BURTON C DOSSIL, RICHARD D

KEY (CORRECT ANSWERS)

1.	B	11.	A
2.	A	12.	C
3.	D	13.	C
4.	D	14.	D
5.	C	15.	C
6.	B	16.	B
7.	B	17.	B
8.	D	18.	A
9.	C	19.	C
10.	D	20.	C

21. A
22. C
23. C
24. D
25. A

TEST 6

DIRECTIONS: For each of the following, you are given a name above and three other names in alphabetical order below. The letters A, B, C, and D stand for spaces where you could file the name. Find the CORRECT space for the name given above so that it will be in alphabetical order with the names below it. The letter that stands for that space is the answer to the question.

1. HATFIELD, NICOLA
A HATCHER, JOHN B HATELY, BRIAN C HATGIS, ELLEN D
1._____

2. IVANOFF, HELENA
A IVAN, LEONARD B IVANOV, SERGE C IVANY, EMERY D
2._____

3. KELKER, NORMAN
A KELFER, STEPHANE B KELING, JAY C KELISON, ABE D
3._____

4. ROGGENBURG, LEE
A ROGERS, SHARON B ROGET, ALLAN C ROGGERO, MORGAN D
4._____

5. SMITH, ALENA
A SMITH, AARON B SMITH, AGNES C SMITH, ALBERT D
5._____

6. ZOLOR, RONALD
A ZOLNAK, SUSANNA B ZOLOTH, SAMUEL C ZOLOTO, PEARL D
6._____

7. ERRICH, GRETCHEN
A ERREICH, RENE B ERRERA, STEVEN C ERRETT, ALICE D
7._____

8. CARDWELL, MELASAN
A CARDUCCI, RONALD B CARDULLO, MIKE C CARDY, FREDRIK D
8._____

9. MOFFAT, SARAH
A MOFFET, JONATHAN B MOFFIE, LISA C MOFFITT, LAUREN D
9._____

10. PARRINO, WAYNE
A PARRETTA, MICHELE B PARRILLA, BERNIE C PARRINELLO, CARRIE D
10._____

11. PINSLEY, SETH
A PINSKY, GLORIA B PINSON, BENNET C PINTADO, MARIE D
11._____

12. FREEMAN, ELMIRA
A FREEMAN, EDITH B FREEMAN, ERIC C FREEMAN, ETHEL D
12._____

13. BERLINGER, SOPHIE
A BERLEY, DAVID B BERLIND, ARNOLD C BERLINGER, FREDA D
13._____

14. ANIELLO, JOSEPH
A ANGULO, ADOLFO B ANHALT, LINDA C ANIBAL, VINCENT D
14._____

15. LACHER, LEO
A LACHET, MARGARET B LACHINI, KAY C LACHIVER, ANDREA D
15._____

16. ROBINSON, MARION
    <u>A</u> ROBINSON, MARCIA <u>B</u> ROBINSON, MARGARET <u>C</u> ROBINSON, MARIETTA <u>D</u>

17. ULRICH, DENNIS
    <u>A</u> ULMAN, CANDY <u>B</u> ULMER, TED <u>C</u> ULRIED, RICHARD <u>D</u>

18. ASHINSKY, ROSS
    <u>A</u> ASHKAR, MICHAEL <u>B</u> ASHKE, PAUL <u>C</u> ASHKIN, ROBERTA <u>D</u>

19. LITVAK, DARRELL
    <u>A</u> LITUCHY, BEVERLY <u>B</u> LITVIN, SAM <u>C</u> LITWACK, MARTIN <u>D</u>

20. SLATTERY, GERALD
    <u>A</u> SLATER, NELLIE <u>B</u> SLATKIN, HEIDI <u>C</u> SLATKY, IRVING <u>D</u>

21. MCCANTS, GEORGIA
    <u>A</u> MCCANN, CHERYL <u>B</u> MCCANNA, THOMAS <u>C</u> MCCARDELL, GARY <u>D</u>

22. HARMER, AVA
    <u>A</u> HARLOW, JULES <u>B</u> HARLSON, NORMAN <u>C</u> HARMEL, SHARON <u>D</u>

23. CALDERONE, PHILIP
    <u>A</u> CALDERIN, ANA <u>B</u> CALDON, WALTER <u>C</u> CALDRON, MICHELE <u>D</u>

24. GINSBURG, ISAAC
    <u>A</u> GINSBURG, EDWARD <u>B</u> GINSBURG, GERALD <u>C</u> GINSBURG, HILDA <u>D</u>

25. LEE, LEIGH
    <u>A</u> LEE, LELA <u>B</u> LEE, LELAND <u>C</u> LEE, LEON <u>D</u>

KEY (CORRECT ANSWERS)

1. C		11. B	
2. B		12. B	
3. D		13. D	
4. C		14. D	
5. D		15. A	
6. B		16. D	
7. D		17. C	
8. C		18. A	
9. A		19. B	
10. D		20. D	

21. C
22. D
23. B
24. D
25. A

TEST 7

DIRECTIONS: For each of the following, you are given a name above and three other names in alphabetical order below. The letters A, B, C, and D stand for spaces where you could file the name. Find the CORRECT space for the name given above so that it will be in alphabetical order with the names below it. The letter that stands for that space is the answer to the question.

1. POWERS, PHYLLIS
   A POWELL, HATTIE B POWER, EDWARD C POWLETT, WENDY D   1._____

2. SILVERA, IRWIN
   A SILVA, ANGEL B SILVANO, FRANK C SILVERIA, ANNA D   2._____

3. BACHRACH, DAN
   A BACHMANN, DONNA B BACHNER, LESTER C BACHOWSKI, JEWEL D   3._____

4. RIVERA, RAMON
   A RIVAS, ERICA B RIVES, SHARON C RIVIER, CLAUDE D   4._____

5. WEINSTOCK, JEFFREY
   A WEINSTEIN, PAUL B WEINSTONE, ALAN C WEINTRAUB, MARCI D   5._____

6. AMANDA, STEPHAN
   A AMADO, DANIELLO B AMALIA, JOSE C AMAR, LISA D   6._____

7. HERRON, LOUIS
   A HERSCH, JACK B HERSCHELL, GREGORY C HERSCHER, GAIL D   7._____

8. REEDY, ARTHUR
   A REED, ALEX B REESE, JOHN C REEVE, DAVE D   8._____

9. FLORIN, RAYMOND
   A FLORENTINO, PAULA B FLORES, MITCHEL C FLORIAN, CARLO D   9._____

10. HOROWITZ, ELLIOT
    A HOROWITZ, FRANKLIN B HOROWITZ, IRA C HOROWITZ, JOAN D   10._____

11. KNOPFLER, WOODY
    A KNOBLER, HENRY B KNOLL, GEORGE C KNOPF, LAURA D   11._____

12. OTIN, JENNIFER
    A OTERO, ALBERT B OTHON, DOROTHY C OTIS, JAMES D   12._____

13. SACHA, IRENE
    A SACCO, HEATHER B SACHNER, JULIE C SACHS, DAVID D   13._____

14. WORTHY, PRISCILLA
    A WORTH, ROBERT B WORTHINGTON, SUSAN C WORTMAN, MYRA D   14._____

15. ZUCKERMAN, GARY
    A ZUKER, JEROME B ZUKOWSKI, CHRIS C ZULACK, JOHN D   15._____

16. BRIEGER, CLARENCE 16._____
    A BRIEF, SIGMUND B BRIELLE, JEAN C BRIELOFF, SAUL D

17. FOSTER, AGNES 17._____
    A FOSTER, ADDIE B FOSTER, ALBERT C FOSTER, ALICE D

18. LIBERSTEIN, MIRIAM 18._____
    A LIBERMAN, HERMAN B LIBERSON, RUBIN C LIBERT, NAT D

19. PRICKETT, DELORES 19._____
    A PRICE, WILLIAM B PRICHARD, STEPHANY C PRITCHETT, KENNETH D

20. TRIBBLE, RITA 20._____
    A TRIAS, JOSE B TRIBBIT, CHARLES C TRIBE, SIENNA D

21. ZOBEL, MAX 21._____
    A ZOBACK, DERRICK B ZOBALI, KIERSTAN C ZOBERG, STUART D

22. HOTRA, WALTER 22._____
    A HOTT, NELL B HOTTENSEN, ROBERT C HOTTON, BRUCE D

23. MICHELL, CARL 23._____
    A MICHELE, KAREN B MICHELMAN, BERTHA C MICHELS, GLORIA D

24. RAFFERTY, GEORGE 24._____
    A RAFFERTY, HAROLD B RAFFERTY, KEVIN C RAFFERTY, LUCILLE D

25. OLIVIERI, ALLAN 25._____
    A OLIVIERO, FRANK B OLIVRY, RAUL C OLIZEIRA, CHARLES D

KEY (CORRECT ANSWERS)

1. C
2. C
3. D
4. B
5. B

6. C
7. A
8. B
9. D
10. A

11. D
12. C
13. B
14. C
15. A

16. B
17. B
18. C
19. C
20. C

21. C
22. A
23. B
24. A
25. A

NAME AND NUMBER CHECKING
EXAMINATION SECTION
TEST 1

DIRECTIONS: Questions 1 through 17 consist of sets of names and addresses. In each question, the name and address in Column II should be an exact copy of the name and address in Column I.
If there is:
a mistake only in the name, mark your answer A;
a mistake only in the address, mark your answer B;
a mistake in both name and address, mark your answer C;
No mistake in either name or address, mark your answer D.

Sample Question

Column I
Christina Magnusson
288 Greene Street
New York, N.Y. 10003

Column II
Christina Magnusson
288 Greene Street
New York, N.Y. 10013

Since there is a mistake only in the address (the zip code should be 10003 instead of 10013), the answer to the sample question is B.

COLUMN I

COLUMN II

1. Ms. Joan Kelly
   313 Franklin Avenue
   Brooklyn, N.Y. 11202

   Ms. Joan Kielly
   318 Franklin Ave.
   Brooklyn, N.Y. 11202

   1.____

2. Mrs. Eileen Engel
   47-24 86 Road
   Queens, N.Y. 11122

   Mrs. Ellen Engel
   47-24 86 Road
   Queens, New York 11122

   2.____

3. Marcia Michaels
   213 E. 81 St.
   New York, N.Y. 10012

   Marcia Michaels
   213 E. 81 St.
   New York, N.Y. 10012

   3.____

4. Rev. Edward J. Smyth
   1401 Brandeis Street
   San Francisco, Calif. 96201

   Rev. Edward J. Smyth
   1401 Brandies Street
   San Francisco, Calif. 96201

   4.____

5. Alicia Rodriguez
   24-68 82 St.
   Elmhurst, N.Y. 11122

   Alicia Rodriguez
   2468 81 St.
   Elmhurst, N.Y. 11122

   5.____

2 (#1)

COLUMN I	COLUMN II	
6. Ernest Eisemann 21 Columbia St. New York, N.Y. 10007	Ernest Eisermann 21 Columbia St. New York, N.Y. 10007	6._____
7. Mr. & Mrs. George Petersson 87-11 91st Avenue Woodhaven, N.Y. 11421	Mr. & Mrs. George Peterson 87-11 91st Avenue Woodhaven, N.Y. 11421	7._____
8. Mr. Ivan Klebnikov 1848 Newkirk Avenue Brooklyn, N.Y. 11226	Mr. Ivan Klebikov 1848 Newkirk Avenue Brooklyn, N.Y. 11622	8._____
9. Mr. Samuel Rothfleisch 71 Pine Street New York, N.Y. 10005	Samuel Rothfleisch 71 Pine Street New York, N.Y. 100005	9._____
10. Mrs. Isabel Tonnessen 198 East 185th Street Bronx, N.Y. 10458	Mrs. Isabel Tonnessen 189 East 185th Street Bronx, N.Y. 10348	10._____
11. Esteban Perez 173 Eighth Street Staten Island, N.Y. 10306	Estaban Perez 173 Eighth Street Staten Island, N.Y. 10306	11._____
12. Esta Wong 141 West 68 St. New York, N.Y. 10023	Esta Wang 141 West 68 St. New York, N.Y. 10023	12._____
13. Dr. Alberto Grosso 3475 12th Avenue Brooklyn, N.Y. 11218	Dr. Alberto Grosso 3475 12th Avenue Brooklyn, N.Y. 11218	13._____
14. Mrs. Ruth Bortias 482 Theresa Ct. Far Rockaway, N.Y. 11691	Ms. Ruth Bortlas 482 Theresa Ct. Far Rockaway, N.Y. 11169	14._____
15. Mr. & Mrs. Howard Fox 2301 Sedgwick Ave. Bronx, N.Y. 10468	Mr. & Mrs. Howard Fox 231 Sedgwick Ave. Bronx, N.Y. 10468	15._____
16. Miss Marjorie Black 223 East 23 Street New York, N.Y. 10010	Miss Margorie Black 223 East 23 Street New York, N.Y. 10010	16._____

COLUMN I | COLUMN II

17. Michelle Herman   Michelle Hermann   17.____
    806 Valley Rd.   806 Valley Dr.
    Old Tappan, N.J. 07675   Old Tappan, N.J. 07675

KEY (CORRECT ANSWERS)

1.	C	7.	A	13.	D
2.	A	8.	C	14.	C
3.	D	9.	D	15.	B
4.	B	10.	B	16.	A
5.	B	11.	A	17.	C
6.	A	12.	D		

TEST 2

DIRECTIONS: Questions 1 through 15 are to be answered SOLELY on the instructions given below. *PRINT THE LETTER OF THE CORRECT ANSWER IN THE SPACE AT THE RIGHT.*

INSTRUCTIONS

In each of the following questions, the 3-line name and address in Column I is the master-list entry, and the 3-line entry in Column II is the information to be checked against the master list. If there is one line that does not match, mark your answer A; if there are two lines that do not match, mark your answer B; if all three lines do not match, mark your answer C; if the lines all match exactly, mark your answer D.

Sample Question

Column I
Mark L. Field
11-09 Price Park Blvd.
Bronx, N.Y. 11402

Column II
Mark L. Field
11-99 Prince Park Way
Bronx, N.Y. 11401

The first lines in each column match exactly. The second lines do not match since 11-09 does not match 11-<u>99</u>; and Blvd. does not match <u>Way</u>. The third lines do not match either since 1140<u>2</u> does not match 1140<u>1</u>. Therefore, there are two lines that do not match, and the CORRECT answer is B.

COLUMN I | COLUMN II

1. Jerome A. Jackson
   1243 14th Avenue
   New York, N.Y. 10023

   Jerome A. Johnson
   1234 14th Avenue
   New York, N.Y. 10023

   1.____

2. Sophie Strachtheim
   33-28 Connecticut Ave.
   Far Rockaway, N.Y. 11697

   Sophie Strachtheim
   33-28 Connecticut Ave.
   Far Rockaway, N.Y. 11697

   2.____

3. Elisabeth N.T. Gorrell
   256 Exchange St.
   New York, N.Y. 10013

   Elizabeth N.T. Gorrell
   256 Exchange St.
   New York, N.Y. 10013

   3.____

4. Maria J. Gonzalez
   7516 E. Sheepshead Rd.
   Brooklyn, N.Y. 11240

   Maria J. Gonzalez
   7516 N. Shepshead Rd.
   Brooklyn, N.Y. 11240

   4.____

5. Leslie B. Brautenweiler
   21 57A Seiler Terr.
   Flushing, N.Y. 11367

   Leslie B. Brautenwieler
   21-75A Seiler Terr.
   Flushing, N.J. 11367

   5.____

2 (#2)

	COLUMN I	COLUMN II	
6.	Rigoberto J. Peredes 157 Twin Towers, #18F Tottenville, S. I., N.Y,	Rigoberto J. Peredes 157 Twin Towers, #18F Tottenville, S.I., N.Y.	6.____
7.	Pietro F. Albino P.O. Box 7548 Floral Park, N.Y. 11005	Pietro F. Albina P.O. Box 7458 Floral Park, N.Y. 11005	7.____
8.	Joanne Zimmerman Bldg. SW, Room 314 532-4601	Joanne Zimmermann Bldg. SW, Room 314 532-4601	8.____
9.	Carlyle Whetstone Payroll Div. –A, Room 212A 262-5000, ext. 471	Carlyle Whetstone Payroll Div. –A, Room 212A 262-5000, ext. 417	9.____
10.	Kenneth Chiang Legal Council, Room 9745 (201) 416-9100, ext. 17	Kenneth Chiang Legal Counsel, Room 9745 (201) 416-9100, Ext. 17	10.____
11.	Ethel Koenig Personnel Services Division, Room 433; 635-7572	Ethel Hoenig Personal Services Division, Room 433; 635-7527	11.____
12.	Joyce Ehrhardt Office of the Administrator, Room W56; 387-8706	Joyce Ehrhart Office of the Administrator, Room W56; 387-7806	12.____
13.	Ruth Lang EAM Bldg., Room C101 625-2000, ext. 765	Ruth Lang EAM Bldg., Room C110 625-2000, ext. 765	13.____
14.	Anne Marie Ionozzi Investigations, Room 827 576-4000, ext. 832	Anna Marie Ionozzi Investigation, Room 827 566-4000, ext. 832	14.____
15.	Willard Jameson Fm C Bldg., Room 687 454-3010	Willard Jamieson Fm C Bldg., Room 687 454-3010	15.____

KEY (CORRECT ANSWERS)

1.	B	6.	D		C
2.	D	7.	B	12.	B
3.	A	8.	D	13.	A
4.	A	9.	B	14.	C
5.	C	10.	A	15.	A

TEST 3

DIRECTIONS: Questions 1 through 10 are to be answered on the basis of the following instructions. *PRINT THE LETTER OF THE CORRECT ANSWER IN THE SPACE AT THE RIGHT.*

INSTRUCTIONS

For each such set of names, addresses, and numbers listed in Columns I and II, select your answer from the following options:
The names in Columns I and II are different,
The addresses in Columns I and II are different,
The numbers in Columns I and II are different,
The names, addresses, and numbers in Columns I and II are identical.

	COLUMN I	COLUMN II	
1.	Francis Jones 62 Stately Avenue 96-12446	Francis Jones 62 Stately Avenue 96-21446	1.____
2.	Julio Montez 19 Ponderosa Road 56-73161	Julio Montez 19 Ponderosa Road 56-71361	2.____
3.	Mary Mitchell 2314 Melbourne Drive 68-92172	Mary Mitchell 2314 Melbourne Drive 68-92172	3.____
4.	Harry Patterson 25 Dunne Street 14-33430	Harry Patterson 25 Dunne Street 14-34330	4.____
5.	Patrick Murphy 171 West Hosmer Street 93-81214	Patrick Murphy 171 West Hosmer Street 93-18214	5.____
6.	August Schultz 816 St. Clair Avenue 53-40149	August Schultz 816 St. Claire Avenue 53-40149	6.____
7.	George Taft 72 Runnymede Street 47-04033	George Taft 72 Runnymede Street 47-04023	7.____
8.	Angus Henderson 1418 Madison Street 81-76375	Angus Henderson 1318 Madison Street 81-76375	8.____

2 (#3)

COLUMN I	COLUMN II	
9. Carolyn Mazur 12 Riverview Road 38-99615	Carolyn Mazur 12 Rivervane Road 38-99615	9.____
10. Adele Russell 1725 Lansing Lane 72-91962	Adela Russell 1725 Lansing Lane 72-91962	10.____

KEY (CORRECT ANSWERS)

1. C   6. B
2. C   7. C
3. D   8. D
4. C   9. B
5. C   10. A

TEST 4

DIRECTIONS: Questions 1 through 20 test how good you are at catching mistakes in typing or printing. In each question, the name and address in Column II should be an exact copy of the name and address in Column I. Mark your answer
A. If there is no mistake in either name or address;
B. If there is a mistake in both name and address;
C. If there is a mistake only in the name;
D. If there is a mistake only in the address.
PRINT THE LETTER OF THE CORRECT ANSWER IN THE SPACE AT THE RIGHT.

COLUMN I

COLUMN II

1. Milos Yanocek
33-60 14 Street
Long Island City, N.Y. 11011

   Milos Yanocek
   33-60 14 Street
   Long Island City, N.Y. 11001

   1.____

2. Alphonse Sabattelo
24 Minnetta Lane
New York, N.Y. 10006

   Alphonse Sabbattelo
   24 Minetta Lane
   New York, N.Y. 10006

   2.____

3. Helen Steam
5 Metropolitan Oval
Bronx, N.Y. 10462

   Helene Stearn
   5 Metropolitan Oval
   Bronx, N.Y. 10462

   3.____

4. Jacob Weisman
231 Francis Lewis Boulevard
Forest Hills, N.Y. 11325

   Jacob Weisman
   231 Francis Lewis Boulevard
   Forest Hills, N.Y. 11325

   4.____

5. Riccardo Fuente
134 West 83 Street
New York, N.Y. 10024

   Riccardo Fuentes
   134 West 88 Street
   New York, N.Y. 10024

   5.____

6. Dennis Lauber
52 Avenue D
Brooklyn, N.Y. 11216

   Dennis Lauder
   52 Avenue D
   Brooklyn, N.Y. 11216

   6.____

7. Paul Cutter
195 Galloway Avenue
Staten Island, N.Y. 10356

   Paul Cutter
   175 Galloway Avenue
   Staten Island, N.Y. 10365

   7.____

8. Sean Donnelly
45-58 41 Avenue
Woodside, N.Y. 11168

   Sean Donnelly
   45-58 41 Avenue
   Woodside, N.Y. 11168

   8.____

9. Clyde Willot
1483 Rockaway Avenue
Brooklyn, N.Y. 11238

   Clyde Willat
   1483 Rockaway Avenue
   Brooklyn, N.Y. 11238

   9.____

2 (#4)

COLUMN I	COLUMN II	
10. Michael Stanakis 419 Sheriden Avenue Staten Island, N.Y. 10363	Michael Stanakis 419 Sheraden Avenue Staten Island, N.Y. 10363	10.____
11. Joseph DiSilva 63-84 Saunders Road Rego Park, N.Y. 11431	Joseph Disilva 64-83 Saunders Road Rego Park, N.Y. 11431	11.____
12. Linda Polansky 2224 Fendon Avenue Bronx, N.Y. 20464	Linda Polansky 2255 Fenton Avenue Bronx, N.Y. 10464	12.____
13. Alfred Klein 260 Hillside Terrace Staten Island, N.Y. 15545	Alfred Klein 260 Hillside Terrace Staten Island, N.Y. 15545	13.____
14. William McDonnell 504 E. 55 Street New York, N.Y. 10103	William McConnell 504 E. 55 Street New York, N.Y. 10108	14.____
15. Angela Cipolla 41-11 Parson Avenue Flushing, N.Y. 11446	Angela Cipola 41-11 Parsons Avenue Flushing, N.Y. 11446	15.____
16. Julie Sheridan 1212 Ocean Avenue Brooklyn, N.Y. 11237	Julia Sheridan 1212 Ocean Avenue Brooklyn, N.Y. 11237	16.____
17. Arturo Rodriguez 2156 Cruger Avenue Bronx, N.Y. 10446	Arturo Rodrigues 2156 Cruger Avenue Bronx, N.Y. 10446	17.____
18. Helen McCabe 2044 East 19 Street Brooklyn, N.Y. 11204	Helen McCabe 2040 East 19 Street Brooklyn, N.Y. 11204	18.____
19. Charles Martin 526 West 160 Street New York, N.Y. 10022	Charles Martin 526 West 160 Street New York, N.Y. 10022	19.____
20. Morris Rabinowitz 31 Avenue M Brooklyn, N.Y. 11216	Morris Rabinowitz 31 Avenue N Brooklyn, N.Y. 11216	20.____

KEY (CORRECT ANSWERS)

1.	D	11.	B
2.	B	12.	D
3.	C	13.	A
4.	A	14.	B
5.	B	15.	B
6.	C	16.	C
7.	D	17.	C
8.	A	18.	D
9.	B	19.	A
10.	D	20.	D

TEST 5

DIRECTIONS: In copying the addresses below from Column A to the same line in Column B, an Agent-in-Training made some errors. For Questions 1 through 5, if you find that the agent made an error in
only one line, mark your answer A;
only two lines, mark your answer B;
only three lines, mark your answer C;
all four lines, mark your answer D.

EXAMPLE

COLUMN A	COLUMN B
24 Third Avenue	24 Third Avenue
5 Lincoln Road	5 Lincoln Street
50 Central Park West	6 Central Park West
37-21 Queens Boulevard	21-37 Queens Boulevard

Since errors were made on only three lines, namely the second, third, and fourth, the CORRECT answer is C.
PRINT THE LETTER OF THE CORRECT ANSWER IN THE SPACE AT THE RIGHT.

COLUMN A   COLUMN B

1. 57-22 Springfield Boulevard   75-22 Springfield Boulevard   1._____
    94 Gun Hill Road   94 Gun Hill Avenue
    8 New Dorp Lane   8 New Drop Lane
    36 Bedford Avenue   36 Bedford Avenue

2. 538 Castle Hill Avenue   538 Castle Hill Avenue   2._____
    54-15 Beach Channel Drive   54-15 Beach Channel Drive
    21 Ralph Avenue   21 Ralph Avenue
    162 Madison Avenue   162 Morrison Avenue

3. 49 Thomas Street   49 Thomas Street   3._____
    27-21 Northern Blvd.   21-27 Northern Blvd.
    86 125th Street   86 125th Street
    872 Atlantic Ave.   872 Baltic Ave,

4. 261-17 Horace Harding Expwy.   261-17 Horace Harding Pkwy.   4._____
    191 Fordham Road   191 Fordham Road
    6 Victory Blvd.   6 Victoria Blvd.
    552 Oceanic Ave.   552 Ocean Ave.

5. 90-05 38th Avenue   90-05 36th Avenue   5._____
    19 Central Park West   19 Central Park East
    9281 Avenue X   9281 Avenue X
    22 West Farms Square   22 West Farms Square

KEY (CORRECT ANSWERS)

1. C
2. A
3. B
4. C
5. B

TEST 6

DIRECTIONS: For Questions 1 through 10, choose the letter in Column II next to the number which EXACTLY matches the number in Column I. *PRINT THE LETTER OF THE CORRECT ANSWER IN THE SPACE AT THE RIGHT.*

<u>COLUMN I</u>   <u>COLUMN II</u>

1. 14235
   - A. 13254
   - B. 12435
   - C. 13245
   - D. 14235

   1.____

2. 70698
   - A. 90768
   - B. 60978
   - C. 70698]
   - D. 70968

   2.____

3. 11698
   - A. 11689
   - B. 11986
   - C. 11968
   - D. 11698

   3.____

4. 50497
   - A. 50947
   - B. 50497
   - C. 50749
   - D. 54097

   4.____

5. 69635
   - A. 60653
   - B. 69630
   - C. 69365
   - D. 69635

   5.____

6. 1201022011
   - A. 1201022011
   - B. 1201020211
   - C. 1202012011
   - D. 1021202011

   6.____

7. 3893981389
   - A. 3893891389
   - B. 3983981389
   - C. 3983891389
   - D. 3893981389

   7.____

8. 4765476589
   - A. 4765476598
   - B. 4765476588
   - C. 4765476589
   - D. 4765746589

   8.____

70

9. 8679678938   A. 8679687938   9.____
                           B. 8679678938
                           C. 8697678938
                           D. 8678678938

10. 6834836932   A. 6834386932   10.____
                           B. 6834836923
                           C. 6843836932
                           D. 6834836932

Questions 11-15.

DIRECTIONS: For Questions 11 through 15, determine how many of the symbols in Column Z are exactly the same as the symbol in Column Y.
If none is exactly the same, answer A;
If only one symbol is exactly the same, answer B;
If two symbols are exactly the same, answer C;
If three symbols are exactly the same, answer D.

COLUMN Y	COLUMN Z	
11. A123B1266	A123B1366 A123B1266 A133B1366 A123B1266	11.____
12. CC28D3377	CD22D3377 CC38D3377 CC28C3377 CC28D2277	12.____
13. M21AB201X	M12AB201X M21AB201X M21AB201Y M21BA201X	13.____
14. PA383Y744	AP383Y744 PA338Y744 PA388Y744 PA383Y774	14.____
15. PB2Y8893	PB2Y8893 PB2Y8893 PB3Y8898 PB2Y8893	15.____

KEY (CORRECT ANSWERS)

1.	D	6.	A	11.	C
2.	C	7.	D	12.	A
3.	D	8.	C	13.	B
4.	B	9.	B	14.	A
5.	D	10.	D	15.	D

CODING

EXAMINATION SECTION

COMMENTARY

An ingenious question-type called coding, involving elements of alphabetizing, filing, name and number comparison, and evaluative judgment and application, has currently won wide acceptance in testing circles for measuring clerical aptitude and general ability, particularly on the senior (middle) grades (levels).

While the directions for this question usually vary in detail, the candidate is generally asked to consider groups of names, codes, and numbers, and then, according to a given plan, to arrange codes in alphabetic order; to arrange these in numerical sequence; to re-arrange columns of names and numbers in correct order; to espy errors in coding; to choose the correct coding arrangement in consonance with the given directions and examples, etc.

This question-type appear to have few parameters in respect to form, substance, or degree of difficulty.

Accordingly, acquaintance with, and practice in, the coding question is recommended for the serious candidate.

TEST 1

DIRECTIONS: Questions 1 through 8 are to be answered on the basis of the code table and the instructions given below.

Code Letter for Traffic Problem	B	H	Q	J	F	L	M	I
Code Number for Action Taken	1	2	3	4	5	6	7	8

Assume that each of the capital letters on the above chart is a radio code for a particular traffic problem and that the number immediately below each capital letter is the radio code for the correct action to be taken to deal with the problem. For instance, "1" is the action to be taken to deal with problem "B", "2" is the action to be taken to deal with problem "H", and so forth.

In each question, a series of code letters is given in Column 1. Column 2 gives four different arrangements of code numbers. You are to pick the answer (A, B, C, or D) in Column 2 that gives the code numbers that match the code letters in the same order.

SAMPLE QUESTION

Column 1
BHLFMQ

Column 2
A. 125678
B. 216573
C. 127653
D. 126573

According to the chart, the code numbers that correspond to these code letters are as follows: B – 1, M – 2, L – 6, F – 5, M – 7, Q – 3. Therefore, the right answer is 126573. This answer is D in Column 2.

2 (#1)

      <u>Column 1</u>   <u>Column 2</u>

1. BHQLMI
   - A. 123456
   - B. 123567
   - C. 123678
   - D. 125678

   1.____

2. HBJQLF
   - A. 214365
   - B. 213456
   - C. 213465
   - D. 214387

   2.____

3. QHMLFJ
   - A. 321654
   - B. 345678
   - C. 327645
   - D. 327654

   3.____

4. FLQJIM
   - A. 543287
   - B. 563487
   - C. 564378
   - D. 654378

   4.____

5. FBIHMJ
   - A. 518274
   - B. 152874
   - C. 528164
   - D. 517842

   5.____

6. MIHFQB
   - A. 872341
   - B. 782531
   - C. 782341
   - D. 783214

   6.____

7. JLFHQIM
   - A. 465237
   - B. 456387
   - C. 4652387
   - D. 4562387

   7.____

8. LBJQIFH
   - A. 614382
   - B. 6134852
   - C. 61437852
   - D. 61431852

   8.____

KEY (CORRECT ANSWERS)

1. C
2. A
3. D
4. B
5. A
6. B
7. C
8. A

TEST 2

DIRECTIONS: Each question or incomplete statement is followed by several suggested answers or completions. Select the one that BEST answers the question or completes the statement. *PRINT THE LETTER OF THE CORRECT ANSWER IN THE SPACE AT THE RIGHT.*

Questions 1-5.

DIRECTIONS: Questions 1 through 5 are based on the following list showing the name and number of each of nine inmates.

1. Johnson   4. Thompson   7. Gordon
2. Smith   5. Frank   8. Porter
3. Edwards   6. Murray   9. Lopez

Each question consists of 3 sets of numbers and letters. Each set should consist of the numbers of three inmates and the first letter of each of their names. The letters should be in the same order as the numbers. In at least two of the three choices, there will be an error. On your answer sheet, mark only that choice in which the letters correspond with the numbers and are in the same order. If all three sets are wrong, mark choice D in your answer space.

SAMPLE QUESTION
A. 386 EPM
B. 542 FST
C. 474 LGT

Since 3 corresponds to E for Edwards, 8 corresponds to P for Porter, and 6 corresponds to M for Murray, choice A is correct and should be entered in your answer space. Choice B is wrong because letters T and S have been reversed. Choice C is wrong because the first number, which is 4, does NOT correspond with the first letter of choice C, which is L. It should have been T. If choice A were also wrong, then D would be the correct answer.

1. A. 382 EGS   B. 461 TMJ   C. 875 PLF   1._____

2. A. 549 FLT   B. 692 MJS   C. 758 GSP   2._____

3. A. 936 LEM   B. 253 FSE   C. 147 JTL   3._____

4. A. 569 PML   B. 716 GJP   C. 842 PTS   4._____

5. A. 356 FEM   B. 198 JPL   C. 637 MEG   5._____

Questions 6-10.

DIRECTIONS: Questions 6 through 10 are to be answered on the basis of the following information:

2 (#3)

In order to make sure stock is properly located, incoming units are stored as follows:

STOCK NUMBERS	BIN NUMBERS
00100 – 39999	D30, L44
40000 – 69999	14L, D38
70000 – 99999	41L, 80D
100000 and over	614, 83D

Using the above table, choose the answer A, B, C, or D, which lists the correct Bin Number for the Stock Number given.

6. 17243
 A. 41L B. 83D C. 14L D. D30 6.____

7. 9219
 A. D38 B. L44 C. 614 D. 41L 7.____

8. 90125
 A. 41L B. 614 C. D38 D. D30 8.____

9. 10001
 A. L44 B. D38 C. 80D D. 83D 9.____

10. 200100
 A. 41L B. 14L C. 83D D. D30 10.____

KEY (CORRECT ANSWERS)

1. B   6. D
2. D   7. B
3. A   8. A
4. C   9. A
5. C   10. C

TEST 3

DIRECTIONS: Each question or incomplete statement is followed by several suggested answers or completions. Select the one that BEST answers the question or completes the statement. *PRINT THE LETTER OF THE CORRECT ANSWER IN THE SPACE AT THE RIGHT.*

Questions 1-9.

DIRECTIONS: Assume that the Police Department is planning to conduct a statistical study of individuals who have been convicted of crimes during a certain year. For the purpose of this study, identification numbers are being assigned to individuals in the following manner:

The first two digits indicate the age of the individual.
The third digit indicates the sex of the individual:
    1. Male
    2. Female
The fourth digit indicates the type of crime involved:
    1. criminal homicide
    2. forcible rape
    3. robbery
    4. aggravated assault
    5. burglary
    6. larceny
    7. auto theft
    8. other
The fifth and sixth digits indicate the month in which the conviction occurred:
    01. January
    02. February, etc.

Questions 1 through 9 are to be answered SOLELY on the basis of the above information and the following list of individuals and identification numbers.

Name	Number	Name	Number
Abbott, Richard	271304	Morris, Chris	212705
Collins, Terry	352111	Owens, William	231412
Elders, Edward	191207	Parker, Leonard	291807
George, Linda	182809	Robinson, Charles	311102
Hill, Leslie	251702	Sands, Jean	202610
Jones, Jackie	301106	Smith, Michael	42108
Lewis, Edith	402406	Turner, Donald	191601
Mack, Helen	332509	White, Barbara	242803

1. The number of women on the above list is
    A. 6   B. 7   C. 8   D. 9

1._____

2. The two convictions which occurred during February were for the crimes of
   A. aggravated assault and auto theft
   B. auto theft and criminal homicide
   C. burglary and larceny
   D. forcible rape and robbery

3. The ONLY man convicted of auto theft was
   A. Richard Abbott
   B. Leslie Hill
   C. Chris Morris
   D. Leonard Parker

4. The number of people on the list who were 25 years old or older is
   A. 6   B. 7   C. 8   D. 9

5. The OLDEST person on the list is
   A. Terry Collins
   B. Edith Lewis
   C. Helen Mack
   D. Michael Smith

6. The two people on the list who are the same age are
   A. Richard Abbott and Michael Smith
   B. Edward Elders and Donald Turner
   C. Linda George and Helen Mack
   D. Leslie Hill and Charles Robinson

7. A 28-year-old man who was convicted of aggravated assault in October would have identification number
   A. 281410   B. 281509   C. 282311   D. 282409

8. A 33-year-old woman convicted in April of criminal homicide would have identification number
   A. 331140   B. 331204   C. 332014   D. 332104

9. The number of people on the above list who were convicted during the first six months of the year is
   A. 6   B. 7   C. 8   D. 9

Questions 10-19.

DIRECTIONS: The following is a list of patients who were referred by various clinics to the laboratory for tests. After each name is a patient identification number. Questions 10 through 19 are to be answered on the basis of the information contained in this list and the explanation accompanying it.

The first digit refers to the clinic which made the referral:
1. cardiac
2. Renal
3. Pediatrics
4. Ophthalmology
5. Orthopedics
6. Hematology
7. Gynecology
8. Neurology
9. Gastroenterology

The second digit refers to the sex of the patient:
1. male
2. female

The third and fourth digits give the age of the patient

The last two digits give the day of the month the laboratory tests were performed

LABORATORY REFERRALS DURING JANUARY

Adams, Jacqueline	320917	Miller, Michael	511806
Black, Leslie	813406	Pratt, William	214411
Cook, Marie	511616	Rogers, Ellen	722428
Fisher, Pat	914625	Saunders, Sally	310229
Jackson, Lee	923212	Wilson, Jan	416715
James, Linda	624621	Wyatt, Mark	321326
Lane, Arthur	115702		

10. According to the list, the number of women referred to the laboratory during January was
    A. 4   B. 5   C. 6   D. 7

11. The clinic from which the MOST patients were referred was
    A. Cardiac
    B. Gynecology
    C. Ophthalmology
    D. Pediatrics

12. The YOUNGEST patient referred from any clinic other than Pediatrics was
    A. Leslie Black
    B. Marie Cook
    C. Arthur Lane
    D. Sally Saunders

13. The number of patients whose laboratory tests were performed on or before January 16 was
    A. 7   B. 8   C. 9   D. 10

14. The number of patients referred for laboratory tests who are under age 45 is
    A. 7   B. 8   C. 9   D. 10

15. The OLDEST patient referred to the clinic during January was
    A. Jacqueline Adams
    B. Linda James
    C. Arthur Lane
    D. Jan Wilson

16. The ONLY patient treated in the Orthopedics clinic was
    A. Marie Cook
    B. Pat Fisher
    C. Ellen Rogers
    D. Jan Wilson

17. A woman, age 37 was referred from the Hematology clinic to the laboratory. Her laboratory tests were performed on January 9. Her identification number would be
    A. 610937   B. 623709   C. 613790   D. 623790

18. A man was referred for lab tests from the Orthopedics clinic. He is 30 years old 18._____
    and his tests were performed on January 6.
    His identification number would be
    A. 413006   B. 510360   C. 513006   D. 513060

19. A 4-year-old boy was referred from the Pediatrics clinic to have laboratory 19._____
    tests on January 23.
    His identification number was
    A. 310422   B. 310423   C. 310433   D. 320403

KEY (CORRECT ANSWERS)

1.	B	11.	D
2.	B	12.	B
3.	B	13.	A
4.	D	14.	C
5.	D	15.	D
6.	B	16.	A
7.	A	17.	B
8.	D	18.	C
9.	C	19.	B
10.	B		

TEST 4

DIRECTIONS: Each question or incomplete statement is followed by several suggested answers or completions. Select the one that BEST answers the question or completes the statement. *PRINT THE LETTER OF THE CORRECT ANSWER IN THE SPACE AT THE RIGHT.*

Questions 1-10.

DIRECTIONS: Questions 1 through 10 are to be answered on the basis of the information and directions given below.

Assume that you are a Senior Stenographer assigned to the personnel bureau of a city agency. Your supervisor has asked you to classify the employees in your agency into the following five groups:

- A. Employees who are college graduates, who are at least 35 years of age but less than 50, and who have been employed by the City for five years or more;
- B. Employees who have been employed by the City for less than five years, who are not college graduates, and who earn at least $32,500 a year but less than $34,500;
- C. Employees who have been City employees for five years or more, who are at least 21 years of age but less than 35, and who are not college graduates;
- D. Employee who earn at least $34,500 a year but less than $36,000 who are college graduates, and who have been employed by the City for less than five years;
- E. Employees who are not included in any of the foregoing groups.

NOTE: In classifying these employees you are to compute age and period of service as of January 1, 2003. In all cases, it is to be assumed that each employee has been employed continuously in City service. In each question, consider only the information which will assist you in classifying each employee Any information which is of no assistance in classifying an employee would not be considered.

SAMPLE: Mr. Brown, a 29-year-old veteran, was appointed to his present position of Clerk on June 1, 2000. He has completed two years of college. His present salary is $33,050.

The correct answer to this sample is B, since the employee has been employed by the City for less than five years, is not a college graduate, and earn at least $32,500 a year but less than $34,500.

Questions 1 through 10 contain excerpts from the personnel records of 10 employees in the agency. In the correspondingly numbered space at the right print the capital letter preceding the appropriate group into which you would place each employee.

1. Mr. James has been employed by the City since 1993, when he was graduated from a local college. Now 35 years of age, he earns $36,000 a year.   1._____

2. Mr. Worth began working in City service early in 1999. He was awarded his college degree in 1994, at the age of 21. As a result of a recent promotion, he now earns $34,500 a year.   2._____

2 (#4)

3. Miss Thomas has been a City employee since August 1, 1998. Her salary is $34,500 a year. Miss Thomas, who is 25 years old, has had only three years of high school training.

3.____

4. Mr. Williams has had three promotions since entering City service on January 1, 1991. He was graduated from college with honors in 1974, when he was 20 years of age. His present salary is $37,000 a year.

4.____

5. Miss Jones left college after two years of study to take an appointment to a position in the City service paying $33,300 a year. She began work on March 1, 1997 when she was 19 years of age.

5.____

6. Mr. Smith was graduated from an engineering college with honors in January 1998 and became a City employee three months later. His present salary is $35,810. Mr. Smith was born in 1976.

6.____

7. Miss Earnest was born on May 31, 1979. Her education consisted of four years of high school and one year of business school. She was appointed as a typist in a City agency on June 1, 1997. Her annual salary is $33,500.

7.____

8. Mr. Adams, a 24-year-old clerk, began his City service on July 1, 1999, soon after being discharged from the U.S. Army. A college graduate, his present annual salary is $33,200.

8.____

9. Miss Charles attends college in the evenings, hoping to obtain her degree is 2004, when she will be 30 years of age. She has been a City employee since April 1998, and earns $33,350.

9.____

10. Mr. Dolan was just promoted to his present position after six years of City service. He was graduated from high school in 1982, when he was 18 years of age, but did not go on to college. Mr. Dolan's present salary is $33,500.

10.____

KEY (CORRECT ANSWERS)

1.	A	6.	D
2.	D	7.	C
3.	E	8.	E
4.	A	9.	B
5.	C	10.	E

TEST 5

DIRECTIONS: Questions 1 through 4 each contain five numbers that should be arranged in numerical order. The number with the lowest numerical value should be first and the number with the highest numerical value should be last. Pick that option which indicates the CORRECT order of the numbers.

Examples: A. 9; 18; 14; 15; 27
B. 9; 14; 15; 18; 27
C. 14; 15; 18; 27; 9
D. 9; 14; 15; 27; 18

The correct answer is B, which contains the proper arrangement of the five numbers.

1. A. 20573; 20753; 20738; 20837; 20098
   B. 20098; 20753; 20573; 20738; 20837
   C. 20098; 20573; 20753; 20837; 20738
   D. 20098; 20573; 20738; 20753; 20837

2. A. 113492; 113429; 111314; 113114; 131413
   B. 111314; 113114; 113429; 113492; 131413
   C. 111314; 113429; 113492; 113114; 131413
   D. 111314; 113114; 131413; 113429; 113492

3. A. 1029763; 1030421; 1035681; 1036928; 1067391
   B. 1030421; 1029763; 1035681; 1067391; 1036928
   C. 1030421; 1035681; 1036928; 1067391; 1029763
   D. 1029763; 1039421; 1035681; 1067391; 1036928

4. A. 1112315; 1112326; 1112337; 1112349; 1112306
   B. 1112306; 1112315; 1112337; 1112326; 1112349
   C. 1112306; 1112315; 1112326; 1112337; 1112349
   D. 1112306; 1112326; 1112315; 1112337; 1112349

KEY (CORRECT ANSWERS)

1. D
2. B
3. A
4. C

TEST 6

DIRECTIONS: The phonetic filing system is a method of filing names in which the alphabet is reduced to key code letters. The six key letters and their equivalents are as follows:

KEY LETTERS	EQUIVALENTS
b	p, f, v
c	s, k, g, j, q, x, z
d	t
l	none
m	n
r	none

A key letter represents itself.
Vowels (a, e, i, o, and u) and the letters w, h, and y are omitted.
For example, the name GILMAN would be represented as follows:
  G is represented by the key letter C.
  I is a vowel and is omitted.
  L is a letter and represents itself.
  M is a key letter and represents itself.
  A is a vowel and is omitted.
  N is represented by the key letter M.

Therefore, the phonetic filing code for the name GILMAN is CLMM.

Answer Questions 1 through 10 based on the information below.

1. The phonetic filing code for the name FITZGERALD would be
   A. BDCCRLD   B. BDCRLD   C. BDZCRLD   D. BTZCRLD

2. The phonetic filing code CLBR may represent any one of the following names EXCEPT
   A. Calprey   B. Flower   C. Glover   D. Silver

3. The phonetic filing code LDM may represent any one of the following names EXCEPT
   A. Halden   B. Hilton   C. Walton   D. Wilson

4. The phonetic filing code for the name RODRIGUEZ would be
   A. RDRC   B. RDRCC   C. RDRCZ   D. RTRCC

5. The phonetic filing code for the name MAXWELL would be
   A. MCLL   B. MCWL   C. MCWLL   D. MXLL

6. The phonetic filing code for the name ANDERSON would be
   A. AMDRCM   B. ENDRSM   C. MDRCM   D. NDERCN

7. The phonetic filing code for the name SAVITSKY would be
   A. CBDCC   B. CBDCY   C. SBDCC   D. SVDCC

8. The phonetic filing code CMC may represent any one of the following names EXCEPT
   A. James   B. Jayes   C. Johns   D. Jones

9. The ONLY one of the following names that could be represented by the phonetic filing code CDDDM would be
   A. Catalano   B. Chesterton   C. Cittadino   D. Cuttlerman

10. The ONLY one of the following names that could be represented by the phonetic filing code LLMCM would be
    A. Ellington   B. Hallerman   C. Inslerman   D. Willingham

KEY (CORRECT ANSWERS)

1.	A	6.	C
2.	B	7.	A
3.	D	8.	B
4.	B	9.	C
5.	A	10.	D

ARITHMETICAL REASONING
EXAMINATION SECTION
TEST 1

DIRECTIONS: Each question or incomplete statement is followed by several suggested answers or completions. Select the one that BEST answers the question or completes the statement. *PRINT THE LETTER OF THE CORRECT ANSWER IN THE SPACE AT THE RIGHT.*

Questions 1-4.

DIRECTIONS: In answering questions 1-4, assume that you are working in a medical facility and are responsible for maintaining inventory and stock.

1. The following quantities of disposable syringes were used during the first six weeks of the year: 840, 756, 772, 794, 723, and 789.
   If the cost of a disposable syringe is seventy cents, the average weekly cost for disposable syringes is MOST NEARLY

   A. $550   B. $780   C. $850   D. $3,270   1.____

2. Four pieces of glass tubing measuring 4 feet 3 inches, 6 feet 8 inches, 7 feet 2 inches, and 7 feet 6 inches are to be cut into 5-inch pieces.
   The TOTAL number of 5-inch pieces that can be cut from the four pieces is

   A. 60   B. 61   C. 62   D. 63   2.____

3. Assume that a 55-gallon drum of disinfectant is to be distributed equally among eight work stations.
   The amount of disinfectant that each work station should receive is

   A. 7.5 gallons   B. 27.5 pints
   C. 55 pints   D. 55 quarts   3.____

4. On June 30, an inventory indicated that there were 13 dozen petri dishes in the stockroom. During the next four weeks in July, the following quantities of petri dishes were given out by the stockroom: 23, 56, 37, and 31. On August 1, no petri dishes were given out, but 9 dozen were delivered to the stockroom.
   The number of petri dishes in the stockroom AFTER delivery on August 1 is

   A. 18   B. 108   C. 110   D. 117   4.____

5. A table of composition of foods lists the protein value of a 100 gram portion of hamburger at 22 grams. The protein value of a 45 gram portion of hamburger is, therefore, _____ grams.

   A. 5   B. 9.9   C. 11.3   D. 12.4   5.____

6. To cover a room 15' x 18' with wall-to-wall carpeting requires _____ square yards.

   A. 25   B. 30   C. 35   D. 90   6.____

7. Assume that you are in a hospital whose x-ray department is open from 8 A.M. to 12 Noon and from 1 P.M. to 6 P.M. You have assigned one of your technicians to schedule all the x-ray appointments for the clinic cases. Your instructions to him are not to make more than 12 appointments per half hour in the morning session and not more 15 per hour for the afternoon session.
The GREATEST number of patients he can schedule in the entire day will be

   A. 75   B. 96   C. 123   D. 171

8. 1,000,000 may be represented as

   A. 10^3 B. 10^5 C. 10^6 D. 10^{10}

9. 35° Centigrade equals

   A. 70° F   B. 95° F   C. 100° F   D. 120° F

10. $10^3 \times 10^4$ equals

    A. 10^7 B. 10^{12} C. 100^7 D. 100^{12}

11. If a mixture is made up of one part Substance A, 3 parts Substance B, and 12 parts Substance C, the proportion of Substance A in the mixture is

    A. 4%   B. 6 1/4%   C. 16%   D. 62 1/2%

12. If 5 grams of a chemical are enough to perform a certain laboratory test 9 times, the quantity of the chemical needed to perform this test 1,350 times would be _____ grams.

    A. 30   B. 150   C. 270   D. 750

13. If it takes 7 grams of a certain substance to make 5 liters of a solution, the quantity of the substance needed to make 4 liters of the solution is _____ grams.

    A. 2.85   B. 4.70   C. 5.60   D. 8.75

14. If it takes 3 grams of Substance A and 7 grams of Substance B to make 4 liters of a solution, how many grams of Substances A and B does it take to make 5 liters of the solution?
    _____ of Substance A and _____ of Substance B.

    A. 3.35; 6.65   B. 3.50; 7.50
    C. 3.75; 8.75   D. 4; 7

15. A certain type of laboratory test can be performed by a laboratory technician in 20 minutes.
Three laboratory technicians can perform 243 such tests in _____ hours.

    A. 16   B. 20   C. 27   D. 81

16. Pairs of shatterproof plastic safety glasses cost $38.00 each, but an 8% discount is given on orders of six pairs or more. Pairs of straight blade dissecting scissors cost $144 a dozen with a 12% discount on orders of two dozen or more.
The TOTAL cost of eight pairs of safety glasses and 30 pairs of dissecting scissors is MOST NEARLY

    A. $596.50   B. $621.00   C. $664.00   D. $731.50

17. On July 1, your laboratory has 280 usable 20-gauge needles on hand. On August 1, 15% of these needles have been lost or damaged beyond repair. On August 15, a new shipment of 50 needles is received by the laboratory, but 10% of these arrive damaged and are returned to the seller.
At this point, the number of usable 20-gauge needles on hand would be

    A. 238 B. 283 C. 288 D. 325

17.____

18. A certain laboratory procedure can be completed by a laboratory technician in 15 minutes.
If your lab is assigned 30 such tests, and they must be completed within 3 hours, the MINIMUM number of technicians that would have to be assigned to this task is

    A. 2 B. 3 C. 4 D. 5

18.____

19. A patient's hospital bill is $24,600. The patient has three different medical insurance plans, each of which will make partial payment toward his bill. One plan will pay $6,500 of the patient's bill, another will pay $7,300 of the bill, and the third will pay $8,832 of the bill.
The percentage of the bill that the patient's three insurance plans combined do NOT pay for is

    A. 5% B. 8% C. 10% D. 20%

19.____

20. A patient has stayed at a hospital for which the all-inclusive daily rate is $205.00. The patient was hospitalized for 27 days. The patient is covered by a private insurance plan that will pay the hospital 2/3 of the patient's total hospital bill.
The one of the following that MOST NEARLY indicates how much of the patient's hospital bill would NOT be covered by this insurance plan is

    A. $1,845 B. $2,078 C. $3,690 D. $3,156

20.____

21. A hospital charges a flat daily rate for all hospital services. In February 2000, the hospital charged a patient $2,772 for 14 days of hospitalization. In April 2002, the same patient was charged for 16 days of hospitalization at the same hospital.
If the daily rate charged by the hospital increased by $7 between the patient's 2000 hospitalization and his 2002 hospitalization, the total amount that the patient must pay for the 2002 hospitalization is

    A. $3,296 B. $3,280 C. $3,264 D. $3,248

21.____

22. A hospital insurance plan that previously covered 3/5 of the total hospital charges for its subscribers has recently been improved, and coverage for total hospital charges has been increased by 25% of the previous rate. A subscriber to this plan has just completed a hospital stay and has received a bill for total hospital charges of $6,200.
Assuming that the hospital stay is covered by the recently improved plan, the one of the following that MOST NEARLY indicates how much the plan now provides the patient toward the payment of the hospital bill is

    A. $1,550 B. $3,720 C. $4,650 D. $5,270

22.____

Questions 23-25.

DIRECTIONS: Questions 23 through 25 are to be answered on the basis of the following situation.

You have been asked to keep records of the time spent with each patient by the doctors in the clinic where you are assigned. Your notes show that Dr. Jones spent the following amount of time with each patient he examined on a certain day: Patient A - 14 minutes, Patient B - 13 minutes, Patient C - 34 minutes, Patient D - 48 minutes, Patient E - 26 minutes, Patient F - 20 minutes, Patient G - 25 minutes.

23. The average number of minutes spent by Dr. Jones with each patient is MOST NEARLY

   A. 20 B. 25 C. 30 D. 35

24. If Dr. Jones is to take care of the seven patients mentioned above at one session, the number of hours he will have to remain at the clinic is MOST NEARLY _____ hour(s).

   A. 1 B. 2 C. 3 D. 4

25. The one of the following groups of patients that required the LEAST time to examine is Patients _____ and _____.

   A. A, C; E B. B, D; F C. C, E; G D. A, D; G

KEY (CORRECT ANSWERS)

1. A		11. B	
2. B		12. D	
3. C		13. C	
4. D		14. C	
5. B		15. C	
6. B		16. A	
7. D		17. B	
8. C		18. B	
9. B		19. B	
10. A		20. A	

21. B
22. C
23. B
24. C
25. A

SOLUTIONS TO PROBLEMS

1. $(840+756+772+794+723+789) \div 6 = 779$. Then, $(779)(.70) = \$545.30 \approx \$550$

2. 4'3" + 6'8" + 7'2" + 7'6" = 25'7" = 307". Then, $307 \div 5 = 61.4$, so 61 5-inch pieces exist.

3. $55 \div 8 = 6.875$ gallons = 55 pints

4. $(13)(12) - 23 - 56 - 37 - 31 + (9)(12) = 117$ dishes

5. Let x = protein value. Then, Solving, x = 9.9 grams

6. (15')(18') = 270 sq.ft. = 30 sq.yds.

7. Maximum number of appointments = $(12)(8) + (15)(5) = 171$

8. $1,000,000 = 10^6$

9. $F = 9/5\, C + 32$. If C = 35, $F = (9/5)(35) + 32 = 95$

10. $10^3 \times 10^4 = 10^7$. When multiplying with like bases, add the exponents.

11. $\dfrac{1}{1+3+2} = \dfrac{1}{16} = 6\dfrac{1}{4}\%$

12. Let x = grams needed. Then, $5/9 = x/1350$. Solving, x = 750

13. Let x = grams needed. Then, $7/5 = x/4$ Solving, x = 5.6

14. Let x = grams of A needed and y = grams of B needed.
    Then, $3/4 = x/5$ and $7/4 = y/5$ Solving, x = 3.75, y = 8.75

15. The test requires 1/3 technician-hrs. Now, $(243)(1/3) = 81$ technician-hrs., and $81 \div 3 = 27$ hours

16. $(8)(\$38.00)(.92) + (2\,1/2)(\$144)(.88) = \$596.48 \approx \$596.50$

17. $280 - (.15)(280) + 50 - (.10)(50) = 283$ needles on hand

18. The test requires 1/4 technician-hrs., so 30 tests require 7 1/2 technician-hrs. Since 3 hrs. is the time limit for these 30 tests, $7\,1/2 \div 3 = 2.5$ or 3 technicians at a minimum are needed.

19. $\$24,600 - (\$6500+\$7300+\$8832) = \$1968$, and $1968/24,600 = 8\%$

20. Amount not covered = $(1/3)(\$205)(27) = \$1845$

21. Daily rate for 2000 = $\$2772 \div 14 = \$198$, so for 2002 the daily rate = $\$205$. Finally, $(\$205)(16) = \$3280$

22. The new plan covers $(.60)(1.25) = .75$ or 75% of the bill. Then, $(.75)(\$6200) = \$4650$

23. (14+13+34+48+26+20+25) ÷ 7 ≈ 26 min., closest to 25 min.

24. 180 min. = 3 hours

25. Patients A, C, E: 74 min.; patients B, D, F: 81 min.; patients C, E, G: 85 min.; patients A, D, G: 87 min. So, the 1st group requires the least time.

TEST 2

DIRECTIONS: Each question or incomplete statement is followed by several suggested answers or completions. Select the one that BEST answers the question or completes the statement. *PRINT THE LETTER OF THE CORRECT ANSWER IN THE SPACE AT THE RIGHT.*

1. A stack of cartons containing pesticides is 10 cartons long, 9 cartons wide, and 5 cartons high.
   The number of cartons in the stack is

   A. 24   B. 55   C. 95   D. 450

   1.____

2. Assume that you have bags of corn meal, each of the same weight. The total weight of 25 bags is 125 pounds.
   How many of these bags would it take to make a TOTAL weight of 50 pounds?

   A. 2   B. 5   C. 6   D. 10

   2.____

3. You are working in the sub-basement of a project building, and the foreman tells you to get two boards from the maintenance shop to stand on. One of the boards is 5 yards long, and the other 3 1/2 feet long.
   The TOTAL length, in feet, of the two boards is

   A. 8 1/2   B. 9 1/2   C. 17 1/2   D. 18 1/2

   3.____

4. Three hundred plastic bags of rat-mix, each bag weighing four ounces, are packed in a carton. The carton weighed one pound before the rat-mix was packed in it.
   The TOTAL weight of the filled carton is _____ pounds.

   A. 37 1/2   B. 38 1/2   C. 75   D. 76

   4.____

5. Of 180 families that relocated in a given month, 1/5 moved into Finder's Fee apartments, 1/4 moved into tenant-found apartments, 1/3 moved into public housing, and the rest moved out of the city.
   How many moved out of the city?

   A. 36   B. 39   C. 45   D. 60

   5.____

6. If a space treatment device covers 1,000 cubic feet in six seconds, how long should it run in order to treat a room that is 30 feet long, 20 feet wide, and 15 feet high?

   A. 18 seconds   B. 54 seconds
   C. 1 minute 24 seconds   D. 1 minute 48 seconds

   6.____

7. If you have to prepare five gallons of 0.5 Diazinon emulsion using water and 20% Diazinon emulsifiable concentrate, what is the amount of concentrate that is necessary?
   _____ ounces.

   A. 1.6   B. 3.2   C. 16.0   D. 64.0

   7.____

8. Suppose you have 15 5/6 ounces of a certain chemical on hand.
   If you later receive shipments of 6 1/2 ounces and 8 3/4 ounces of this chemical, the TOTAL number of ounces you should then have on hand is

   A. 29 7/8   B. 30 5/6   C. 31 1/12   D. 31 3/4

   8.____

9. You are told to prepare 60 pounds of 2% pyrethrum dust using talc and 5% pyrethrum dust concentrate.
   What is the amount of concentrate that is required in the mixture?
   _____ pounds.

   A. 24   B. 28   C. 30 1/2   D. 36

10. In the pest control shop of a certain housing development, there is a supply of 4 one-gallon containers of insecticide. This week, the exterminator will use up five quarts of this insecticide in his work, and for each week thereafter he will use up five quarts. Deliveries are made on the first day of the week.
    Next week, and each week thereafter, the shop will get a delivery of one gallon of insecticide. The exterminator will need an additional supply of insecticide by the end of the _____ week.

    A. 4th   B. 12th   C. 24th   D. 29th

11. There are 22 boxes of rat mix in a certain pest control shop.
    If each box contains 7 1/2 pounds of rat mix, the TOTAL amount of rat mix in the shop is _____ pounds.

    A. 165   B. 172 1/2   C. 180   D. 182 1/2

12. A pest control shop has a supply of 26 one-gallon cans of insecticide.
    If the exterminator works 5 days a week and uses 32 ounces of the liquid a day, the number of work weeks this supply of insecticide will last is MOST NEARLY

    A. 10   B. 20   C. 28   D. 32

13. A certain supplier packs two dozen mousetraps to a box. If the exterminator gets a delivery of 20 boxes and finds that two of these boxes are half-full, the TOTAL number of traps the exterminator received from this supplier is

    A. 408   B. 432   C. 456   D. 480

14. Assume that a truck which contains a shipment of pesticides is parked outside your exterminating shop. You are able to unload the truck in one hour.
    How long would it take four exterminators, starting at the same time and working at the same rate as you, to unload four trucks similar to the one you unloaded?

    A. 15 minutes   B. 1 hour   C. 2 hours   D. 4 hours

15. A certain building in a housing development has 142 apartments. It takes one exterminator an average of six minutes to treat one apartment.
    At that rate, approximately how long should it take him to treat all 142 apartments?
    _____ hours.

    A. 2   B. 14   C. 24   D. 85

16. A crate contains 3 pieces of pesticide equipment weighing 73, 84, and 47 pounds, respectively.
    If the crate is lifted by 4 exterminators, each lifting one corner of the crate, the average number of pounds, in addition to the weight of the crate, lifted by each of the exterminators is

    A. 51   B. 65   C. 71   D. 78

17. Of the following, the pair that is NOT a set of equivalents is 17.____

    A. .014%; .00014   B. 1/5%; .002   C. 1.5%; 3/200   D. 115%; .115

18. 10^{-2} is equal to 18.____

    A. 0.001   B. 0.01   C. 0.1   D. 100.0

19. $10^2 \times 10^3$ is equal to 19.____

    A. 10^5 B. 10^6 C. 100^5 D. 100^6

20. The length of two objects are in the ratio of 2:1. 20.____
If each were 3 inches shorter, the ratio would be 3:1.
The longer object is _____ inches.

    A. 8   B. 10   C. 12   D. 14

21. If the weight of water is 62.4 pounds per cubic foot, the weight of the water that fills a rectangular container 6 inches by 6 inches by 1 foot is pounds. 21.____

    A. 7.8   B. 15.6   C. 31.2   D. 46.8

22. The formula for converting degrees Centigrade to degrees Fahrenheit is as follows: 22.____
    Fahrenheit = 9/5 of Centigrade + 32°, or
    multiply the number of degrees Centigrade by 9, divide by 5 and add 32).
If the Centigrade thermometer reads 25°, the temperature in degrees Fahrenheit is

    A. 13   B. 45   C. 53   D. 77

23. To make a certain preparation, you have been told to mix one ounce of Liquid A and 3 ounces of Liquid B. 23.____
If you have used 18 ounces of Liquid B in preparing a larger amount, the number of ounces of Liquid A you should use is

    A. 6   B. 15   C. 21   D. 54

24. If one inch is equal to approximately 2.5 centimeters, the number of inches in fifteen centimeters is MOST NEARLY 24.____

    A. 1.6   B. 6   C. 12.5   D. 37.5

25. You are in charge of a small lawn area of 1,850 sq. ft. You are asked to apply lime on this lawn at the rate of 40 pounds per 1,000 sq. ft. 25.____
The number of pounds of lime you will need to cover the entire area of the lawn is MOST NEARLY _____ pounds.

    A. 74   B. 86   C. 87   D. 89

KEY (CORRECT ANSWERS)

1. D
2. D
3. D
4. D
5. B

6. B
7. C
8. C
9. A
10. B

11. A
12. B
13. C
14. B
15. B

16. A
17. D
18. B
19. A
20. C

21. B
22. D
23. A
24. B
25. A

SOLUTIONS TO PROBLEMS

1. (10)(9)(5) = 450 cartons

2. Let x = number of bags. Then, 25/125 = x/50. Solving, x = 10

3. 5 yds. + 3 1/2 ft. = 15 ft. + 3 1/2 ft. = 18 1/2 ft.

4. Total weight = 1 + (300) (4/16) = 76 pounds

5. 1-1/5-1/4-1/3=13/60. Then, (180)(13/60) = 39 families

6. (30')(20')(15') = 9000 cu.ft. Let x = number of seconds, Then, $\frac{1000}{6} = \frac{9000}{X}$. Solving, x = 54

7. 1 qt. of concentrate = 16 oz.

8. 15 5/6 + 6 1/2 + 8 3/4 = 29 25/12 = 31 1/12 ounces

9. .05x = .02(60)
   x = 24

10. For the 1st week (end), there will be 16 - 5 = 11 qts. left. For each additional week, since 4 qts. are delivered but 5 qts. are used, there will be a net loss of 1 qt. Thus, at the end of 12 weeks, the supply of insecticide will be gone.

11. (22)(7 1/2) = 165 pounds

12. (26)(128) = 3328 oz., and (32)(5) = 160 oz. used each week. Finally, 3328 ÷ 160 = 20.8, closest to 20 oz.

13. (24) (18) + (12)(2) = 456 mousetraps

14. 4 trucks require 4 man-hours. Then, 4 ÷ 4=1 hour

15. (142)(6) = 852 min. = 14.2 hrs. ≈ 14 hrs.

16. Total weight = 204 lbs. Then, 204 ÷ 4 = 51 lbs.

17. 115% = 1.15, not .115

18. 10^{-2} = 1/100 = .01

19. $10^2 \times 10^3 = 10^5$. When multiplying with like bases, add the exponents.

20. Let x, 1/2x = lengths of the longer and shorter objects. Then, x - 3 = 3(1/2x-3). Simplifying, x - 3 = 3/2x - 9. Solving, x = 12 in.

21. (1/2')(1/2')(1') = 1/4 cu.ft. Then, (62.4)(1/4) = 15.6 pounds

22. F = (9/5)(25°) + 32° = 77°

23. Let x = number of ounces of liquid A. Then, 1/3 = x/18. Solving, x = 6

24. 15 cm. = $\dfrac{15}{\approx 2.5}$ or approx. 6 in.

25. (40)(1850/1000) = 74 pounds

DRUG LAWS OF THE UNITED STATES

CONTENTS

	Page
1. Laws governing pharmacy	1
2. The Federal Food, Drug, and Cosmetic Act	1
a. Adulterated drugs	1
b. Misbranded drugs	1
c. Labeling	2
d. Coal tar colors	2
e. New drugs	2
3. The Durham-Humphrey Act	2
a. Prescription legend drugs	2
b. Telephone prescriptions	2
c. Renewing legend drug prescriptions	3
d. Enforcement of the acts	3
4. The drug efficacy studies	3
5. Controlled substances	4
a. General	4
b. Schedule substances	4
c. Code R and Code K items	5
d. Ordering	5
e. Record keeping	5
f. Filing	6
g. Inventorying	6
h. Security	6
i. Dispensing	6
j. Destruction	8
6. UCMJ	8
7. Prescription ownership	8
8. Confidentiality of prescriptions	8

DRUG LAWS OF THE UNITED STATES

1. **Laws governing pharmacy.** There are Federal laws pertaining to pharmacy which must be followed by everyone practicing pharmacy who is associated with the U.S. Government. There are also State laws which pertain to the practice of pharmacy in a particular state. Any State law may be more stringent or strict than the Federal law, but it may not be less so. The practice of Army pharmacy is also governed by Army Regulations such as AR 40-2, AR 40-4, AR 40-7, AR 40-18, and AR 40-61. In the Army, we must abide by the Federal pharmacy laws and Army Regulations, but we do not have to abide by the State laws. It is a matter of local policy whether a particular installation will also abide by the pharmacy laws of the state in which the installation is located.

2. **The Federal Food, Drug, and Cosmetic Act.** The Federal Food, Drug, and Cosmetic Act first became law in 1906, followed by revision, amendment, and final emergence as our present law in 1965. This act is intended to protect the consumer from adulterated and misbranded food, drugs, devices, and cosmetics, and for other purposes. It directly prohibits adulterated or misbranded items from movement across state lines (interstate commerce).

   a. Adulterated drugs. By provision of the Federal Food, Drug, and Cosmetic Act, a drug or device is construed as being adulterated under the following conditions if:

   (1) It contains any filthy, putrid, or decomposed substance, or is packed under conditions which would result in its contamination; if it is a drug and its container is composed of any poisonous or injurious substance which could be passed on to the contents; or if it contains a coal tar color not certified by regulations.

   (2) It is said or advertised to be a drug of official nature and differs from or is not the same quality as the official standard.

   (3) Its strength differs from or the purity and quality fall below that indicated on the label.

   (4) It is a drug and any other drug has been substituted for it or mixed with it to reduce its quality or strength.

   b. Misbranded drugs. A drug or device is misbranded if—

   (1) The labeling is not truthful or is misleading.

   (2) It is in a package and does not contain the name and address of the manufacturer, packager, or distributor, and an accurate statement of the weight, measure, or numerical count of the contents.

   (3) Any word or information required by the Act to appear on the label is not prominently placed (in comparison with the rest of the label) so that it is likely to be read and understood by ordinary individuals.

   (4) It is intended for human use and contains any quantity of a substance which is habit-forming, unless the label shows the name and quantity of that substance and adjacent to it, the statement "Warning: May be habit-forming."

   (5) It is a drug and is not labeled by a name official in our compendia (USP and NF), unless it bears the common name, if one exists; and if it is made of two or more ingredients, the common or usual name of each active ingredient.

   (6) It is a drug of one or more active ingredients and the name, quantity, and proportion of any alcohol contained is not specified on the label.

   (7) It is a drug and the label does not specify the name and quantity or proportion of any bromides, ether, chloroform, acetanilid, acetophenetidin, aminopyrine, antipyrine, atropine, hyoscine, hyoscyamus, arsenic, digitalis, digitalis glucosides, mercury, ouabain, strophanthin, strychnine, thyroid, or any derivative or preparation of any such substances. If compliance with this item or items *(5)* and *(6)* above is impracticable, exemptions may be established by regulation.

   (8) The labeling does not bear adequate directions for use and appropriate warnings against use under specific circumstances (for example, laxatives where abdominal pain is present).

(9) It is stated or advertised to be an official preparation and is not packaged and labeled according to the official directions in the monograph.

(10) The packaging is such that it is misleading; it is an imitation of another drug; or it is offered under the name of another drug.

(11) It is dangerous to health when used as recommended by the label on it.

(12) It is, or is stated to be, made of or in part of insulin or antibiotic unless it be from a batch certified by this law.

 c. Labeling. All drugs leaving the pharmacy must be labeled adequately.

 (1) Labeling drugs dispensed on prescription. Drugs dispensed on prescription must bear the proper information on a prescription-type label—including the name and location of the facility, the name of the patient, the date of issuance, the number assigned to the prescription, the directions for use, the prescriber's name, and the initials of the person typing the label. In the Army, AR 40-2 also requires us to place the name and strength of the drug on the label, except when the prescriber directs otherwise, and also the legend "KEEP OUT OF THE REACH OF CHILDREN" in boldface type on all prescription labels. In addition, the labels for controlled substances must contain the legend, "CAUTION: FEDERAL LAW PROHIBITS THE TRANSFER OF THIS DRUG TO ANY PERSON OTHER THAN THE PATIENT FOR WHOM IT WAS PRESCRIBED" in boldface type.

 (2) Labeling drugs dispensed to patients without a prescription. Drugs dispensed by the pharmacy without a prescription as provided in AR 40-2 must be properly labeled. According to law, the label must show the name of the medication; adequate directions for use; the quantity contained; the name of the facility and location; special notes or warnings; and if any habit-forming drugs are contained in any amount, the name of such drug and the amount per unit must be stated on the label as well as the statement—"Warning: May be habit-forming." Items which have an expiration date or deteriorate after mixing must bear a label stating such information. AR 40-2 also states that the legend "KEEP OUT OF THE REACH OF CHILDREN" must appear in boldface type on the label.

 (3) Labels of drug stock in using activities. It is the duty of pharmacy personnel to insure that the stock in wards and in treatment rooms is labeled properly. A little bottle on the shelf in a treatment room marked "Achromycin—250 mg" is not adequate and is in direct violation of the law. When possible, drugs dispensed for ward stock should remain in their original container and with their original labeling. If labeled by pharmacy personnel, the label should contain such things as the name of the drug; trade name, if applicable; strength; quantity; date; name of manufacturer and manufacturer's lot number; and expiration date.

 d. Coal tar colors. A list of certified coal tar colors for the purpose of coloring foods or drugs is set forth in this law. These coloring agents must be proved harmless and suitable for the purpose for which they are intended. A list of these coal tar colors can be found in *Remington's Practice of Pharmacy.*

 e. New drugs. Before being introduced into interstate commerce, all new drugs must be first approved by the Secretary of the Department of Health, Education, and Welfare. Only "approved" drugs will be procured, prescribed, or dispensed except those unapproved drugs authorized by The Surgeon General to save life or prevent suffering. Investigational drugs may be used within the provisions of AR 40-2 (sec. 15) and AR 40-7.

3. The Durham-Humphrey Act. The Durham-Humphrey Act (Durham-Humphrey Amendment) is nothing more than a set of changes to the Food, Drug, and Cosmetic Act. This amendment groups drugs into two main classes—those which may be dispensed only on prescription, and those which may be sold over-the-counter (OTC); that is, without a prescription.

 a. Prescription legend drugs. The Durham-Humphrey Act rules that drugs which by their nature are unsafe, or require medical supervision or advice with their use, must bear the legend "Caution: Federal Law Prohibits Dispensing Without a Prescription." Any drug so labeled is known as a prescription legend drug (sometimes called a legend drug) and cannot be sold without a prescription. Conversely, all drugs considered safe to use without medical supervision must not bear the caution and may be sold OTC.

 b. Telephoned prescriptions. The Durham-Humphrey Amendment permits a physician to prescribe medication in the legend category by telephone. The pharmacist must reduce the prescription to writing and include the medication, strength, dose or directions for use, the name of the patient, and all other data given him by the physician. AR 40-2 states that all prescriptions will be signed by an authorized prescriber and that prescriptions for potentially harmful drugs (legend drugs) will be dispensed only upon receipt of a *written* prescription.

    c. Renewing legend drug prescriptions. One of the most important stipulations of the Durham-Humphrey Act is that prescriptions for legend drugs may not be renewed (refilled), except when authorized by the prescriber. Such authorization may be made at the time of writing the prescription by stating the number of times the prescription may be refilled. The interpretation of this act, like all the others, must be in accordance with good professional judgment and good faith.

    d. Enforcement of the acts. The Food, Drug, and Cosmetic Act and the Durham-Humphrey Act are enforced by the Food and Drug Administration (FDA) of the Department of Health, Education, and Welfare. Violations of the acts are misdemeanors and are punishable by "imprisonment for not more than one year, or a fine of not more than $1,000, or both."

4. The drug efficacy studies

    a. As a result of the 1962 Kefauver-Harris New Drug Amendments to the Food, Drug, and Cosmetics Act of 1938, it was ruled that *drugs must not only have proof of "safety," but also proof of "effectiveness."* This was the basis for the commissioner of the Food and Drug Administration (FDA) requesting the National Academy of Sciences/National Research Council (NAS/NRC) to make a comprehensive survey of effectiveness for all drugs marketed under new drug applications (NDA) approved between 1938 and October 1962. Their findings are called the *Drug Efficacy Study.* Each drug after review is classified in one of four categories:

    (1) Effective. The drug is effective for the presented indications.

    (2) Probably effective. The effectiveness of the drug is probable for the indications presented but additional evidence of effectiveness is required of the manufacturer within 12 months before it can be classified *effective.*

    (3) Possibly effective. There is little evidence of effectiveness for presented indications; however, the manufacturer is allowed 6 months to submit additional data to provide substantial evidence of effectiveness.

    (4) Ineffective. There is no acceptable evidence to support a claim of effectiveness, and immediate administrative action by the FDA is justified in withdrawing the drug from the market or deleting the claimed indication(s) from the label. The manufacturer has 30 days to submit pertinent data bearing on this regulatory proposal.

    b. As a direct result of the Drug Efficacy Study and FDA enforcement and regulatory action, the Department of Defense established the following policy regarding the procurement and prescribing of three of the above categories of drugs:

    (1) Category 1A, "Ineffective" drugs.
- These drugs have definitely been determined to be ineffective by the FDA.
- No further procurement or issue is authorized for those items that have been withdrawn from the market.
- Remaining stocks of standard and nonstandard items will be destroyed or other appropriate action taken.

    (2) Category 1B, "Ineffective" drugs.
- These drugs have been determined to be ineffective by the FDA; however, manufacturers have been given time to refute the FDA decision.
- Authorization for central or local procurement is suspended until final action is taken by FDA.
- These drugs will be suspended from use and issue until final status of drug is resolved.

    (3) Category 2, "Possibly Effective" drugs.
- Standard and local procurement of these items are no longer authorized. Remaining stocks may be used until exhausted. Exception: continued therapeutic use of these drugs will depend upon the decision of the medical facility Therapeutic Agents Board (TAB). Local procurement is authorized if the TAB decides no alternate means of therapy are available.
- Requisitioning of "possibly effective" drugs (if approved by TAB) is minimized to no more than 60 days stock on hand in the medical facility.

    (4) Category 3, "Probably Effective" drugs.
- All central and local procurement of these items

is minimized so that there is no more than 60 days stock on hand in the medical facility.

• Continued issue and use is authorized until further change in classification by FDA.

  c. Information concerning the classification of a drug within these categories is not specifically included in this manual. If further information is needed, a consolidated listing of drugs classified as "Ineffective," "Possibly Effective," or "Probably Effective" was summarized in SB 8-75-4, 18 January 1972. An updating of this list and current "Drug Safety and Effectiveness Information" will be published periodically in the SB 8-75 series.

5. Controlled substances

  a. *General.* The ordering, dispensing, and destruction of controlled substances in the United States is governed by the "Comprehensive Drug Abuse Prevention and Control Act of 1970" (also known as the Controlled Substances Act or Public Law (PL) 91-513, October 27, 1970). Essentially, this act combines the control of drugs formerly known as Class A, B, X, and M narcotics and DACA (Drug Abuse Control Amendment of 1965, which identified those drugs that have potential for high abuse) into one statute, with responsibility for enforcement placed on one agency, the Bureau of Narcotics and Dangerous Drugs (BNDD), of the U.S. Department of Justice. Most states have their own laws which supplement the Federal law. Although the practice of pharmacy on a military installation is not governed by the law of the state in which the installation is located, it is subject to the provisions of the "Comprehensive Drug Abuse Prevention and Control Act," PL 91-513. The Army does have regulations governing the handling of controlled substances which, in essence, are comparable to state laws. Army regulations are often more stringent than, or at least parallel to, the Federal law, but they are never less stringent than the Federal law. The question of which law or regulation to follow in a given situation then arises. The following rule of thumb should be followed if Army's regulations and Federal law differ, "the more stringent law or regulation is applicable." Regarding the handling of controlled substances, differences between the Federal law and Army regulation will be seen in several areas, such as labeling requirements and filing and destruction procedures. Where these differences exist, the more stringent requirements will be covered here.

  b. *Schedule substances.* The Controlled Substances Act designated controlled drugs into five schedules based on their potential for abuse. As pharmacy specialists, it is easy for you to determine which schedule a given drug belongs to simply by examining the commercial container in which the drug is supplied. The container will bear an identification symbol indicating the schedule in which the drug belongs. The symbol can appear in either of two ways: a capital C followed by the roman numeral indicating the schedule number (for example, C-II), or a capital C with the Roman numeral inside of it (for example, Ⓘ). The five schedules are defined as follows:

  (1) Schedule I substances. Have no accepted medical use in the United States. Some examples are heroin, marihuana, LSD, peyote, mescaline, psilocybin, tetrahydrocannabinols, ketobemidone, levomoramide, racemoramide, benzylmorphine, dihydromorphine, morphine methylsulfonate, nicocodeine, nicomorphine, and others.

  (2) Schedule II substances. Have a high abuse potential with severe psychic or physical dependence liability. Many have been known in the past as Class A Narcotic Drugs. Non-narcotic substances are currently included in this schedule. Some examples are: amphetamines, methamphetamines, methylphenidate, phenmetrazine, opium, morphine, codeine, dihydromorphinone, methadone, pantopon, meperidine, cocaine, anileridine, oxymorphone, and any other substance so designated by amendments to the Controlled Substances Act. The first difference between Federal law and Army regulations is encountered with Schedule II substances. By Army regulation, paregoric (which by Federal law is classified in Schedule III) and ethyl alcohol and alcoholic beverages (which by Federal law are not included in any schedule), must be received, dispensed, and accounted for in Army hospitals in the same manner as Schedule II substances. (However, commercial containers of paregoric, alcohol, or alcoholic beverages will *not* be imprinted with the C-II or Ⓘ symbol when you receive them.) You must be aware of the fact that these substances are being controlled by the Army in this manner because the Army Regulation, which in this case is more stringent than the Federal law, has to be followed.

  (3) Schedule III substances. Have an abuse potential less than those in Schedules I and II, and includes those drugs formerly known as Class B Narcotics and, in addition, non-narcotic

drugs, such as glutethimide, methyprylon, chlorhexadol, phencyclidine, sulfondiethylmethane, sulfonmethane, nalorphine, and some barbiturates, and any other items so designated by amendments to the Controlled Substances Act.

(4) Schedule IV substances. Have an abuse potential less than those listed in Schedule III and include drugs such as barbital, phenobarbital, methylphenobarbital, chloral betaine, chloral hydrate, ethchloruynol, ethinamate, meprobamate, paraldehyde, pentaetythritol chloral, methohexital, chlordiazepoxide, diazepam, and any other items so designated by amendments to the Controlled Substances Act.

(5) Schedule V substances. Have an abuse potential less than those listed in Schedule IV, and consist of those preparations formerly known as Exempt Narcotics, with the exception of paregoric. Paregoric is now listed as a Schedule III Controlled Substance but, as you have seen in *(2)* above, is received, dispensed, and accounted for in the Army as a Schedule II substance.

c. *Code R and Code K items.* Another method of classifying controlled substances is used in military medical supply channels and the Federal Supply Catalog: classification as Code R or Code K items. To be sure you are fully aware of the relationship between these items and the schedules, each term will be defined.

(1) Code R item is defined as those controlled substances classified in Schedule II, plus ethyl alcohol, alcoholic beverages, and paregoric.

(2) Code K item is defined as those controlled substances classified in Schedules III, IV, and V.

d. *Ordering.*

(1) The Controlled Substances Act outlines general guidelines which must be followed by everyone who orders and dispenses controlled substances. In the Army, the specific methods by which these guidelines are carried out are outlined in AR 40-2.

(2) While a special BNDD order form is used by medical supply to locally purchase Schedule II substances, all schedule substances are normally ordered by the pharmacy from medical supply by using a DA Form 2765-1 (Request for Issue or Turn-In). This policy may vary with installation policy, and other forms may be used.

e. *Record keeping.*

(1) When any controlled substance is received from medical supply, you will also receive a numbered voucher which shows the date and quantity of the substance you received. This voucher must be filed and will serve as your debit record when accounting for that substance. By law, Schedule II vouchers must be filed separately from Schedule III, IV, and V vouchers. The date, quantity received, and voucher number will be entered in the appropriate column of the DA Form 3862 (Controlled Substances Stock Record) which is maintained for that specific item. A separate DA Form 3862 must be maintained for each form in which the controlled substance is supplied. The metric system must be used for all entries where appropriate. When you receive controlled substances from medical supply, you will be required to sign a voucher, which is retained by medical supply, showing that these controlled substances have been delivered to you. Make sure that everything ordered is present, or deleted as appropriate, and that all items received are the exact items ordered before you sign for them.

(2) Individual prescriptions serve as your credit record for subtracting from DA Form 3862 the control substance dispensed. The manner in which specific preparations are accounted for depends on the schedule to which the preparation belongs.

(3) For Schedule II substances, ethyl alcohol, alcoholic beverages, and paregoric, each order for stock expended will be subtracted from the balance on hand shown on the DA Form 3862 maintained for that item. Each entry will show the date expended, the prescription number, and the amount expended. The *last* figure in the "Balance on Hand" column of the DA Form 3862 for that item will always reflect the *actual* amount on hand.

(4) Entries for Code R items will be made on DA Form 3862 on a daily basis with each prescription and/or voucher being recorded.

(5) For Schedule III, IV, and V controlled substances (and any other items designated by the commander), expenditures for each item will be summarized weekly and subtracted from the balance on hand shown on the DA Form 3862 maintained for that item. Concurrently, an inventory of all the stocks on hand will be conducted by pharmacy personnel and the inventory balance compared with the balance shown on DA Form 3862. An adjustment for minor overages and shortages caused by

operational handling or undiscoverable posting errors will be made by posting an inventory adjustment to the stock record since a series of small losses over an extended period of time could result in a major inventory shortage. All major inventory shortages will be investigated immediately and remedial action taken. Records of all investigations and remedial actions should be maintained in the pharmacy records.

(6) In event an error is made in posting, one line must be drawn through the incorrect entry and initialed and the correct entry made.

f. Filing.

(1) While the Controlled Substances Act provides three general methods by which persons receiving and dispensing controlled substances may maintain their prescription files, AR 40-2 provides one specific method by which prescriptions will be numbered and filed in Army pharmacies.

(2) At least three series of numbers will be used to number prescriptions filled in Army pharmacies–one for Schedule II substances, ethyl alcohol, alcholic beverages, and paregoric; one for Schedule III, IV, and V substances; and one for all other prescriptions. A corresponding file will be established for each series of numbers.

g. Inventorying.

(1) AR 40-2 requires that at least once each month a disinterested officer or senior noncommissioned officer be designated by the commander to inspect the stock records for controlled substances. He will conduct an inventory of each Schedule II substance, and all ethyl alcohol, alcoholic beverages, and paregoric, and verify that the amount of each drug or preparation actually in stock is the same amount show in the "Balance on Hand" column of the DA Form 3862 maintained for that item. At the same time he will verify all other entries. His findings, together with the date of the inspection and action taken, will be noted over his signature and grade immediately below the last entry on the card. Any discrepancies noted will be reported immediately in writing to the commander. Concurrently, he will inspect the stock records for at least 10 percent of the Schedule III, IV, and V items and include in his report to the commander any unusual expenditures or any major inventory discrepancies.

(2) If controlled substances are used in the manufacture of pharmaceutical preparations, a DD Form 1289 (Prescription Form) with the R_x symbol lined out will be used to account for their expenditure. Such orders will be authenticated and signed by the officer in charge of the pharmacy. The quantity expended will be subtracted from the DA Form 3862 maintained for that item, and the order will be filed in the appropriate prescription file.

h. Security. The Controlled Substances Act directs that Schedule II substances be stored in at least a securely locked, substantially constructed cabinet, and Schedule III, IV, and V substances be either stored in such a locked cabinet or dispersed throughout the stock of noncontrolled drugs in such a manner as to obstruct their theft or diversion. In the Army, controlled substances must be safeguarded at each storage location within a medical facility by placing stocks in appropriate security devices such as a vault, safe, locked cabinet, or locked cage. At least annually, the installation provost marshal must be requested to survey the adequacy of the security provided, and corrective action must be taken as indicated. In other words, in an Army hospital pharmacy all controlled substances must be securely locked in the pharmacy vault or stored in some other secure area.

i. Dispensing.

(1) The dispensing process must be examined from two aspects, inpatient dispensing and outpatient dispensing. The Controlled Substances Act sets guidelines for dispensing controlled substances which deal mostly with the outpatient situation. More specific and stringent guidance on how controlled substances are to be dispensed, labeled, and handled within an Army hospital can be found in AR 40-2.

(2) Controlled substances will be dispensed in bulk to inpatient agencies only upon receipt of a properly written and authenticated prescription (DD Form 1289) with the R_x symbol lined out. This order must be signed by an individual authorized to write prescriptions or by a registered nurse. The order will show the name of the agency receiving the controlled substance and the date. This prescription will be used as a credit voucher to deduct the quantity dispensed from the DA Form 3862 maintained for that item. Labeling requirements for controlled substances issued in bulk to wards, clinics, and other authorized agencies will be prescribed locally by the commander.

(3) While the Controlled Substances Act allows oral-prescription orders for Schedule III and IV substances (and Schedule II substances in an emergency), AR 40-2 states that all prescriptions filled in Army pharmacies will be stamped, typed, or written in ink and will be signed by the prescriber. Thus, no oral prescriptions are authorized in military pharmacies.

(4) Both the Controlled Substances Act and AR 40-2 require prescriptions for schedule drugs to contain the date of issue; name, rank, corps, organization, and address of the patient; and signature of the prescriber. The Controlled Substances Act does state that the physician's BNDD registration number has to appear on prescriptions for schedule drugs. Military physicians are exempt from the requirement to register, but by regulation they must place their service identification number, in lieu of the registration number, on all prescriptions for controlled substances. AR 40-2 also requires that the name of the prescriber be typed, handprinted, or stamped on a controlled prescription in addition to his signature.

(5) Both the Controlled Substances Act and AR 40-2 require that the label on the container of controlled substance dispensed to individual patient will contain:

(a) Prescription number.

(b) Identity of the facility dispensing the controlled substance.

(c) Name of the prescriber.

(d) Name of the patient.

(e) Date of dispensing.

(f) Directions for use and any caution or statement (such as "shake well" or "refrigerate") if needed.

(g) Transfer warning or legend "CAUTION: FEDERAL LAW PROHIBITS THE TRANSFER OF THIS DRUG TO ANY PERSON OTHER THAN THE PATIENT FOR WHOM IT WAS PRESCRIBED" in boldface type.

(6) In addition to these seven requirements, AR 40-2 also requires that all prescription labels contain the name and strength of the drug, except when the prescriber directs otherwise; the initials of the person typing the prescription label; and the legend "KEEP OUT OF REACH OF CHILDREN" in boldface type.

(7) Both by law and by regulation, prescriptions for Schedule II substances cannot be refilled. In addition, AR 40-2 extends this restriction to ethyl alcohol, alcoholic beverages, and paregoric, and prohibits personnel who are authorized to write prescriptions for Code R items from prescribing them for themselves or for members of their family.

(8) If the pharmacy does not have enough of a Schedule II item to fill a prescription order completely, partial filling of the prescription is permitted provided the balance is supplied to the patient within 72 hours. When a prescription for a Schedule II substance is partially filled, a notation of the fact must be made on the prescription and the prescriber must be notified of the action taken.

(9) Prescriptions for Schedules III through V controlled substances (and any other drug designated by the commander) cannot be refilled unless such refilling is authorized by the prescriber on the original prescription. These prescriptions cannot be refilled more than five times and cannot be refilled more than six months after the date of issue. When a prescription for any controlled substance in Schedule III or IV is refilled, the pharmacist will enter his initials, the date of refilling, and the amount of drug refilled on the back of the original prescription form or another appropriate uniformly maintained record which indicates prescription refills.

(10) The partial dispensing of Schedules III, IV, and V controlled substances is authorized provided that each partial dispensing is recorded in the same manner as a renewal, the total quantity dispensed in all partial orders does not exceed the total quantity prescribed, and no dispensing occurs six months after the issuance of the prescription order. Although authorized by law, the partial dispensing of Schedule III through V substances in Army hospitals would be a relatively rare situation such as this: the pharmacy temporarily runs out of stock of the item prescribed and dispenses only enough drug to hold the patient over until new stocks can be obtained from medical supply.

(11) While the Controlled Substances Act authorized the dispensing of Schedule V substances without a prescription provided certain conditions are met, AR 40-2 limits nonprescription dispensing to small quantities of noncontrolled pharmaceuticals suitable for relief of distress due to conditions such as simple headache and mild indigestion. Thus, as a pharmacy technician, you need not become concerned with the details of over-the-counter dispensing of Schedule V drugs.

(12) When a pharmacy does not have a controlled substance required by a patient and the patient has no alternative source of that drug reasonably available to him, the pharmacy may obtain it from a second pharmacy. In such a

situation neither pharmacy need register as a distributor. Records of the transaction must be kept, however, and the amount transferred may not exceed that necessary for immediate dispensing. The transaction is recorded as a dispensing by the pharmacy providing the drug and as a receipt by the pharmacy receiving it. Each must retain a signed receipt of the transaction which, if it involves a Schedule II drug, must be an official order form. Since the Pharmacy Service does not have official order forms for controlled substances, arrangement will have to be through medical supply for the transfer of a Schedule II substance.

j. Destruction. Under the provisions of AR 40-2, whenever controlled substances have deteriorated to the point where they are not usable for the purpose originally intended, are of questionable potency, or have had their identity compromised, they will be reported to the commander for a determination of disposition. Commanders will take such action as may be appropriate and, when indicated, will investigate negligence or carelessness and will direct appropriate disposition of the reported items. If destruction is directed, it will be accomplished in the presence of a witnessing officer and such other officials as may be required by regulations. A record of such destruction, signed by the witnessing officer, will be filed in the controlled substances file as authority for dropping the items from the records of the accounts. (AR 40-61 gives procedures for and documentation of this action.)

6. **UCMJ.** In addition to the specific Federal Statutes referred to above, pharmacy technicians are subject to the Uniform Code of Military Justice, Article 134, which includes the wrongful possession or use of habit-forming narcotic drugs.

7. **Prescription ownership.** From the time a patient receives his prescription from the prescriber and surrenders it to the pharmacist for filling, there is no doubt that the patient is the rightful owner of that prescription. Once a prescription has been turned over to the pharmacy for filling and the patient has received his medication, the prescription is a necessary legal document for the pharmacy's records and legally belongs to the pharmacy. The courts also say that if a patient brings a prescription for filling but decides after the medication has been compounded that he does not want it, the written prescription still belongs to him and he may demand that it be returned.

8. **Confidentiality of prescriptions.** Much confidential and privileged information is contained in the prescription file regarding the people of a given community. The nature of prescriptions must not be discussed with unauthorized persons nor may they be permitted to examine the files. If it is important that a person know the contents of a prescription for legal or other reasons, he can obtain a court order to obtain the necessary information. People must not be allowed to examine the files unless they are acting within their official capacity, such as the issuing physician, inventory officer, auditor, or member of an IG team. From the standpoint of pharmaco-medical ethics, it is bad to let one physician examine the prescriptions of another physician; it may also be an invasion of privacy.

9. **Prescription copies.** Frequently, a patient will ask for a copy of his prescription when he is moving to a different area or going on vacation. You may legally provide a patient with a copy of his prescription IF you adhere to the following:

a. All copies must plainly, and in large letters, be marked or stamped "COPY."

b. Prescriptions which cannot be refilled should, in addition to "COPY," bear the words "NOT TO BE REFILLED." Some pharmacists add the notation "FOR INFORMATION ONLY."

c. Those prescriptions which can be legally refilled (that is, those which do not require a prescription initially) or those which are marked to be refilled a specified number of times must bear a marking instructing future pharmacists regarding the number of times the medication may still be refilled.

d. You must be alert for those asking for copies of narcotic, barbiturate, or amphetamine type drugs. It may be wise to ask the prescriber for his consent before doing so. Whenever possible, avoid issuing copies of this type of prescription.

BASIC FUNDAMENTALS OF THE PRESCRIPTION

CONTENTS
Page

SECTION I : PRESCRIPTION LANGUAGE-PHARMACEUTICAL LATIN

1.	Latin in pharmacy and medicine	1
2.	Commonly used Latin abbreviations, words, and translations	1
3.	Common names of drugs and the Latin counterpart	3

SECTION II : THE PRESCRIPTION 3

4.	Superscription	3
5.	Inscription	3
6.	Subscription	4
7.	Signa (signatura)	4
8.	Abbreviation of names of drugs	4
9.	Abbreviation in subscription and signa	4
10.	Prescription examples	4
11.	Importance of pharmaceutical calculations	6
12.	Fractions	7
13.	Rules applying to all fractions	7
14.	Working with fractions	8
15.	Lowest terms	8
16.	Lowest common denomincator (LCD)	8
17.	Adding fractions	9
18.	Subtracting fractions	9
19.	Multiplying fractions	10
20.	Dividing fractions	11
21.	Decimals	12
22.	Adding decimals	12
23.	Subtracting decimals	13
24.	Multiplication of decimals	13
25.	Division of decimals	13
26.	Roman numerals	14
27.	Weights and measures	14
28.	Metric system	15
29.	Apothecary system	17
30.	Avoirdupois system	21
31.	Relationship and approximate equivalents	21
32.	Ratio and proportion	22
33.	Percentage preparations	23
34.	Ratio preparations	25
35.	Specific gravity	26
36.	Specific gravity of liquids	26
37.	Specific gravity of solids	28
38.	Application of specific gravity to pharmaceutical Problems	29
39.	Specific volume	31
40.	Density	31
41.	Temperature	31
42.	Temperature calculation	32
43.	Temperature conversion	32
44.	Dosage	33
45.	Concentration and dilution	36
46.	Alligation	36

BASIC FUNDAMENTALS of the PRESCRIPTION

Section I. PRESCRIPTION LANGUAGE–PHARMACEUTICAL LATIN

1. Latin in pharmacy and medicine. Latin in prescription writing is centuries old. Although more and more of the prescription is being written in English today, most prescriptions are in part written in Latin or use the Latin abbreviations. As long as physicians continue to use Latin and Latin abbreviations in prescription writing, the pharmacist will have to be able to read and fully understand the terms that are used. Latin used in medicine and prescription writing may be intended to conceal the nature of the medication from the patient, to reduce the possibility of a patient's tampering with a prescription, or to make the prescription universally legible to pharmacists regardless of their national language. Probably the most outstanding reason for the use of Latin in medicine and pharmacy is through force of habit. It has been done for so long that it is hard to break away from the trend. Medical and pharmacy colleges teach the physician to write prescriptions in Latin and the pharmacist to be able to interpret them.

2. Commonly used Latin abbreviations, words, and translations. Since it would be extremely time consuming and of doubtful value to present an entire course in Pharmaceutical Latin here, it is strongly suggested that you read, learn, and *memorize* the words, abbreviations, and meanings on the right. This will familiarize you with the more common terms and phrases used in prescription writing and enable you to understand the physician's or other prescriber's orders. Later, when you have time and a desire to improve your command of Latin, as pertinent to pharmacy, procure a copy of an authoritative pharmacy text. With the aid of such a text, the average individual may become familiar with Latin as it applies to the professions of medicine and pharmacy.

Latin	*Abbreviation*	*English Translation*
ad	ad	to; up to
ad libitum	ad lib.	at pleasure
adde, addendus	add.	add, let them be added
agitata ante usum	agit. ant. us.	shake before using
albus	alb.	white
alternus horis	alt. hor.	alternate hours
amplus	amplus	large
ana	aa.	of each
ante	a.	before
ante cibos; ante cibum	a.c.	before meals; before food
ante meridiem	A.M.	before noon
applicandus	applicand.	to be applied
aqua	aq.	water
aqua bullions	aq. bull.	boiling water
aqua destillata	aq. dest.	distilled water
aqua fervens	aq. ferv.	hot water
aqua frigida	aq. frig.	cold water
aqua forte	aq. fort.	nitric acid
aromaticus	arom.	aromatic
argentum	arg.	silver
aurio	aur.	ear
bene	ben.	well
bibe	bib.	drink
bis in die	b.i.d.	twice a day
bolus	bol.	a large pill
capeat	cap.	let him take
capsula	cap.	a capsule
charta	chart.	paper (powder)
charta cerati	chart. cerat.	waxed paper
cibus	cib.; c.	food
cochleare amplum	coch. amp.	tablespoonful
cochleare infans	coch. inf.	teaspoonful
cochleare magnum	coch. mag.	tablespoonful
cochleare maximum	coch. max.	tablespoonful
cochleare medium	coch. med.	dessertspoonful
cochleare minimum	coch. min.	teaspoonful
cochleare modicum	coch. mod.	dessertspoonful
cochleare parvum	coch. parv.	teaspoonful
cochleare paulus	coch. paul.	teaspoonful
cochleare plenum	coch. plen.	tablespoonful
cola, colatus	col.	strain, strained
collunarium	collun.	nasal douche
collutorium	collut.	mouthwash
collyrium	collyr.	eye lotion
compositus	comp.	compound,

Latin	Abbreviation	English Translation	Latin	Abbreviation	English Translation
		compounded	misce	M.	Mix
congius	cong.	gallon	mistura	mist.	mixture
continuentur remedia	cont. rem.	continue the medication	mitte	mitt.	send
			modo praescripto	mod. praes.	in the manner prescribed
creta	cret.	chalk			
cum	c.; c̄	with	mollis	moll.	soft
da	d.	give	nasus	n.	nostril
decem	decem	ten	nebula	nebul.	a spray
dentur	dent.; d.	let be given; give	niger	nig.	black
dentur tales doses	d.t.d.	give of such doses	nocte	noct.	at night
dexter	dext.	right			
dies	d.	day	nocte maneque	noct. maneq.; n. et m.	night and morning
diebus alternis	dieb. alt.	on alternate days			
diebus secundis	dieb. secund.	every second day	non	non	not
diebus tertiis	dieb. tert.	every three days	non repetatur	non rep.	do not repeat
diluo; dilutus	dil.	dilute	octarius	O.; oct.	a pint
dispensa; dispensatur	disp.	dispense; let be dispensed	oculus	ocul.	the eye
			oculo dextro	O.D.; ocul. dext.	the right eye, in the
dividatur	div.	divide	oculo sinistro	O.S.; ocul. sinist.	the left eye, in the
dividatur in partes aequales	div. in par. aeq.	divide into equal parts	oculo laevo	O.L.; ocul. laev.	the left eye, in the
			oculo utro	O.U.; ocul. utro	in each eye
dosis	dos.; d.	a dose	oleum	ol.	oil
drachma	ʒ	a drachm	omnis	omn.	every
dura	dur.	hard	omni altera hora	omn. alt. hor.	every alternate hour
e	e	out of; in			
et	et	and	omni hora	omn. hor.	every hour
e lacte	e lact.	in milk	omni mane	omn. man.	every morning
ex modo praescripto	e.m.p.	in the manner prescribed	omni quarta hora	omn. 4 hor.	every four hours
			parvus	parv.	small
fac; fiat; fiant	ft.	make; let be made	per	per	by means of
ferrum	ferr.	iron	per os	per os	by mouth
filtra	filtra	filter	phiala	phial.; p.	a bottle
flavus	flav.	yellow	phiala fusca	phial. fusc.	a brown bottle
folium; folia	fol.	leaf; leaves	phiala prius agitata	p.p.a.	the bottle first being shaken
fortis; fortior	fort.	strong; stronger			
gargarisma	garg.	a gargle	placebo	placebo	I please
gradatim	grad.	gradually	plumbum	plumb.	lead
grossus	gros.	large	ponderosus	pond.	heavy
gramma	Gm.	gram	post aurum	post aur.	behind the ear
granum	gr.	grain	post cibum; post cibos	p.c.	after food; after meals
gutta; guttae	gtt.	drop; drops			
hora	hor.; h	an hour	post meridiem	P.M.	afternoon
hora somni	h.s.	at bedtime	praecipitatus	ppt.	precipitated
hydrargyrum	hydrarg.	mercury	pro capillis	pro capil.	for the hair
in aurem sinistram	in aur. sinist.	in the left ear	pro recto	pro rect.	rectal
			pro re nata	p.r.n.	as occasion arises
in die	in d.	in a day	pro usa externo	pro us. ext.	for external use
in dies	ind.	daily	pulvis	pulv.	powder
in oculo laevo	in ocul. laev; O.L.	in the left eye	quantitatim sufficientum	q.s.	a sufficient quantity
inter	inter	between			
inter cibos	int. cib.	between meals	quaque	qq.	each, every
inter noctem	int. noct.	during the night	quaque die	q.d.	every day
in vitro	in vit.	in glass	quaque hora	q.h.	every hour
lac	lac	milk	quater in diem	q.i.d.	four times a day
levis	lev.	light	repetatur	rep.	let it be repeated
libra	lb.	pound	recipe	Rx; ℞	take thou
liquor	liq.	liquid; solution	ruber	rub.	red
lotio	lot.	lotion	scrupulus	℈	scruple
luteus	lut.	yellow	secundum artem	s.a.	according to the art
magnus	mag.	large	secundum legem	s.l.	according to law
mane	man.	morning, in the	semi	sem.	one-half
massa	mass.	a mass	semissem	ss	one-half
milligramma	mg.; mgm.	a milligram	sesqui	sesqui	one and a half
minimum	♏	a minim			

Latin	Abbreviation	English Translation
signa	sig.; S.	write
simul	simul	at one time
sine	s̄	without
sine aqua	sin. q.; s̄ aq.	without water
si opus sit	s.o.s.	if there is need
solve	solv.	dissolve
spiritus frumenti	sp. frum.	whiskey
spiritus vini rectificatus	S.V.R.	alcohol
spiritus vini tenuis	S.V.T.	diluted alcohol
spiritus vini vitis	sp. vin. vit.	brandy
statim	stat.	immediately
succus	suc.	juice
syrupus	syr.	syrup
tabella	tab.	tablet
talis	tal.; t.	of such
ter in die	t.i.d.	three times a day
tres; trium	tres; trium	three
tussis	tuss.	cough
uncia	℥	ounce
unguentum	ung.; ungt.	ointment
ut dictum	ut dict.	as directed
viridis	vir.	green

3. Common names of drugs and the Latin counterpart

Common Name	Latin
Acid	Acidum
Alcohol	Spiritus Vini Rectificatus (SVR)
Belladonna Leaf	Belladonna Folium
Belladonna Root	Belladonna Radix
Bitter	Amari
Cascara	Rhamnus Purshiana
Castor Oil	Oleum Ricini
Charcoal	Carbo
Wood Charcoal	Carbo Ligni
Clove Oil	Oleum Caryophylli
Coal Tar	Pix Carbonis
Coal Tar Solution	Liquor Carbonis Detergens; Liquor Picis Carbonis
Cod Liver Oil	Oleum Morrhuae
Corn Oil	Oleum Maydis
Cottonseed Oil	Oleum Gossypie Seminis
Earth	Terra
Hard Soap	Sapo Duris
Juice	Succus
Lard	Adeps
Lime	Calx
Linseed Oil	Oleum Lini
Medicinal Soft Soap	Sapo Mollis Medicinalis
Oil	Oleum
Ointment	Unguentum
Orange	Aurantium
Peppermint	Mentha Piperita
Peppermint Oil	Oleum Menthal Piperitae
Purified Cotton	Gossypium Purificatum
Rosin	Resina
Seed	Semen
Sherry Wine	Vinum Xericum
Solution	Liquor
Spearmint Oil	Oleum Menthae Viridis
Spermaceti	Cetaceum
Starch	Amylum
Sucrose	Surcrosum; Saccharum
Sweet	Dulcis
Syrup	Syrupus
Turpentine	Terebinthinae
Wax	Cera
Wild Cherry	Prunus Virginiana
Whiskey	Spiritus Frumenti
White Ointment	Ungunentum Alba
White Wax	Cera Alba
Wool Fat	Adeps Lanae
Yellow Ointment	Unguentum Flavum
Yellow Wax	Cera Flava

Section II. THE PRESCRIPTION

The word prescription is a derivation of two Latin words; namely, "prae," meaning "before," and "scribo," meaning "I write." Therefore, the prescription is something written beforehand, hence a rule or direction. It is a written order to the pharmacist by a physician, dentist, veterinarian, or other licensed practitioner, instructing him to compound and/or dispense a specific medication for a specific patient. Through common misuse, the word prescription has also come to mean the completed medication itself. The completed prescription is generally divided into four subdivisions: Superscription, Inscription, Subscription, and Signa. These four parts, in addition to the patient's name, address, and age; the date of writing; and the prescriber's signature, address, and registry number, make up the correct completed prescription.

4. Superscription. The superscription is that which is written above. The superscription always consists of, and is in fact represented by the symbol R_x. This symbol is most frequently printed as part of the prescription blank. R_x is taken from the Latin "recipe," meaning "take thou." It is also thought that the slash across the "R" is a sign for Jupiter and is a carry-down of an invocation to the god.

5. Inscription. The inscription, or what is written within, contains the actual ingredients and their respective amounts. Each ingredient is placed on a separate line, and all important words are

capitalized. Quantities are written, as will be seen in section III (Pharmaceutical Calculations), in either the metric or the apothecary system. In the apothecary system, the amount is shown by a symbol followed by a roman numeral, e.g., ℥ viii (eight ounces). In the metric system, a symbol is not used, grams or milliliters being written or understood. The inscription may be further subdivided into base, adjuvant, corrective, and vehicle.

  a. Base. The base is the main or active ingredient or ingredients designed to restore the patient to health.

  b. Adjuvant. The adjuvant is a substance which increases the efficiency of the base.

  c. Corrective. The corrective modifies or counteracts any undesirable effects of the base or adjuvant.

  d. Vehicle. The vehicle may serve several purposes. It may give proper dosage form (producing a liquid, suppository, capsule, etc.). It may dilute so that the patient may take one capsule or one teaspoonful rather than a few grains or a few drops. It may be used to improve taste or appearance. Or it may aid the patient in receiving the proper amount of a potent drug.

6. **Subscription.** The subscription, or that written below, follows the inscription. It tells the pharmacist the manner of compounding and what the finished product shall be. For example: *M. Fiant solutio* means to mix and let a solution be made. The order of the ingredients on the prescription is not necessarily the order in which they are incorporated into the medication. This is up to the pharmacist and is done according to the art of pharmacy. As you will see later in the course, order of mixing has a pronounced effect on many prescriptions and can be the cause of incompatibilities.

7. **Signa (signatura).** The signa follows the subscription and means literally to write. It tells the pharmacist the directions to the patient which will be typed on the label. An example of a signa is: ℨ i t. i. d. Since most individuals have no idea of the meaning of a drachm (ℨ), it must be changed to its approximate equivalent, one teaspoonful. The label would then read: "Take one teaspoonful three times a day." Prescriptions should bear exact instructions to the patient as in figure 2-1 rather than the overused "ut dict," which means "as directed." When directions are specified exactly, there is no doubt that the patient understands how much of the medication he is to take, and at what intervals. Also, by using the directions, the pharmacist is able to check more accurately for excessive dosage. Study figure 2-1 to see the relationship of the superscription, the inscription and its parts, the subscription, and the signa.

8. **Abbreviations of names of drugs.** In writing a prescription, it is always desirable that the official names of agents be used and spelled out completely. Abbreviations or chemical symbols are confusing and can lead to serious error. An abbreviation such as Hyd. Chlor. is not clear. It could be taken for chloral hydrate, for calomel (mercurous chloride), or for mercuric chloride. Chloral hydrate is a hypnotic, used to induce sleep. Calomel is a purgative. Mercuric chloride is a deadly poison even in the smallest doses, and is intended for use as an antiseptic in external preparations to be used on inanimate objects. You can readily see what would happen if one agent were mistaken for another! Imagine the possibilities of confusion with HgCl and $HgCl_2$. HgCl is calomel, the purgative; $HgCl_2$ is mercuric chloride, the poison.

9. **Abbreviations in subscription and signa.** The more important abbreviations for use in the subscription and the signa are given on the preceding pages.

10. **Prescription examples.** Read each of the prescriptions shown in figure 2-2 in English and try to pick out the prescription parts previously described in the text and shown in figure 2-1. Note that the prescriptions in figure 2-2 are written in longhand and use abbreviations. This is the form in which you will most likely see them in the pharmacy.

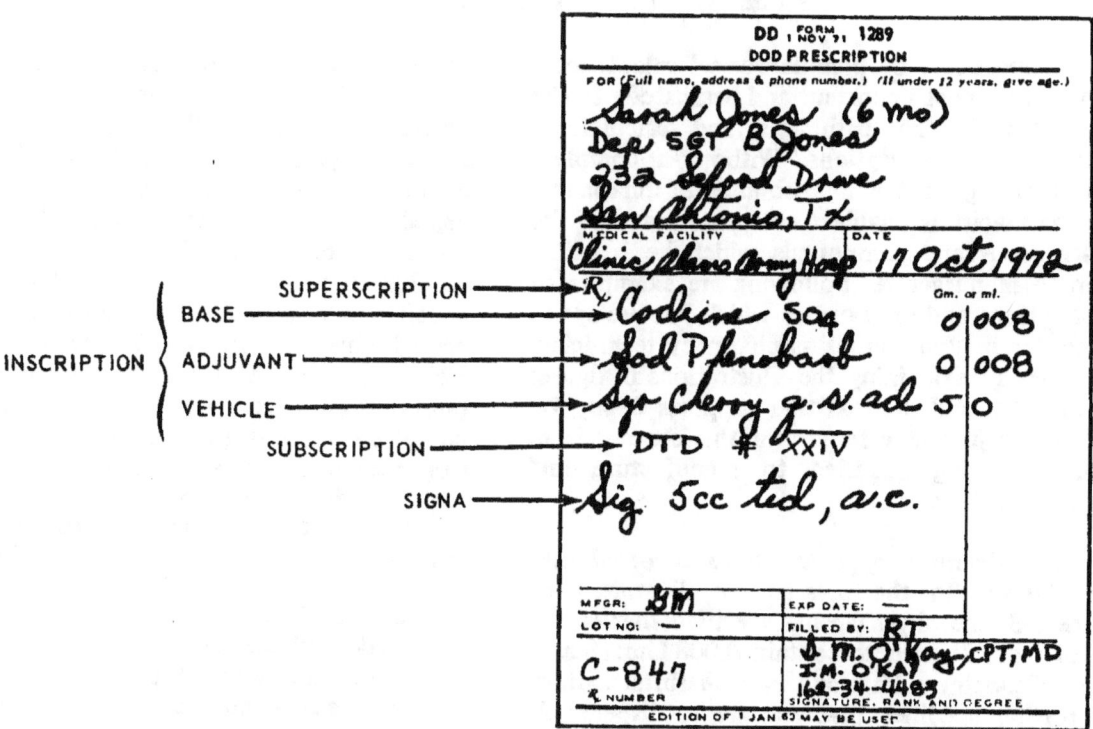

Figure 1. Components of a prescription.

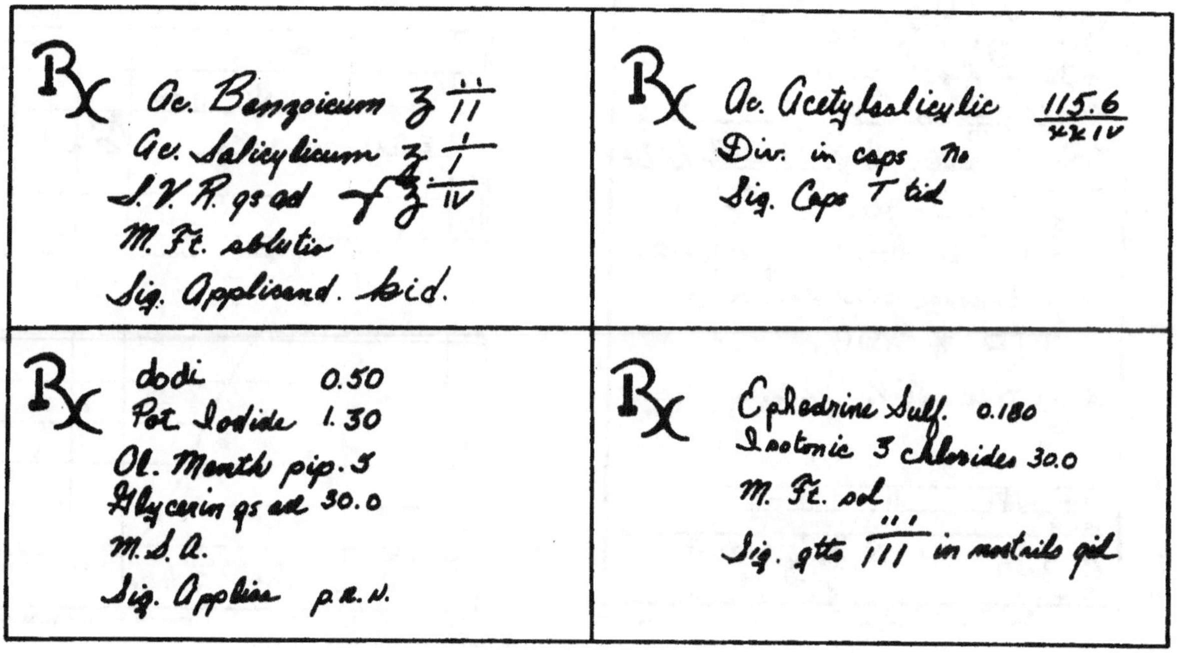

Figure 2. Prescription examples.

Section III. PHARMACEUTICAL CALCULATIONS

11. Importance of pharmaceutical calculations. Perhaps the most important and basic study to the pharmacist is the arithmetic and calculations pertinent to prescriptions. Without a complete understanding of the mathematics of pharmacy, the pharmacist is unable to dispense many of the prescriptions and compounds which he is called upon to manufacture. Following are examples of prescriptions and drug orders which you are apt to encounter in your duties as pharmacy technician. By carefully examining the illustrations in figures 2-3 and 2-4, and the text that supports them, you will realize just how important this chapter is to your becoming qualified to manufacture and dispense medicinals.

    a. Example of calculations involved in a prescription. In the prescription illustrated by figure 2-3, the physician has specified that each 5 ml. of medication is to contain 0.008 Gm. (8 mg.) each of codeine sulfate and phenobarbital sodium. He further specifies that you are to dispense 24 doses of this completed medication. How much codeine sulfate, phenobarbital sodium, and cherry syrup will you use in compounding this preparation? What will the total volume of the completed prescription be and what size bottle will be used to contain it? Are the doses of each ingredient safe for this 6-month-old child? When you have completed this chapter, you will readily be able to arrive at the answer: 192 mg. each of codeine sulfate and phenobarbital sodium, and enough cherry syrup to make the product measure 120 ml. are necessary in compounding this prescription correctly. The total volume of the completed prescription will be 120 ml. and will be dispensed in a 4-ounce bottle. The doses are safe for this patient. In addition, you will know that the label for this medication should direct that one teaspoonful be given 3 times a day before meals.

    b. Example of calculations involved in a bulk order. Figure 2-4 shows a bulk order for an instrument sterilizer solution. The pharmacist has to calculate how much concentrated benzalkonium chloride solution will be necessary to make 4000

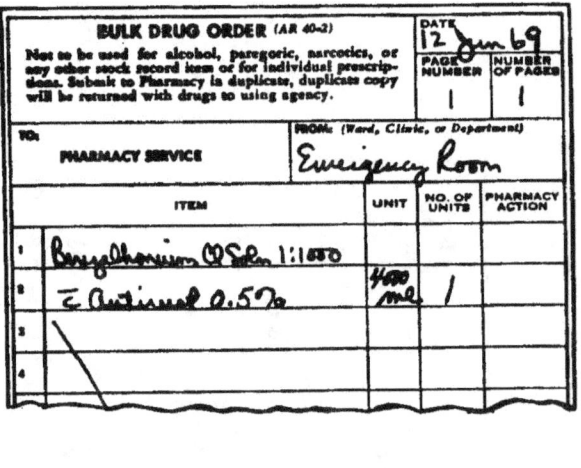

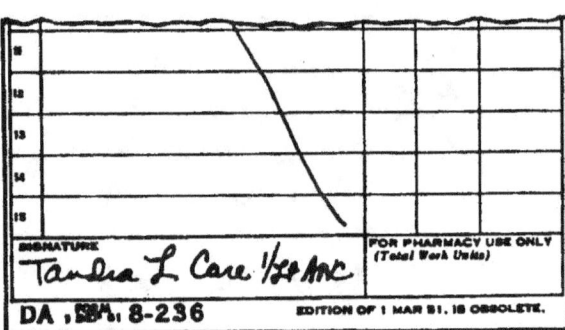

Figure 3. Example of calculations involved in a prescription.

Figure 4. Example of calculations involved in a bulk order.

ml. of a 1:1000 dilution. He will also have to be able to calculate the number of grams of antirust to be used to obtain a 0.5 percent concentration. Upon completing this chapter, it will not be difficult for you to calculate the necessary quantities as being 40 ml. of 10-percent benzalkonium chloride concentrate and 20 Gm. of antirust to make up 4000 ml. of finished solution. These have been but two examples of the absolute necessity of a sound understanding of pharmaceutical arithmetic in pharmacy. As you progress through this chapter, many more will be illustrated and solved.

c. Ground work for pharmaceutical calculations. At first the material that is forthcoming may seem juvenile to you, and you may be inclined to skip over some of the basic aspects. DON'T! Mistakes occur every day in simple addition, subtraction, multiplication, and division. Have you ever caught yourself making such an error? Well, in some places, errors can be allowed for and are not of too much significance, but in pharmacy there is no place for error. First, then, before delving in to the new material, let's begin with a review of fractions and decimals. Here is the place to check yourself on your work. If you work all the problems in fractions and decimals presented in the next few pages, you are well on your way to success in pharmaceutical calculations.

12. Fractions. A fraction represents a simple division problem. It expresses one or more of the equal parts into which a whole number is divided. The fraction $\frac{4}{5}$, then, means five divided into four equal parts of a possible five.

a. Numerator. The number above the separating line is called the numerator. It tells how many parts of the whole are used. In our example $\frac{4}{5}$, four parts of the whole are used.

b. Denominator. The denominator is the number below the separating line and represents the number of parts into which the whole is divided. Again using $\frac{4}{5}$ as an example, the whole (1) is broken into five equal parts, four of which remain.

c. Mixed numbers. Numbers made up of a whole number plus a fraction are called mixed numbers. For example, $1\frac{4}{5}$ has the whole number, 1, and the fraction, $\frac{4}{5}$, and is consequently a mixed number. It means that we have a whole of 1, plus 4 of the 5 parts of another whole.

d. Proper fractions. A fraction having a numerator which is smaller than its denominator is a proper fraction. It always is less than a whole number. Again, $\frac{4}{5}$ is a proper fraction.

e. Improper fractions. A fraction having a numerator larger than or equal to its denominator is an improper fraction, and it is always equal to or greater than a whole number. For example, $\frac{5}{4}$ is an improper fraction. It is the same as $1\frac{1}{4}$ ($\frac{5}{4} = \frac{4}{4}$ and $\frac{1}{4}$; $\frac{4}{4} = 1$).

f. Relative values of fractions. Let's compare the relative values of several fractions. Of $\frac{1}{5}$, $\frac{1}{6}$, $\frac{1}{3}$, and $\frac{1}{4}$, the smallest is $\frac{1}{6}$. Thus, if fractions have the same numerator, but different denominators, the one with the largest denominator is the smallest in value. Comparing $\frac{2}{5}$, $\frac{3}{5}$, and $\frac{4}{5}$; the largest is $\frac{4}{5}$. Thus, in fractions having the same denominator but different numerators, the one with the largest numerator is the largest. To compare fractions with different numerators and different denominators is more difficult.

13. Rules applying to all fractions. Fractions are division problems and follow three basic rules—

a. Value of fractions maintained. If the numerator and denominator are both multiplied or divided by the same number, the value of the fraction is *not* changed. *Example:* Multiplying both the numerator and denominator of $\frac{1}{3}$ by 3, you get $\frac{3}{9}$ which equals $\frac{1}{3}$; $\frac{3}{9}$ divided by 3 (both numerator and denominator) equals $\frac{1}{3}$ which is equal to $\frac{3}{9}$.

b. *Multiplying the value of fractions.* If the numerator is multiplied or the denominator divided by a number, the value of the fraction is *multiplied* by that number. *Example:* Multiplying the numerator of $\frac{1}{3}$ by 3 you have $\frac{3}{3}$ which is three times as large; or if you divide the denominator of $\frac{3}{3}$ by 3 you have $\frac{1}{1}$ or 1, which is three times as large.

c. *Dividing the value of fractions.* If the numerator is divided or the denominator multiplied by a number, the value of the fraction is divided by that number. *Example:* Dividing the numerator of $\frac{3}{9}$ by 3 you have $\frac{1}{9}$, or by multiplying the denominator of $\frac{3}{9}$ by 3 you have $\frac{3}{27}$ which is also $\frac{1}{9}$.

14. Working with fractions. When working with fractions, you often have to reduce a whole number to an improper fraction or reduce an improper fraction to a whole or mixed number.

a. *Reducing a whole or mixed number to an improper fraction.*
(1) *Whole number reduction.* To reduce a whole number to an improper fraction, it is necessary to know into how many parts you want to divide the whole (the denominator). If you wish to convert 6, for instance, to an improper fraction having 5 parts, you will have 5 as the denominator. If you reduce 1 to an improper fraction having 5 parts, you would have $\frac{5}{5}$. The whole number, 6, when converted to an improper fraction with 5 as the denominator, would be 6 times as large, or $\frac{5}{5} \times 6 = \frac{30}{5}$.

(2) *Mixed number reduction.* A mixed number is handled in the same manner. To reduce $8\frac{2}{10}$ to 10ths: $1 = \frac{10}{10}$; then $\frac{10}{10} \times 8 = \frac{80}{10}$ and $\frac{80}{10}$ plus the original $\frac{2}{10} = \frac{82}{10}$, the number of 10ths in $8\frac{2}{10}$.

b. *Reducing an improper fraction to a whole or mixed number.* As previously stated, a fraction is simply a division problem. For this reason, by dividing the denominator into the numerator, you will get a whole number if the division is even, or a mixed number (whole number plus a remaining fraction) if the division is not even. *Example:* Reduce $\frac{20}{2}$: $\frac{20}{2} = 20 \div 2 = 10$, a whole number; or reduce $\frac{35}{4}$: $\frac{35}{4} = 35 \div 4 = 8\frac{3}{4}$, a mixed number.

15. Lowest terms. A fraction is said to be in its lowest terms when the numerator and denominator cannot be divided by the same number. To illustrate: $\frac{3}{9}$, $\frac{6}{27}$, and $\frac{9}{36}$ are NOT in their lowest terms, for both the numerator and denominator can be divided by a common number. The 3 and 9 in $\frac{3}{9}$ can each be divided by 3 to give $\frac{1}{3}$ which is the lowest terms; the 6 and 27 in $\frac{6}{27}$ by 3 to give $\frac{2}{9}$, the lowest terms; and the 9 and 36 in $\frac{9}{36}$ by 9 to give $\frac{1}{4}$, the lowest terms. These final numbers, then, $\frac{1}{3}$, $\frac{2}{9}$, and $\frac{1}{4}$ are fractions in their lowest terms.

16. Lowest common denominator (LCD). When you add, subtract, or compare fractions, it is necessary to have them in common terms. As apples cannot be added to oranges or automobiles to airplanes, fractions with different denominators cannot be added. By changing apples and oranges to fruit, their common denominator, they can be added. This is also true of fractions. The common denominator can be found by two methods: by multiplying the denominators together, and by a "visual method."

a. *Multiplying denominators to find a common denominator.* When all the different denominators of the fractions with which you are dealing are multiplied together, the resulting number is common to all. It is not, however, always the lowest number common to all. For example, to find a denominator common to $\frac{1}{4}, \frac{1}{3}, \frac{1}{2}, \frac{1}{8}$, and $\frac{1}{16}$: Multiply the denominators (all of which are different)— 4 x 3 x 2 x 8 x 16—you get 3072, the common denominator.

   b. *Visual method.* Visually you can see that 48 is also a denominator common to all the fractions in the preceding example and is much smaller and easier to work with than 3072; 48 is also the *lowest* common denominator. Obtaining the LCD by the visual method is not always easy. The best starting point is to try the denominator which is largest; if it does not work, double it. If doubling the largest denominator does not work, triple it; eventually you will arrive at a common denominator. You must always change the denominators to their LCD before adding, subtracting, or comparing fractions.

   c. *Expressing fractions in terms of the LCD.* After you have established the lowest common denominator for the fractions with which you are working, you must express each fraction in terms of the LCD. This is accomplished by dividing the denominator of the fraction into the LCD and then multiplying both the numerator and denominator by the resulting number. After this has been done for all the fractions involved, you may proceed to add, subtract, or compare.

17. **Adding fractions.** In the preceding paragraphs we have defined fractions, stated the rules applying to fractions, and given you the necessary information to work with fractions. Now you will work with examples which have been broken down in step procedures to show how this information is used.

   a. *Proper fractions.*

   Example: Add $\frac{3}{4}, \frac{1}{8}$, and $\frac{5}{6}$.

● *Step 1.* Find the LCD. Visually, you find the LCD to be 24, since 4 will divide into 24, 6 times; 8 will divide into 24, 3 times; and 6 will divide into 24, 4 times.

● *Step 2.* Convert each fraction to similar terms using the LCD. $24 \div 4 = 6$; therefore, $\frac{3}{4} \times \frac{6}{6} = \frac{18}{24}$; $24 \div 8 = 3$; therefore, $\frac{1}{8} \times \frac{3}{3} = \frac{3}{24}$; $24 \div 6 = 4$; therefore, $\frac{5}{6} \times \frac{4}{4} = \frac{20}{24}$.

● *Step 3.* Add the numerators and place the resulting sum over the common denominator. Thus: $18 + 3 + 20 = 41$. Therefore, the sum is $\frac{41}{24}$, which, when reduced to lowest terms, is $1\frac{17}{24}$.

   b. *Mixed numbers and fractions.*

   Example: Find the sum of $1\frac{1}{3}, 2\frac{1}{4}$, and $\frac{1}{2}$.

● *Step 1.* When working with mixed numbers, add all the whole numbers first. $1 + 2 = 3$.

● *Step 2.* Find the LCD for the fractions. By the visual method, you arrive at the LCD as being 12. Change the fractions to common terms. $\frac{1}{3} = \frac{4}{12}; \frac{1}{4} = \frac{3}{12}; \frac{1}{2} = \frac{6}{12}$.

● *Step 3.* Add the numerator. $4 + 3 + 6 = 13$. Place the resulting number (13) over the LCD: $\frac{13}{12}$, which, reduced to lowest terms, is $1\frac{1}{12}$.

● *Step 4.* Add the $1\frac{1}{12}$ to the whole number from step 1: $1\frac{1}{12} + 3 = 4\frac{1}{12}$.

18. **Subtracting fractions**

   a. *Basic method.* The procedure for subtracting fractions is basically the same as adding them.

   Example: Subtract $\frac{3}{4}$ from $\frac{9}{10}$.

● *Step 1.* Find the LCD. By the multiplication method you find a common denominator to be 40 (4 x 10). On visual examination, however, you see that 20 is the *lowest* common denominator.

● *Step 2.* Convert each fraction to similar terms using the LCD. Dividing the 4 into 20 you get 5, which when multiplied by the numerator (5 x 3 = 15) gives $\frac{15}{20}$. Doing the same with the $\frac{9}{10}$, 20 divided by 10 = 2; 2 x 9 = 18, therefore, $\frac{18}{20}$.

● *Step 3.* Subtract the two numerators, 18 − 15 = 3. Place this number (3) over the LCD and arrive at the answer: $\frac{3}{20}$.

   b. *Subtracting larger from smaller.* A problem arises in mixed numbers when the fraction portion of the number being subtracted is larger than the fraction portion of the bigger number.

   Example: Subtract $1\frac{2}{3}$ from $3\frac{1}{2}$.

● *Step 1.* Find the LCD. Visually, you see that it is 6.

● *Step 2.* Express both fractions in terms of the LCD. $3\frac{1}{2} = 3\frac{3}{6}$; $1\frac{2}{3} = 1\frac{4}{6}$.

● *Step 3.* Subtract:
$$3\frac{3}{6}$$
$$-1\frac{4}{6}$$

You can't take $\frac{4}{6}$ from $\frac{3}{6}$. Therefore, you will have to convert the whole number (part of it in this case) to a fraction so that you may subtract. By taking 1 from $3\frac{3}{6}$ and changing it to $\frac{6}{6}$ and adding it to the $\frac{3}{6}$ you already have, you get $2\frac{9}{6}$.

You can now subtract:
$$2\frac{9}{6}$$
$$-1\frac{4}{6}$$
$$1\frac{5}{6}$$

   c. *Alternate method.* An alternate method is to change *all* whole numbers to fractions before subtracting and then reduce the answer to its lowest terms.

   Example: Subtract $2\frac{1}{2}$ from $4\frac{1}{4}$.

● *Step 1.* Find the LCD visually, or by the multiplication method, and you arrive at the LCD of 4.

● *Step 2.* Express all numbers (including the whole number portions) in terms of the LCD: $2\frac{1}{2} = \frac{10}{4}$ and $4\frac{1}{4} = \frac{17}{4}$.

● *Step 3.* Subtract:
$$\frac{17}{4}$$
$$-\frac{10}{4}$$
$$\frac{7}{4}$$

● *Step 4.* Reduce to lowest terms: $\frac{7}{4} = 1\frac{3}{4}$, answer.

19. **Multiplying fractions.** Going back to the three general rules, you know that multiplying the numerator or dividing the denominator by a given number, multiplies the value of the fraction by that number.

   a. *Multiplying fractions by multiplying the numerator.*

   Example: Applying the rule, multiply $\frac{3}{4}$ by 8.

● *Step 1.* Multiply the numerator: 3 x 8 = 24. Place the resulting number (24) over original denominator: $\frac{24}{4}$

● *Step 2.* Reduce to lowest terms: $\frac{24}{4} = \frac{6}{1} = 6$, answer.

   b. *Multiplying fractions by dividing the denominator.*

   Example: Applying the rule, multiply $\frac{3}{4}$ by 2.

● *Step 1.* Divide the denominator: 4 ÷ 2 = 2. Placing the original numerator (3) over the new denominator, you have $\frac{3}{2}$.

● *Step 2.* Reduce to lowest terms: $\frac{3}{2} = 1\frac{1}{2}$, answer.

c. *Multiplying fractions by fractions.* To multiply two or more fractions, multiply the numerators and denominators separately and reduce the obtained fraction to lowest terms.

Example: Multiply $\frac{7}{9}$ by $\frac{6}{14}$.

- *Step 1.* Multiply the numerators: 7 × 6 = 42, the new numerator.

- *Step 2.* Multiply the denominators: 9 × 14 = 126, the new denominator.

- *Step 3.* Make a fraction of the new numbers: $\frac{42}{126}$.

- *Step 4.* Reduce to lowest terms: $\frac{42}{126} = \frac{1}{3}$, answer.

d. *Multiplying fractions by fractions using cancellation.* Cancellation is a process of dividing both numerator and denominator of fractions by the same number. It is like reducing to lowest terms. When two or more fractions are to be multiplied (or divided), cancellation between the numerators and denominators not only works, but is time saving in most cases.

Example: Multiply the following: $\frac{7}{9} \times \frac{6}{14} \times \frac{1}{2}$.

- *Step 1.* Here you will divide seven into both numerator and denominator, making the 7 a 1 and the 14 a 2: $\frac{1}{9} \times \frac{6}{2} \times \frac{1}{2} =$

- *Step 2.* Here you will divide both the numerator and denominator by two, making the 6 a 3 and 2 a 1: $\frac{1}{9} \times \frac{3}{2} \times \frac{1}{1} =$

- *Step 3.* Here you will divide both numerator and denominator by three as before. No more such division is possible, so you multiply the numerators together and the denominators together, and if necessary, reduce to lowest terms: $\frac{1}{3} \times \frac{1}{2} \times \frac{1}{1} =$

- *Step 4.* Multiply the numerators and denominators: $\frac{1}{3} \times \frac{1}{2} \times \frac{1}{1} = \frac{1}{6}$, the answer.

In this example, you have made individual steps out of each of the division steps. In a real situation, you would do all of this in one step, as shown in the next two examples.

Example: Multiply $\frac{7}{9} \times \frac{6}{14} \times \frac{1}{2}$; $\frac{\cancel{7}}{\cancel{9}} \times \frac{\cancel{6}}{\cancel{14}} \times \frac{1}{2} = \frac{1}{6}$, answer.

Example: Multiply $\frac{3}{10} \times \frac{9}{26} \times \frac{26}{54}$; $\frac{\cancel{3}}{10} \times \frac{9}{\cancel{26}} \times \frac{\cancel{26}}{\cancel{54}} = \frac{1}{20}$, answer.

e. *Multiplying two or more numbers, one or more of which is a mixed number.* To multiply mixed numbers, you must change them first to improper fractions, then proceed as with regular fractions.

Example: Multiply $\frac{1}{4} \times 1\frac{5}{8} \times 1\frac{1}{2} \times 5\frac{1}{3}$.

- *Step 1.* Change all mixed numbers to improper fractions: $\frac{1}{4} \times \frac{13}{8} \times \frac{3}{2} \times \frac{16}{3}$

- *Step 2.* Cancel and reduce to lowest terms:

$\frac{1}{4} \times \frac{13}{\cancel{8}} \times \frac{\cancel{3}}{\cancel{2}} \times \frac{\cancel{16}}{\cancel{3}} = \frac{13}{4} = 3\frac{1}{4}$.

20. **Dividing fractions**

a. Again going back to the three general rules, "If the numerator is divided or the denominator multiplied by a given number, the value of the fraction is divided by that number," you have the basis for division among fractions. In order to avoid error, it is best to put a 1 over the whole number, so that you do not inadvertently multiply the numerator instead of the denominator.

Example: Divide $\frac{3}{4}$ by 3. Multiply the denominator of the fraction by 3: $\frac{3}{4} \times \frac{1}{3} = \frac{3}{12} = \frac{1}{4}$.

   b. To divide a whole number or a fraction by a fraction, *invert* the divisor (the number by which you are dividing). This has the effect of placing a 1 over the fraction. Thus, inverting $\frac{2}{3}$ gives us $\frac{3}{2}$, or: $\frac{1}{\frac{2}{3}} = \frac{\frac{3}{3}}{\frac{2}{3}} = \frac{3}{2}$.

      (1) Example: Divide 4 by $\frac{1}{3}$. Invert the fraction by which you are dividing: $4 \times \frac{3}{1} = \frac{12}{1} = 12$.

      (2) Example: Divide $\frac{1}{4}$ by $\frac{1}{8}$. Invert the $\frac{1}{8}$; $\frac{1}{4} \times \frac{\cancel{8}^2}{1} = 2$.

      (3) Example: Divide $2\frac{1}{2}$ by $1\frac{1}{4}$. Here you must first change the mixed numbers to improper fractions, then proceed as before.

$2\frac{1}{2} = \frac{5}{2}; 1\frac{1}{4} = \frac{5}{4}$.

$\frac{5}{2} \div \frac{5}{4} = \frac{\cancel{5}^1}{\cancel{2}_1} \times \frac{\cancel{4}^2}{\cancel{5}_1} = \frac{2}{1} = 2$.

21. Decimals

   a. Writing decimals. Fractions that have 10 or any power of 10 for denominators are called decimal fractions. *For example,* $\frac{1}{10}$, $\frac{3}{100}$, $\frac{126}{1000}$, and $\frac{1234}{10000}$ are decimal fractions. In writing decimals, the denominators can be omitted and a decimal point (.) placed in the numerator to show what the denominator is. There are as many digits *after* the decimal point as there were zeros in the denominator. Taking the examples above—

$\frac{1}{10} = 0.1$, $\frac{3}{100} = 0.03$, $\frac{126}{1000} = 0.126$, $\frac{1234}{10000} = 0.1234$.

Where there are less digits in the numerator than there are zeros in the denominator, zeros must be placed between the decimal point and the numerator as in $\frac{25}{10,000} = 0.0025$, and $\frac{21}{100,000} = 0.00021$. Be very careful to place the zeros to the right of the decimal and before (to the left of) the numerator.

   b. Movement of decimal point. Any error in the placement of the decimal is serious, for each movement of the decimal point to the right or left produces an error of tenfold. To illustrate what happens, consider the difference between $1.00, $10.00, $100.00, and $1,000.00. In each case, the decimal has been moved one place to the right and in each case, the amount of money represented has been multiplied ten times. Similarly, the dose of nitroglycerin is 0.4 mg.; to give a patient 4.0 mg. is a serious error. For this reason, be extremely cautious and exact when working with decimals.

22. Adding decimals

   a. When adding decimals, *always* make sure the decimal points are directly under each other. The actual addition is then the same as with whole numbers.

   b. The following three examples demonstrate the necessity of having the decimal points in line under each other. Compare examples (1) and (2) with example (3).

      (1) Example: Add $100.25, $50.69, and $18.10.

$$\begin{array}{r} \$100.25 \\ 50.69 \\ 18.10 \\ \hline \$169.04 \end{array}$$

      (2) Example: Add 21.25, 36.17, 18.19, and 7.03.

$$\begin{array}{r} 21.25 \\ 36.17 \\ 18.19 \\ 7.03 \\ \hline 82.64 \end{array}$$

(3) Example: Add 1.324, 2347.1, 0.68235, and 11.0001. Remember to line up the decimal points!

```
     1.324
  2347.1
     0.68235
    11.0001
  ─────────
  2360.10645
```

23. Subtracting decimals

a. Again the decimal points must be placed directly beneath each other, and again the procedure is the same as with whole numbers.

b. The following two examples also demonstrate the necessity of having the decimal points in line. Study example (2) carefully. Here we must add zeros at the end of the shorter numbers so that we have something to subtract from. Adding zeros at the right of the number after the decimal point has no effect on the value of the number. Zeros cannot, however, be added before the number after a decimal point, or after a number before a decimal point.

(1) Example: Subtract 11.59 from 102.21.

```
  102.21
   11.59
  ──────
   90.62
```

(2) Example: Subtract .675061 from 2.31.

```
  2.310000
   .675061
  ────────
  1.634939
```

Thus, 2.31 is the same as 2.310000. But 2.31 is NOT equal to 2.0031 or 20.31.

24. Multiplication of decimals. The basic principle in multiplication of decimals is that the number of places to the right of the decimal point in the product (answer) is the *sum* of the decimal points in the factors (numbers being multiplied).

Example: 43.789 (3 places to right of decimal)
            x .02   (2 places to right of decimal)

Product: .87578 (3 + 2 = 5 places to right of decimal)

25. Division of decimals

a. How would you go about determining how much of a powder to pack into each of 12 capsules to evenly divide 64.8 grains of medication? You would divide 64.8 by 12. This division is shown below.

```
       5.4
    ──────
  12)64.8
     60
     ──
      4 8
      4 8
```

b. Above you have divided and placed a decimal one place from the right because there was one place in the amount of powder. Division of a decimal by another decimal is basically the same except for one modification. We know that multiplying the numerator and the denominator each by the same number has no effect on the fraction. For this reason, we can eliminate the decimal from the divisor.

(1) Example: Divide 225.6648 by 0.8.

● *Step 1.* Multiply both the numbers by 10 (simply moving the decimal one place to the right in each case): 08)2256.648.

● *Step 2.* Now the decimal will be correctly situated simply by placing it directly above the other decimal.

```
          282.081
        ─────────
   08)2256.648
      16
      ──
       65
       64
       ──
        16
        16
        ──
         064
         064
         ───
          08
          08
```

(2) Example: Divide 1.23456 by 0.02.

0.02)1.23456

● *Step 1.* Multiply both numbers by 100 (simply moving the decimal two places to the right in each case).

002)123.456

● *Step 2.* Now the decimal will be correctly situated simply by placing it directly above the other decimal.

```
         61.728
   002/123.456
         12
         ──
         03
         02
         ──
         14
         14
         ──
          05
          04
          ──
           16
           16
```

26. Roman numerals. Roman numerals are used in writing prescriptions. They are used to specify the amounts of ingredients when the apothecary system is being used, for example, "Codeine Sulfate gr. iii." They are used to specify the number of units (capsules, tablets, powders, or suppositories) to be dispensed, for example, "Disp. xxiv." And, lastly, they are used in the signa or directions to the patient, for example, "tabs. ii stat, then i q iv h." You should therefore be thoroughly familiar with the system of Roman numerals used in pharmacy. The basic symbols or numerals are—

ss or s̄s̄	1/2
i	1
v	5
x	10
L	50
C	100
D	500
M	1000

These basic numerals may be combined to represent *any* number and there are definite rules for the manner in which they are combined. The rules for Roman numerals are as follows:

a. Fractions. Except for "ss" meaning one-half (1/2), all other fractions are represented by the Arabic numeral, for example, 1/4, 3/8, 1/120.

b. Repeating numerals. Numerals may be repeated and when they are, the value of the number is repeated. Thus iii or III is 3, xxx is 30, and ccc is 300. Any numeral that would be the same as another when repeated is NOT repeated. For example, vv is NOT used for 10 (5 + 5) because x is 10. LL is NOT used for 100 (C = 100).

c. Smaller numerals before larger. A smaller numeral placed before a larger one is subtracted from that numeral. Only one number can be subtracted in this way. Thus iv (5 − 1) = 4, ix (10 − 1) = 9; XC (100 − 10) = 90; etc. But 3 is *never* written iiv.

d. Smaller numerals after larger. A smaller numeral placed after a larger one is added to it as viii = (5 + 3) = 8; xiii (10 + 3) = 13; CLX = (100 + 50 + 10) = 160.

e. Smaller numeral between two larger. A smaller numeral between two larger ones is ALWAYS subtracted from the larger numeral which follows it as CXL (100 + (50 − 10)) = 140; MCMLXV (1000 + (1000 − 100) + 50 + 10 + 5) = 1965.

f. Dotting the one. A dot over the numeral representing 1(i) is often used to distinguish it from a portion of the numeral v. When poorly written, \ / and v may be very similar. If the ones are dotted however, \ / can never be mistaken for 5. As a further precaution against error, the last i may be replaced by a j; 3 written in this manner would be written iij.

g. Table of Roman numerals. Table 2-1 shows Roman numerals and their equivalents. Memorize this chart. You must know these numerals as well as you do Arabic numerals.

Table 1. The Roman Numerals

ss	=	½	x	=	10	xx	=	20	li	=	51
i	=	1	xi	=	11	xxi	=	21	lix	=	59
ii	=	2	xii	=	12	xxix	=	29	lx	=	60
iii	=	3	xiii	=	13	xxx	=	30	lxx	=	70
iv	=	4	xiv	=	14	xxxi	=	31	lxxx	=	80
v	=	5	xv	=	15	xxxix	=	39	xc	=	90
vi	=	6	xvi	=	16	xl	=	40	c	=	100
vii	=	7	xvii	=	17	xli	=	41	ci	=	101
viii	=	8	xviii	=	18	xlix	=	49	cxxi	=	121
ix	=	9	xix	=	19	l	=	50	d	=	500
									m	=	1000

27. Weights and measures. Metrology is the study of measurement as applied to length, weight, and volume. During your study of pharmacy in your Army career, you will constantly be dealing with it, weighing, measuring, or transposing. To be effective, both while you are learning and while you are practicing pharmacy, you must have certain tables and equivalents *committed to memory.* The time you spend memorizing the tables of weights and measures now will be repaid with interest a hundredfold. Although there are other systems of weight and measure, there are three with which the pharmacist comes into daily contact; the metric system, apothecary system, and avoirdupois system.

28. Metric system. The metric system of weights and measures is the legal standard in the United States. All other systems are referred to it for official comparisons. It is used as the scientific system of measuring, the world over.

   a. Units of length, weight, and volume.
   (1) Meter. The standard unit of length, the meter, may be defined as a multiple (1,650,763.73) of the wave length of the light produced by a gas-discharge lamp filled with Krypton 86. This standard permits measurements to an error of 1 part in 10 million. This extreme accuracy degree is necessary in today's missile programs.
   (2) Liter. The unit of volume in the metric system, the liter, is the volume occupied by a kilogram of water at its greatest density (4° C.), and weighed in a vacuum.
   (3) Gram. The unit of weight, the gram, is the weight of one cubic centimeter of water at its greatest density (4° C.), and weighed in a vacuum.

NOTE
The internationally recognized symbol for a Gram is "g." This is also the symbol used by *The United States Pharmacopeia*, XVIII, and *The National Formulary*, XIII, which were published in 1970. Previously the official abbreviation for the Gram was "Gm." This was to distinguish the Gram from the grain (gr). Another commonly used abbreviation for the Gram is "gm." The change from the abbreviation "Gm" to "g." for Gram took place while this TM was being revised. The change came too late to convert all the "Gm" abbreviations in this text to "g." As a result, Gram is still abbreviated Gm. throughout even though the accepted abbreviation is "g."

   b. Advantages of the metric system. There are several definite advantages of the metric system over the other systems—
   (1) It has universal use.
   (2) Every weight and measure has a simple relation to the meter.
   (3) Every unit is multiplied or divided by 10 to reach the next higher or lower unit. As in our system of money, it is a system of decimal progression.

   10 mills = 1 cent
   10 cents = 1 dime
   10 dimes = 1 dollar

   (4) It is the only system of weights and measures having a common standard where a unit of weight equals a unit of volume. The common standard is water. Therefore, under the standard conditions of temperature and pressure, 10 ml. of H_2O equals 10 Gm.: 100 ml. of H_2O weighs 100 Gm.

   c. Subdivisions and multiples. Each table of the metric system has a definite unit around which the subdivision and multiples are based; the meter for length, the liter for volume, and the gram for weight. Subdivisions and multiples of these principal units are indicated respectively by Latin and Greek prefixes.
   (1) Subdivisions (from Latin).

   $$\frac{1}{1000} = milli$$

   $$\frac{1}{100} = centi$$

   $$\frac{1}{10} = deci$$

   (2) Multiples (from Greek).
   10 times = Deka
   100 times = Hecto
   1000 times = Kilo

   d. Learning the metric system. When you have learned the subdivisions and multiples above, the metric system will not be difficult for you to understand or to learn. Remember that it works just like our money system. Using tables 2-2, 2-3, and 2-4, those of lengths, weights, and liquid measure, memorize the metric system.

   e. Metric weights set. Figure 2-5 depicts the standard weight set you will be using in the pharmacy. It consists of weights from 10 milligrams to 100 grams. By combining these weights, it is possible to weight substances between 10 mg. and 201 Gm. *For example*, to weigh 20.750 Gm., you would select a 20 Gm. weight, a 500 mg. weight, a 200 mg. weight, and a 50 mg. weight. The combined total of these weights is 20.750 Gm.

Table 2. Metric Table of Lengths

Lengths			Abbreviations		
10 millimeters	=	1 centimeter	10 mm.	=	1 cm
10 centimeters	=	1 decimeter	10 cm.	=	1 dm.
10 decimeters	=	1 meter	10 dm.	=	1 M.
10 Meters	=	1 Dekameter	10 M.	=	1 Dm.
10 Dekameters	=	1 Hectometer	10 Dm.	=	1 Hm.
10 Hectometers	=	1 Kilometer	10 Hm.	=	1 Km.

The metric table may also be written:

1 meter	=	1000 millimeters
	=	100 centimeters
	=	10 decimeters
	=	0.1 Dekameter
	=	0.01 Hectometer
	=	0.001 Kilometer

Table 3. Metric Table of Weights

Weights			Abbreviations		
10 milligrams	=	1 centigram	10 mg.	=	1 cg.
10 centigrams	=	1 decigram	10 cg.	=	1 dg.
10 decigrams	=	1 gram	10 dg.	=	1 Gm.
10 grams	=	1 Dekagram	10 Gm.	=	1 Dg.
10 Dekagrams	=	1 Hectogram	10 Dg.	=	1 Hg.
10 Hectograms	=	1 Kilogram	10 Hg.	=	1 Kg.

The metric table of weights may also be written:

1 gram	=	1000 milligrams
	=	100 centigrams
	=	10 decigrams
	=	0.1 Dekagram
	=	0.01 Hectogram
	=	0.001 Kilogram

Table 4. Metric Table of Liquid Measures

Liquid measures			Abbreviations		
10 milliliters	=	1 centiliter	10 ml.	=	1 cl.
10 centiliters	=	1 deciliter	10 cl.	=	1 dl.
10 deciliters	=	1 liter	10 dl.	=	1 L.
10 liters	=	1 Dekaliter	10 L.	=	1 Dl.
10 Dekaliters	=	1 Hectoliter	10 Dl.	=	1 Hl.
10 Hectoliters	=	1 Kiloliter	10 Hl.	=	1 Kl.

The metric table of liquid weights may also be written:

1 liter	=	1000 milliliters
	=	100 centiliters
	=	10 deciliters
	=	0.1 Dekaliter
	=	0.01 Hectoliter
	=	0.001 Kiloliter

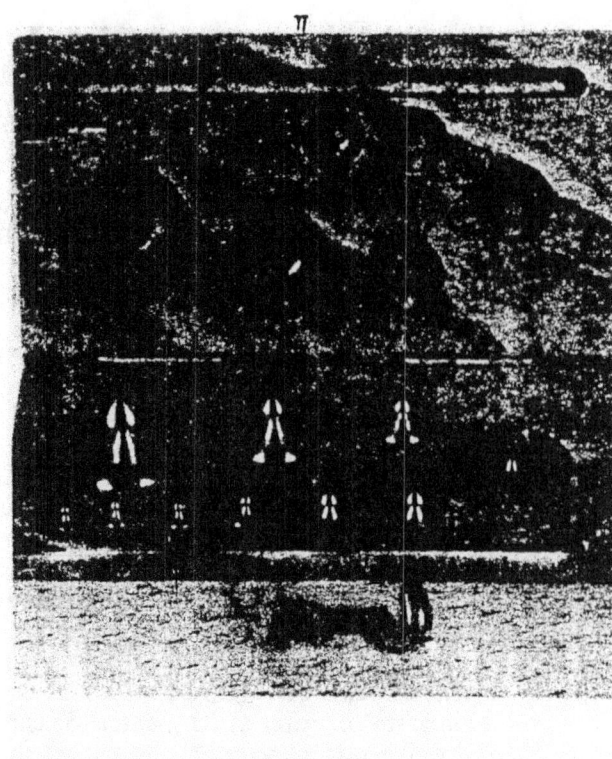

Figure 5. Metric weights.

f. Working with the weights and measures. Now that you have reviewed decimal fractions and have learned the metric system of weights and measures, apply the two as you will be using them in your job.

(1) Example: Addition and subtraction in the metric system. Suppose you dispensed the following amounts of a powder from your stock of 4000 Gm.—28 Gm., 500 mg., 14 cg., and 2 Kg. How much powder would you have remaining?

● *Step 1.* Since you are dealing with four different denominations of weight, you cannot add or subtract until you have a common unit to work with. Since you want the answer in grams (your shelf stock having been specified in grams), it will be simplest to convert all the quantities to grams as follows:

```
    28 Gm. =    28.0  Gm.
   500 mg. =      .5  Gm.
    14 cg. =      .14 Gm.
     2 Kg. =  2000.0  Gm.
            = 2028.64 Gm. amount dispensed
```

● *Step 2.* You started with 4000 Gm. and dispensed a total of 2028.64 Gm., so by subtracting you will determine the balance on hand. Therefore:

$$\begin{array}{r} 4000.00 \text{ Gm.} \\ - \underline{2028.64} \text{ Gm.} \\ \hline 1971.36 \text{ Gm. remaining} \end{array}$$

NOTE

The same method is applied to liquid measure. How many ml. of alcohol would remain if you dispensed 240 from an original liter?

$$\begin{array}{r} 1 \text{ liter} = 1000 \text{ ml.} \\ - \underline{240} \text{ ml.} \\ \hline 760 \text{ ml. remaining} \end{array}$$

(2) Example: Multiplication. How many grams of powder would be necessary to manufacture 20 capsules, each containing 300 mg.?

$$\begin{array}{r} 300 \text{ mg.} \\ \times \underline{20} \\ \hline 6000 \text{ mg.} = 6.0 \text{ Gm.} \end{array}$$

(3) Example: Division. How many 30 ml. bottles of cough syrup can you dispense if you have 3 liters of the syrup on hand?

3 liters = 3000 ml.
3000 ÷ 30 = 100 bottles, answer

29. Apothecary system. Although the Army requires that all Army prescriptions be written in the metric system, the pharmacy technician must also be able to use the apothecary system. In civil practice the apothecary system is widely used and consequently many formulas are specified in terms of apothecary units. Many of the ready-made pharmaceuticals have strength and dosage listed in the apothecary system. Further, you will be filling prescriptions written by civilian prescribers who will use the apothecary system for quantity and dosage. In previous editions of the USP (Revision xiv and before), dosage of the official preparations was listed as an approximation of the apothecary system. The dosage is now completely in the metric system, the apothecary system being completely eliminated.

a. Units of weight and volume.

(1) Apothecary weight. The basic unit in the apothecary system of weight is the grain, which is approximately 64.8 mg. Divisions of the grain are expressed as fractions, for example, $\frac{1}{60}$ gr. Prescriptions will be written with a symbol for the weight denomination and a Roman numeral for the amount of that denomination. Study the table of apothecary weights and abbreviations (table 2-5). Thus, in prescriptions written in the apothecary system, you will see the following written:

Ʒiii   ℥ii   gr iiiss   ℥viii

Table 5. Apothecary Weights and Abbreviations

Apothecary weights			Abbreviations	
20 grains	= 1 scruple		gr. xx	= Ʒi
3 scruples	= 1 drachm	= 60 grains	Ʒ iii	= ℥i
8 drachms	= 1 ounce	= 480 grains	℥viii	= ℥i
12 ounces	= 1 pound	= 5760 grains	℥xii	= 1 lb.

(2) Apothecary liquid measure. The basic unit of the apothecary system of fluid measure is the minim (♏). Study the table of apothecary liquid measure below in table 2-6. Prescriptions are written with a symbol for the denomination to be used. Thus in prescriptions written in the apothecary system for liquids, you will see quantities such as the following:

f ℥ ss   f ℥ ¼   ♏xii   f ℥ viii

(3) Apothecary weights. Apothecary weights used in pharmacy are of two types—cylindrical weights and coin weights.

(a) Apothecary cylindrical weights. The apothecary cylindrical weights are

Table 6. Apothecary Fluid Measure and Abbreviations

Apothecary fluid measure			Abbreviation	
60 minims	= 1 fluidrachm	=	♏lx	= f℥i
8 fluidrachm	= 1 fluidounce	= 480 minims	f℥viii	= f℥i
16 fluidounce	= 1 pint	= 7,680 minims	f℥vxi	= Oi
2 pints	= 1 quart	= 32 fluidounces	Oii	= qt i
4 quarts	= 1 gallon	= 128 fluidounces	qt iv	= Ci

similar to the metric weights depicted in figure 2-5. They usually range from one-half scruple to two drachms. The set contains grain weights in the form of wires; the number of sides indicates the number of grains (fig. 2-6).

    (b) Apothecary coin weights. Coin-type weights which have the weight embossed on their surfaces are particularly subject to error and should not be used.

  b. Converting between denominations. It is often convenient to express a weight or measure in its equivalent in a lower or higher denomination. This can be easily accomplished by either multiplying or dividing the weight by the number of units that equals either the higher or lower measure.

    (1) Example: Express 3/4 quart in its lowest terms in the apothecary system.

● *Step 1.* Since 2 pints = 1 quart; 2 x 3/4 = 1 1/2 pints which can be expressed—pt ii x qt 3/4 = pt iss.

● *Step 2.* Put aside and save the whole number, the one pint, and break the fraction to its next lowest terms.
    1 pint = 16 fluidounces
  so, 16 fluidounces x 1/2 = 8 fluidounces
    or, f ℥ xvi x pt ss = f ℥ viii

● *Step 3.* Continue in this manner, changing each remaining fraction to the next lower denomination. In this case, however, you need go no further, 8 ounces is even. Now you have the whole pint saved from step 2, which equals 16 ounces plus the 8 ounces from step 3, or a total of 24 fluidounces for the answer.

    (2) Example: Express 2/5 gallon in its lowest apothecary terms.

● *Step 1.* 1 gallon = 8 pints.
    8 x 2/5 = 3 1/5 pt
    or, pt viii = gal i
    pt viii x gal 2/5 = pt iii 1/5

● *Step 2.* Continue in this manner, saving the whole and breaking the fraction to its next lowest terms:
    fl ℥ xvi x pt 1/5 = f ℥ iii 1/5
    fl ℨ xviii x fl ℥ 1/5 = fl ℨ i 3/5
    ♏ lx x fl ℨ 3/5 = ♏ xxxvi

● *Step 3.* Putting the numbers previously saved together in sequence, you arrive at the answer: 2/5 gallons = 3 pints, 3 fluidounces, 1 fluidrachm, and 36 minims; or gallon 2/5 = ℴ iii, fl ℥ iii, fl ℨ i, ♏ xxxvi.

    (3) Example: In order to proceed from a lower measure to highest terms, the procedure is just opposite. Divide the measure by the number of units of that measure that equals one unit of the next higher measure. Express 57,688 minims in its highest terms.

● *Step 1.* 60 minims = 1 fluidrachm, therefore

```
          961 ——→ 961 fl ℨ
    60/57688
          540
          ───
          368
          360
          ───
           88
           60
          ───
           28 ——→ 28 minims
```

Save the minims left over and break down the fluidrachms.

● *Step 2.* 8 fluidrachms = 1 fluidounce, therefore

```
          120 ——→ 120 fl ℥
     8/961
          8
         ──
         16
         16
         ──
         01
          0
         ──
          1 ——→ 1 fluid ℨ
```

Save the fluidrachms and break down the fluidounces.

● *Step 3.* 16 fluidounces = 1 pint, therefore

```
            7 ——→ 7 pints
    16/120
       112
       ───
         8 ——→ 8 fluidounces
```

Save the fluidounces and change the pints to the next higher value (quarts).

● *Step 4.* 2 fluid pints = 1 fluid quart, therefore

```
            3 ——→ 3 quarts
      2/7
        6
       ──
        1 ——→ 1 pint
```

● *Step 5.* Now, combine the various quantities you have saved in previous steps. Your answer is:

57,688 minims = 3 qts, 1 pt, 8 fʒ , 1 fʒ , 28 minims.

(4) Checking your answers. You can check your answers in both procedures by just reversing the procedure.

- In example (2), you converted 2/5 gallon to 3 pints, 3 fluidounces, 1 fluidrachm, and 36 minims. Going in reverse to check the accuracy:

  60 minims = 1 fluidrachm

  $\frac{36}{60}$ minims = 3/5 fluidrachm

  3/5 + 1 = 1 3/5 fluidrachms
  8 fluidrachms = 1 fluidounce
  1 3/5 fluidrachms = 1/5 fluidounce
  1/5 + 3 = 3 1/5 fluidounces
  16 fluidounces = 1 pint
  3 1/5 fluidounces = 1/5 pint
  1/5 + 3 = 3 1/5 pints
  8 pints = 1 gallon
  3 1/5 pints = 2/5 gallon—the answer checks.

- In example (3), you converted 57,688 minims to 7 pints, 8 fluidounces, 1 fluidrachm, and 28 minims. To check this answer, you again proceed in reverse.

  7 pt, 8 fʒ, 1 fʒ + 28 minims ⟶ 28 minims
  7 pt, 8 fʒ, 1 fʒ
  1 fʒ = 60 minims ⟶ 60 minims
  7 pt, 8 fʒ
  8 fʒ = 64 fʒ (8 × 8)
  64 fʒ = ⟶ 3,840 minims
  (64 × 60)
  7 pt = 112 fʒ = 896 fʒ = ⟶ 53,760 minims
  (112 × 8) (896 × 60)
  adding the columns of minims ⟶ 57,688 minims
  our answer checks.

c. *Addition and subtraction.* The arithmetic involved in the apothecary system is slightly more involved than that of the metric system. In the metric system, the units increase by multiples of ten. However, the apothecary system has no uniform scale of variation. You are again confronted with the problem that quantities of like denomination must be added or subtracted first, then converted to lowest terms. To illustrate this, look at the following addition problem.

(1) Example:
   4 lb, 3 ʒ , 4 ʒ , 1 ℈ , 18 gr.
 + 8 lb, 2 ʒ , 3 ʒ , 2 ℈ , 19 gr.

- *Step 1.* By simple addition, adding pounds to pounds, ounces to ounces, you get—
   4 lb, 3 ʒ , 4 ʒ , 1 ℈ , 18 gr.
 + 8 lb, 2 ʒ , 3 ʒ , 2 ℈ , 19 gr.
  12 lb, 5 ʒ , 7 ʒ , 3 ℈ , 37 gr.

- *Step 2.* This answer is not in its reduced terms, because 37 grains equals one scruple plus 17 grains, 3 scruples equal a drachm, and so on. To reduce this answer, begin at the right and work to the left, changing each quantity possible to the next higher denomination. Twenty grains equals one scruple, leaving 17 grains and adding 1 scruple to the 3 previously in the column. Likewise, since there are 3 scruples to the drachm, you must convert 3 of the 4 scruples you now have in this column to 1 drachm, leaving 1 ℈ and increasing the drachms to 8. There being 8 drachms to the ounce, you have no drachms remaining, but increase the ounces to 6. The final reduced answer then beomes 12 lb, 6 ʒ , 1 ℈ , 17 gr.

(2) Example: Subtract 4 lb, 6 ℈ , 4 ʒ , 1 ℈ , 19 gr. from 6 lb, 8 ʒ , 5 ʒ , 2 ℈ , 15 gr.

- *Step 1.* Set up for subtraction.
   6 lb, 8 ʒ , 5 ʒ , 2 ℈ , 15 gr.
 − 4 lb, 6 ʒ , 4 ʒ , 1 ℈ , 19 gr.

Since you could not take 19 grains from 15 grains, it is necessary to convert one scruple to grains, reducing the number of scruples in the upper figure to 1 and increasing the grains to 35. You may never have a negative number in subtracting weights and measures.

- *Step 2.* Having converted the scruple to grains, your problem becomes:
   6 lb, 8 ʒ , 5 ʒ , 1 ℈ , 35 gr.
 − 4 lb, 6 ʒ , 4 ʒ , 1 ℈ , 19 gr.
   2 lb, 2 ʒ , 1 ʒ , 0 ℈ , 16 gr.

d. *Multiplication and division.*
(1) Example: Multiplication. Multiplication of compound numbers such as arise in the apothecary system may be accomplished in several ways, the easiest of which is to multiply each denomination individually, then reduce the answer. Multiply 2 gal, 3 qt, 1 pt, 9 fʒ , 7 fʒ , 18 min. by 6.

- *Step 1.*
   2 gal, 3 qt, 1 pt, 9 fʒ , 7 fʒ , 81 min.
                                              × 6
  ───
  12 gal, 18 qt, 6 pt, 54 fʒ , 42 fʒ , 108 min.

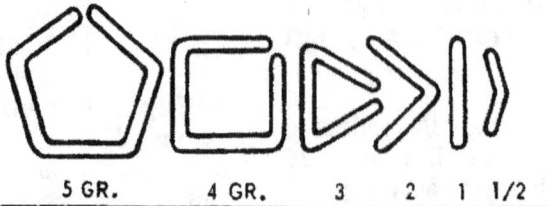

Figure 6. Apothecary grain weights.

Table 7. Approximate Equivalents

Weight

Metric	Approx apothecary	Metric	Approx apothecary	Metric	Approx apothecary
0.1 mg.	1/600 gr.	6 mg.	1/10 gr.	0.1 Gm.	1-1/2 gr.
0.2 mg.	1/300 gr.	8 mg.	1/8 gr.	0.12 Gm.	2 gr.
0.3 mg.	1/200 gr.	10 mg.	1/6 gr.	0.15 Gm.	2-1/2 gr.
0.4 mg.	1/150 gr.	12 mg.	1/5 gr.	0.2 Gm.	3 gr.
0.5 mg.	1/120 gr.	15 mg.	1/4 gr.	0.3 Gm.	5 gr.
0.6 mg.	1/100 gr.	20 mg.	1/3 gr.	0.5 Gm.	7-1/2 gr.
1 mg.	1/60 gr.	25 mg.	3/8 gr.	0.6 Gm.	10 gr.
1.2 mg.	1/50 gr.	30 mg.	1/2 gr.	1 Gm.	15 gr.
2 mg.	1/30 gr.	50 mg.	3/4 gr.	1.5 Gm.	22 gr.
3 mg.	1/20 gr.	60 mg.	1 gr.	2 Gm.	30 gr.
4 mg.	1/15 gr.	75 mg.	1-1/4 gr.	3 Gm.	45 gr.
5 mg.	1/12 gr.	90 mg.	1-1/2 gr.	4 Gm.	60 gr. (1 drachm)
				5 Gm.	75 gr.
				7.5 Gm.	2 drachms
				15 Gm.	4 drachms
				30 Gm.	1 ounce

Liquid Measure

Metric	Approx apothecary	Metric	Approx apothecary	Metric	Approx apothecary
0.03 ml.	1/2 minim	0.6 ml.	10 minims	15 ml.	4 f. drachms (1/2 oz)
0.05 ml.	3/4 minim	0.75 ml.	12 minims	30 ml.	1 f. ounce
0.06 ml.	1 minim	1 ml.	15 minims	60 ml.	2 f. ounces
0.1 ml.	1-1/2 minims	2 ml.	30 minims	120 ml.	4 f. ounces
0.2 ml.	3 minims	3 ml.	45 minims	250 ml.	8 f. ounces
0.25 ml.	4 minims	4 ml.	60 minims	500 ml.	16 f. ounces (1 pint)
0.3 ml.	5 minims	5 ml.	1 f. drachm	1000 ml.	1 quart
0.5 ml.	8 minims	10 ml.	2 f. drachms		

N.B. These are *approximate* equivalents. They may be used to compare prepared dosage forms such as tablets, capsules, and solutions. For converting *specific* quantities as are called for in formulas, use the exact equivalents provided in the U.S.P. For prescription compounding, use the exact equivalents rounded to 3 significant figures.

● *Step 2.* Simply reduce the above answer to the lowest terms as previously explained.
17 gal, 2 qt, 1 pt, 11 f℥, 3 fℨ, 48 min.

(2) Example: Division (usual method). Division of compound numbers is best done by dividing the highest measure first, keeping the whole number obtained and converting any remainder to the next smaller denomination and adding it to the given quantity. Then continue the division. Divide 8 gal, 2 qt, 1 pt by 3.

● *Step 1.*
8 gal ÷ 3 = 2 gal (+ 2 gal remainder)
2 gal = 8 qt + original 2 qt = 10 qt.

● *Step 2.*
10 qt ÷ 3 = 3 qt (+ 1 qt remainder)
1 qt = 2 pt + original 1 pt + 3 pt.

● *Step 3.*
3 pt ÷ 3 = 1 pt.

● *Step 4.* Add the products from all steps (not the remainders!).
2 gal, 3 qt, 1 pt, answer.

(3) Example: Division (alternate method). An alternate method is to convert the amounts to their lowest form; in this case, pints, then convert back to highest terms after dividing. Divide 8 gal, 2 qt, 1 pt by 3.

● *Step 1.*
8 gal = 64 pt
2 qt = 4 pt
1 pt = 1 pt
total = 69 pt

● *Step 2.* Divide.
69 ÷ 3 = 23 pt

● *Step 3.* Convert back to highest terms.
23 pt = 11 qt, 1 pt
11 qt = 2 gal, 3 qt
2 gal, 3 qt, 1 pt, answer.

30. **Avoirdupois system.** In the United States all items sold by weight are commercially bought and sold by avoirdupois weight. Exceptions to this rule include gems and precious metals. The weight which appears on a scale when you weigh yourself is avoirdupois weight. Unless expressly stated, all drugs and chemicals are bought and sold by avoirdupois weight. Therefore, it is *extremely* important to note that in receiving narcotics from the warehouse, an ounce bottle contains 437.5 grains (avoirdupois ounce), not 480 grains (apothecary ounce). As you can readily see, serious error could result in your narcotic records if you did not understand this principle. The grain is common to BOTH the avoirdupois and the apothecary system, *but* the ounces and pounds are different. Study the comparison below.

Apothecary
ounce = 480.0 grains
Avoirdupois
ounce = $\underline{437.5 \text{ grains}}$
= 42.5 grains *difference*
Apothecary
pound = 12 oz × 480 grains = 5760 grains
Avoirdupois
pound = 16 oz × 437.5 grains = $\underline{7000 \text{ grains}}$
1240 grains *difference*

31. **Relationship and approximate equivalents.** The metric system, apothecary system, and avoirdupois system are all used extensively by the pharmacy technician. Because you have and use three separate systems of weight and measure, it is necessary to understand their relationship and know how to convert from one to the other quickly and accurately.

a. Some relationships to remember.
● *Remember:* The pharmacist receives drugs and chemicals by avoirdupois weight at 437.5 grains per ounce, 16 ounces per pound.
● *Remember:* The pharmacist dispenses prescriptions in the metric or apothecary system. The apothecary system has 480 grains per ounce and only 12 ounces per pound.
● *Remember:* One apothecary fluidounce (H_2O) weighs 454.6 grains at 25° C. There are 480 minims in an apothecary fluidounce. It follows, then, that 1 minim of water at 25° C. weighs $\frac{454.6}{480} = 0.95$ grains.

b. Approximate equivalents. Table 2-7 should be thoroughly memorized. These equivalents will allow conversion between systems with a *relative degree of accuracy*. A facsimile of this table should be conspicuously placed near the work area in your pharmacy as a reference and check.

c. *Exact conversion.* Exact accuracy in conversion from one system to another as is needed for compounding prescriptions cannot be accomplished using approximate equivalents. Nearly exact conversion equivalents are given in a table in the USP.

32. Ratio and proportion

a. *Ratio.* Ratio is an expression of the relationship of one thing to another. For the purpose of arithmetic, ratio is the relation showing the amount by which one thing is different from another. Thus, if you have a solution of 9 grams of sodium chloride in 1000 grams of water, the ratio of NaCl to water is 9:1000 or $\frac{9}{1000}$, and is read "9 to 1000." The value of a ratio is the number obtained by dividing the first term (antecedent) by the second term (consequent); therefore, the value of 12:4 is 3.

(1) *Ratios remain constant.* Multiplying or dividing BOTH terms of a ratio does not change its value. Therefore, multiplying both terms of 10:5 by 5 gives us 50:25. In either case, the ratio is the same, 2:1. The terms of a ratio taken together are called a couplet.

(2) *Equal units.* Ratio can exist only between numbers of the same unit value—as ratio of percent to percent or weight to weight—but never weight to percent. (*Exception:* In pharmacy, we often make solutions which are expressed as weight to volume.) The comparing of numbers of the same unit volume follows as certainly as apples can be compared to apples and oranges to oranges, but never oranges to apples.

(3) *Examples of ratio problems:*
- What is the value of the ratio 10:100? Divide the first term by the second to get 1/10.
- Simplify 6:36. Divide both terms by 6 to get 1:6.
- What is the ratio between 18 percent and 9 grams? No ratio! Percent cannot be compared to grams.
- What do the following three ratios have in common? 1:5, 3:15, 5:25. When simplified, each is 1:5 or 1/5.

b. *Proportion.* 15:3 :: 10:2 is a proportion. It is read "15 is to 3 as 10 is to 2." Proportion is a means of showing equality between ratios. 15 ÷ 3 = 5 and 10 ÷ 2 = 5; they have the same value. The first and fourth terms of a proportion are called the *extremes* and the second and third terms are called the *means*. In the example cited above, 15 and 2 are the extremes; 3 and 10 are the means. The product of the extremes (15 x 2) equals the product of the means (3 x 10).

(1) *Example:* 50:10 :: 25:5
50 x 5 = 250;
10 x 25 = 250.

Thus, it is apparent that if one of the numbers were an unknown, it could easily be determined as follows:

(2) *Example:* If it takes 50 grains of powder to make 5 capsules, how many grains are necessary to make 3 capsules? This problem is nothing more than a proportion in which one of the terms is an unknown.

50:x :: 5:3
5x = 150 (arrived at by multiplying the means and extremes)
x = 30 grains, answer (to make 3 capsules)

It is customary to let x or y represent the unknown number in proportions. Thus you find that 30 grains would be necessary to make 3 capsules.

(3) *Example: Rule of Words.* Putting this example into a rule of words—"To find either extreme, multiply the means (2nd and 3rd numbers) and divide by the known extreme." Likewise, "To find either mean, multiply the extremes (1st and 4th numbers) and divide by the known mean." Notice how you progress from a statement of problem to a written proportion. If 500 Gm. of a salt solution contains 10 percent salt, to what weight must you evaporate the solution to make it 20 percent salt?

- *Step 1.* Write down the facts.
500 Gm. is 10%
? Gm. is 20%

- *Step 2.* Let x represent the unknown (?) quantity. Arbitrarily, let x take the fourth position.

- *Step 3.* Since we can compare only like articles, put the number with the same denomination as x in the third position.

- *Step 4.* Determine if the unknown is to be larger or smaller than the third number. In the preceding example, you are evaporating a solution and thus it will be smaller. Since the smaller follows the larger in the 3rd and 4th positions, the *same* must hold true of the 1st and 2d. Therefore, the larger number will be in first position, and the smaller in second position.

- *Step 5.* From the preceding 4 steps, you may conclude that—

    20:10 :: 500:x

- *Step 6.* Cross multiply (multiply the means and extremes).

    20 x = 5000

- *Step 7.* Solve for x.
    x = 5000 ÷ 20
    x = 250 Gm., the weight of the 20% solution, answer.

33. Percentage preparations. Many of the calculations you will be required to make in the pharmacy will be for the compounding and dispensing of percentage preparations (solutions or powders). The most important factor to keep in mind here is that *slight* errors in dilute preparations may be considered negligible, whereas even a slight error in a concentrated preparation may be serious. To firmly impress this in your mind, consider the difference between losing one quarter from your pocket containing ten quarters and losing ten quarters from another pocket containing 100 quarters. The loss in each case is 10 percent. In the first instance, 10 percent loss amounted to only 25 cents, while in the second instance the 10 percent loss amounted to $2.50. Thus, as the percentage of a solution or other preparation becomes greater, the error becomes more severe. The strength of a solution is the ratio of active ingredient to solvent and can be expressed as a percent or as a ratio.

a. *Percent solutions.* The Latin "per centum" literally means "by hundreds." Ten percent, then, refers to 10 hundreds or 10 parts out of 100 parts. A 10-percent solution could be broken down as follows:

Total volume of solution — 100% or 100 parts
Solute (active ingredient) — 10% or 10 parts
Solvent — 90% or 90 parts

In solutions of solids or gases in a liquid, the solid or gas being dissolved is called the solute, and the liquid is the solvent. In solution of liquids in liquids, we arbitrarily say that the liquid present in greater quantity is the solvent and the liquid of lesser quantity is the solute. Thus we say that in mixing 25 percent water and 75 percent alcohol, we obtain a solution of water in alcohol. Reversing the situation, 25 percent alcohol and 75 percent water, we would term a solution of alcohol in water.

(1) *Variable meaning of percentage.* Percentage in solutions can have different meanings under different circumstances. In solution, you are dealing with solids which are weighed, and liquids which can be weighed or measured; thus, it is necessary to define the expression of percentage concentration of solutions. There are three different percentage solutions:

(a) Percent weight in weight (w/w)—expresses the number of grams of a constituent in 100 grams of solution.

(b) Percent weight in volume (w/v)—expresses the number of grams of a constituent in 100 ml. of solution, and is used in prescription practice regardless of whether water or another liquid is used.

(c) Percent volume in volume (v/v)—expresses the number of milliliters of a constituent in 100 ml. of solution.

(2) Rules for percentage solutions. Unless specifically stipulated otherwise, the following rules hold true for prescriptions of percentage solutions:
- Mixtures of solids are weight in weight.
- Solids in liquids are weight in volume.
- Liquids in liquids are volume in volume.
- Gases in liquids are weight in volume.

For example, to make a 10-percent solution, dissolve 10 Gm. of a solid or 10 ml. of a liquid in the amount of solvent necessary (qs) to make 100 ml. of finished solution. In the apothecary system, 45.6 grains of a solid or 48 minims of a liquid dissolved in enough solvent to make 1 fluidounce would yield a 10-percent solution. Slight changes in volume attributable to changes in room temperature are negligible and may be disregarded.

b. Percent weight in volume solutions. Weight in volume (w/v) percentage may be called the "key" to percentage and ratio solutions. You are dissolving a weight of solid in a volume of liquid (water, unless otherwise specified).

(1) Metric system rule. Multiply the specified percentage, expressed as a decimal fraction, times the required number of ml. The resulting number will represent the number of grams of solid in the solution, or percent (decimal) x ml. = grams solute.

(2) Apothecary system rule. Multiply the percent, expressed as a whole number times 4.5457 times fluidounces of solution required. The answer you obtain will be the number of grains of solute to be used. The weight of 1 fluidounce of water at 25° C. is 454.57 grains. Therefore, 4.5457 grains is the amount of solute necessary to prepare a 1-percent solution of 1 ounce. Expressed as a formula, this rule becomes percent (whole number) x 4.5457 x fl oz. required = grains of solute.

(3) Example: Prepare 300 ml. of 20-percent (w/v) solution of sodium thiosulfate. How many grams of solute are necessary? How much solvent is used?

- *Step 1.* Formula.
  % (decimal) x ml. = grams solute

- *Step 2.* Substitute.
  .20 x 300 = 60 grams of solute

- *Step 3.* Since the total solution is to be 300 ml., you add enough water to the 60 grams of solute to make the finished product measure 300 ml. If you assumed that 60 grams took up 60 ml. of volume, you could deduce that 240 ml. of liquid added to the 60 grams of solute would make 300 ml. This does not hold true. Many solids when dissolved do not take up a volume equal to their weight, so you must always add enough water to make the volume up to the required amount. This bringing up to the required volume is expressed in prescriptions as "qs ad" from the Latin, and means "add a sufficient quantity."

(4) Example: Work this similar problem in the apothecary system. Make ℥ iv (4 fluidounces) of a 20-percent solution of sodium thiosulfate.

- *Step 1.* Formula.
  % x 4.5457 x fl. oz. = grains of solute.

- *Step 2.* Substitute.
  20 x 4.5457 x 4 = 363.6 grains = (℥ vi gr iiiss)

The prescription could have been written:
Rx Sod. Thiosulfate grs 363.6
Pur. Water qs ad ℥ iv.

c. Percent volume in volume solutions. To calculate percentage of solutions of one liquid in another, multiply the desired percent, as a decimal fraction, of the active ingredient times the amount of total solution desired.

Example: How many ml. of an active ingredient must be used to produce 480 ml. of a 3-percent solution?
480 x .03 = 34.4 ml., answer

d. Percent weight in weight solution. In some cases, a definite finished weight of solution is required. To find the percent of solid in the solution, multiply the total weight of the finished solution desired by the percent desired, expressed as a decimal. Written as a formula this would be—Gm. total solution x % (decimal) = Gm. of active solute. By subtracting this weight (the weight of the solute) from the weight of the total solution, the weight of the liquid required as solvent is found. This weight may be converted to volume by dividing the weight of liquid required by the specific gravity of the liquid. Specific gravity will be discussed below.

(1) Example: How many grams of acriflavine are required to manufacture 200 Gm. of a 10-percent (w/w) solution? How much glycerin will you use as the solvent? Express the amount of glycerin in both weight and volume (Sp. Gr. glycerin = 1.25).

200 × 0.10 = 20 Gm. acriflavine
200 − 20 = 180 Gm. glycerin
180 ÷ 1.25 = 144 ml. glycerin

(2) *Example:* Prepare 4 fluidounces of a 10-percent (w/w) solution of acriflavine in glycerin. This problem takes on more difficulty in the apothecary system. First reduce the total weight of solution to grains.

- *Step 1.* Reduce solution to grains.
  4 fl oz × 454.6 = 1818.4 grains (total solution)

- *Step 2.* 10 % of 1818.4 = 181.84 grains of acriflavine.

- *Step 3.* 1818.4 − 181.84 = 1636.56 grains of glycerin.

- *Step 4.* 1 fl oz of water weighs 454.6 grains; therefore, 1 fluidounce of glycerin weighs 454.6 × 1.25 = 568.25 gr.

- *Step 5.* Since you need 1636.56 grains of glycerin, by dividing this by the number of grains of glycerin in a fluidounce, you will obtain the volume of glycerin required in terms of fluidounces.
  1636.56 ÷ 568.25 = 2.88 fluidounces or
  f ʒ ii f ʒ vii ♏ii

34. Ratio preparations. Ratio is similar to percent, the entire solution is the total, the active ingredient is a certain part of the total, and the solvent or diluent is the remainder. Ratio solutions are expressed as so much in so much; for example, 1 in 10; 1 in 100; 1 in 1000. It means exactly what it says, 1 part in a total of 10 parts, or 1 part in a total of 100 parts; it does not mean 1 part plus 10 parts to give 11 parts. It is obvious that a 1 in 10 solution, therefore, is identical to a 10 percent solution. A ratio solution is expressed by parts—so many parts in a total of so many parts; 1 part in 10 parts = 1 in 10. The number of parts of active ingredient is taken as 1, and the total parts possible is variable as in 1 in 10, 1 in 20, 1 in 100. You remember in percentage, the total mixture was always 100 and the active part was variable, as 10 percent (10/100), 20 percent (20/100), or 50 percent (50/100).

  a. Weight in volume solution by ratio. The following proportion is used in making ratio solutions of the weight in volume type.

$$\frac{\text{weight of solute}}{\text{wt of given volume of solution if it were water}} :: \frac{\text{one part of solute}}{\text{No. of parts of completed solution containing 1 part of solute}}$$

(1) *Example:* What is the ratio strength (w/v) of a solution containing 25 Gm. of solute in 250 ml. of solution?
Substitute in the preceding formula.

$$\frac{25}{250} :: \frac{1}{x}$$

$$25x = 250$$

x = 10; ratio strength, then, is 1 in 10 (1/10)
Using this formula, any one of the four parts can be found, if the other three are known.

(2) *Example:* If the ratio strength (w/v) of a solution is 1:25, and it contains 50 Gm. of solute, what is the total volume of the solution?
Substitute:

$$\frac{50}{x} :: \frac{1}{25}$$

x = 1250 ml., the total volume of solution.

  b. Volume in volume solution by ratio. Again, a simple proportion can be used to solve this type of problem.

$$\frac{\text{vol. of ingredient}}{\text{vol. of total solution}} :: \frac{\text{parts of ingredient}}{\text{parts of whole}}$$

CAUTION
The two volumes concerned *must* be expressed in the same denomination; that is, if one is expressed in ml., the other must also be ml.

(1) *Example:* What amount of active ingredient must be used to produce 500 ml. of a solution (v/v) with a ratio strength of 1:20?
Substitute:

$$\frac{x}{500} :: \frac{1}{20}$$

$$20x = 500$$

x = 25 ml., answer

(2) *Example:* What is the ratio strength of a solution which contains 5 ml. of active ingredient in a total of 250 ml.? Substitute:

$$\frac{5}{250} :: \frac{1}{x}$$

$$5x = 250$$

$$x = 50$$

strength is 1 in 50 (1:50)

  c. Weight to weight solution by ratio. For w/w solutions, two proportions may be expressed;

one shows the relationship between active ingredient and the total solution, the other between ingredient and diluent.

$$\frac{\text{wt ingredient}}{\text{wt mixture}} :: \frac{\text{parts of ingredient}}{\text{parts total mixture}}$$

or

$$\frac{\text{wt ingredient}}{\text{wt diluent}} :: \frac{\text{parts of ingredient}}{\text{parts of diluent}}$$

(1) Example: What is the weight in grams of a 1:10,000 (w/w) solution containing 150 mg. of active ingredient? Substituting in first formula:

$$\frac{150}{x} = \frac{1}{10,000}$$
$$x = 1,500,000 \text{ mg.}$$
$$x = 1500 \text{ Gm. (wt of solution)}$$

(2) Example: If 8 Gm. of a substance is dissolved in 128 ml. of water, what is the w/w ratio strength of the solution? Substituting in second formula:

$$\frac{8}{128} :: \frac{1}{x}$$
$$8x = 128$$
$$x = 16$$
$$1 \text{ in } 16 \text{ (1:16)}$$

35. Specific gravity. Specific gravity, abbreviated Sp. Gr., is the relation between the weights of two substances, one of which is a standard. Determination of Sp. Gr. is accomplished under specific conditions, namely, 25° C. and normal barometric pressure. Distilled water is the standard for liquids and solids, and air for gases. Specific gravity is always expressed as a decimal; the standard substance has a Sp. Gr. of 1.000. Comparing equal volumes of glycerin and water, for example, we find that glycerin is 1-1/4 times as heavy. Since the Sp. Gr. of water is 1.000, the Sp. Gr. of glycerin is 1.250.

36. Specific gravity of liquids. There are several instruments used for determination of the specific gravity of liquids. We will discuss only two here, the pycnometer and the hydrometer.

a. Pycnometer. The pycnometer (fig. 2-7) is a specific gravity bottle. Pycnometer is derived from the Greek word pykno, meaning dense, and meter, meaning measure. It is, therefore, a device for measuring density. Any small, long-necked flask made of thin glass will serve as a pycnometer. It is preferable for simplicity of calculation that the pycnometer hold some simple unit volume of

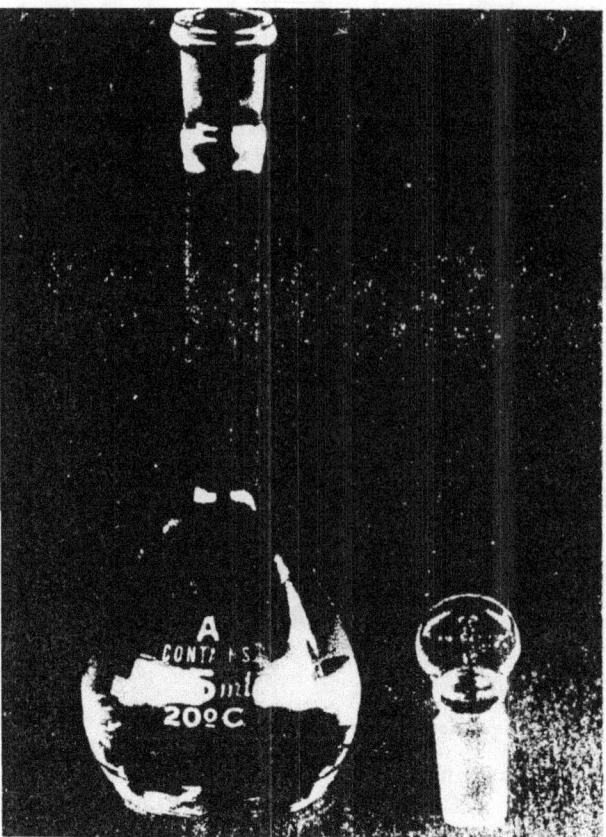

Figure 7. The pycnometer.

water, 25 Gm., 50 Gm., or 100 Gm. You will see the benefit of this in the following paragraphs. To find specific gravity using a pycnometer, proceed as follows:

(1) First, we must know the exact weight of the empty pycnometer. This is called the "tare" or "tare weight." Since dirt and moisture will affect this tare weight, it is important that the vessel be clean and dry. Make a note of the tare weight.

(2) Distilled water is then poured into the pycnometer until it reaches a convenient level in the neck. A line is marked on the pycnometer at the level of the lower edge of the meniscus (concave or convex surface of the liquid).

(3) Note the temperature of the water and record it. Now carefully weigh the pycnometer and its contents and record the combined weight.

(4) The weight of the water alone can be calculated by subtracting the tare weight of the pycnometer from the combined weight recorded in step *(3)* above. This is the weight of the water at the recorded temperature. The tare weight, temperature, and weight of the water may be permanently etched on the side of the flask for

future calculations. These figures will remain constant for all future specific gravity determinations.

(5) When the flask is again clean and dry, the specific gravity of any liquid may be taken by filling it to the same point with the liquid to be tested.

(6) Weigh the pycnometer, now containing a liquid to be tested, and subtract the tare weight of the vessel. The number resulting will be the weight of the liquid you are testing.

(7) Determine the specific gravity by substituting in this formula:

$$\text{Sp. Gr.} = \frac{\text{weight of known volume of substance}}{\text{weight of equal volume of distilled water}}$$

(8) Example: A pycnometer weighs 20.123 Gm. when clean and dry. When filled to a convenient level with water at 25° C., it weighs 44.678 Gm. The same bottle filled to the same level with glycerin at 25° C. weighs 50.816 Gm. What is the specific gravity of the glycerin?

- *Step 1.*

weight of glycerin + bottle =	50.816 Gm.
minus tare weight of bottle	− 20.123 Gm.
the weight of glycerin	30.693 Gm.

- *Step 2.*

weight of water + bottle =	44.678 Gm.
minus tare weight of bottle	− 20.123 Gm.
the weight of water	24.555 Gm.

- *Step 3.* Formula:

$$\text{Sp. Gr.} = \frac{\text{weight substance}}{\text{weight equal volume of water}}$$

- *Step 4.*

$$\text{Sp. Gr.} = \frac{30.693}{24.555} = 1.25 \text{ the Sp. Gr. of glycerin}$$

b. Hydrometer. The hydrometer is an instrument which gives us a quick but not as accurate a determination of specific gravity as the pycnometer. It can also be used to measure density of liquids and percent of solutions, such as the alcoholic content of liquids or the radiator of an automobile. The hydrometer consists of a closed glass tube, blown at one end and having a long stem at the other. The blown end is filled with a heavy weight (usually mercury or shot) to keep it erect when floated in a liquid. The long stem is internally calibrated with a graduated scale. For increased accuracy, there are hydrometers calibrated for use in light liquids and others for heavy liquids.

(1) Theory of the hydrometer. All floating bodies displace their own weight of a liquid in which they are immersed and sink to a depth proportionate to the volume of liquid displaced. Since this volume equals the weight of the immersed object, specific gravity can be determined by comparison of the volumes displaced. Thus a hydrometer is marked 1.000 at the level it sinks in distilled water at normal temperature. The scale is then carried above and below the 1.000 mark. When the instrument is placed in a different liquid, the specific gravity of that liquid can be read directly from the scale.

(2) Testing the hydrometer. Do not accept hydrometers as you receive them. Always test them first. By immersing your hydrometer in a number of liquids of known specific gravity, including water, you can observe its degree of accuracy. In the event a particular hydrometer shows consistent deviation of one or two points, you need not discard it as useless. Make a notation of the deviation on its box and merely add or subtract the error from the reading as you use it.

(3) Hydrometer jar. The hydrometer is generally floated in a hydrometer jar to take the reading (fig. 2-8). This device lessens the amount of liquid necessary for a reading because it is tall and narrow. It also facilitates cooling of the liquid to specified temperature, the jar being easily immersed in ice water.

(4) Other applications of the hydrometer:

(a) Urinometer—this hydrometer has a special scale for the determination of specific gravity of urine.

(b) Saccharometer—generally measures the percent of syrups rather than the specific gravity.

(c) Alcoholometer—determines alcoholic strength of hydroalcoholic solutions.

(d) Lovi's beads—also called specific gravity beads, are balloon-like, hollow globes of glass. They are of different sizes and weights and have a specific gravity number etched on their sides. When dropped into a liquid, those heavier than the liquid sink to the bottom; the ones lighter than the liquid float to the top; and the one which hovers in the liquid, neither floating nor sinking, represents the specific gravity. They must be used at a definite temperature for which they have been calibrated.

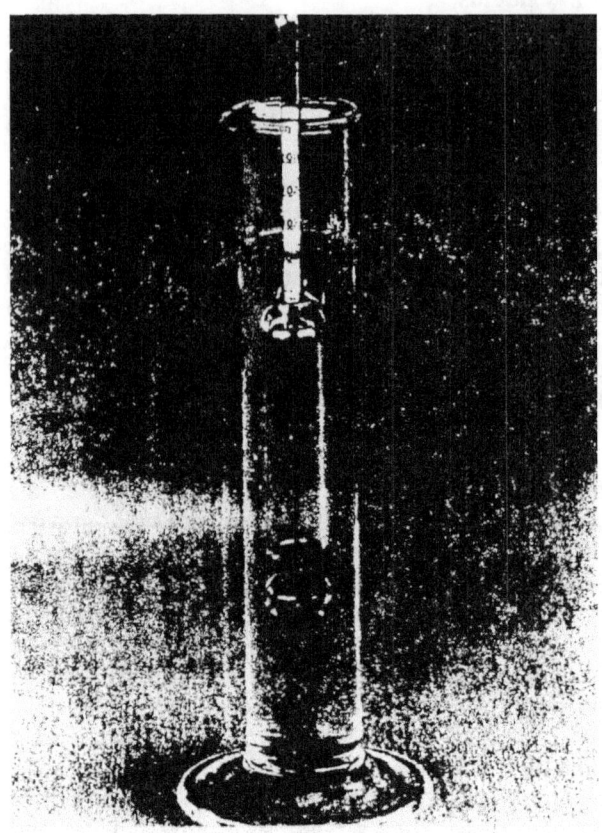

Figure 8. Hydrometer and jar.

37. Specific gravity of solids. Although various procedures must be used for determining the specific gravity of different solids, the formula used is always the same:

$$\text{Sp. Gr.} = \frac{\text{weight of solid in air}}{\text{weight of equal volume of water}}$$

Because of slight variations of technique necessary to establish the specific gravity of solids with different physical properties, we will break solids into groups according to their solubility and weight relative to water. Thus we have—
- Solids insoluble in and heavier than water.
- Solids soluble in and heavier than water.
- Solids insoluble in and lighter than water.
- Solids soluble in and lighter than water.

a. Solids insoluble in and heavier than water.

(1) When solid is a single piece. First, consider a solid in one piece, such as a block of metal or a strip of wire. The easiest method for determining specific gravity of a single piece of solid insoluble in and heavier than water is by using a balance.

● *Step 1.* Accurately weigh the sample to be tested on a good Rx or analytical balance and record this weight as the weight of the substance in air.

● *Step 2.* Attach a horsehair or fine, water-proofed, silk thread to the sample and to the beam of the scale. Immerse the sample in a beaker of water so that it is covered by the water, but not touching the bottom or sides of the beaker. The weight of the sample must be entirely supported by the beam of the balance. Make sure no air bubbles are attached to the sample which would provide buoyancy and make the weighing in water inaccurate. Record the weight of the sample in the water.

● *Step 3.* Apply the formula. *For example,* if a sample of copper weighs 10.52 Gm. in air and 9.34 Gm. when suspended in water, to find the specific gravity of the copper:

Weight in air   = 10.52 Gm.
Weight in water   9.34 Gm.
                  1.18 = loss of weight in water

$$\text{Sp. Gr.} = \frac{\text{weight in air}}{\text{weight of equal volume of water}}$$

Since the loss of weight in water equals the weight of an equal volume of water, substitute in the formula:

$$\text{Sp. Gr.} = \frac{10.52}{1.18}$$

Sp. Gr. = 8.92 (copper)

(2) When solid is fragmentary. Another method of determining the specific gravity of solids insoluble in and heavier than water is by the use of a pycnometer. This method is convenient when the solid is in fragments or smaller particles.

● *Step 1.* Weigh the sample in air and record the weight.

● *Step 2.* Drop the material into a tared pycnometer and fill with distilled water at 25° C. Weigh again, making sure that no water remains on the exterior of the vessel. This weight represents the weight of the pycnometer, the water, and the sample. Subtracting the tare weight, you have the weight of the sample plus the water in the bottle.

● *Step 3.* Apply the formula. *For example,* a sample weighing 10.5 Gm. is placed in a pycnometer which has been determined to hold

100 Gm. of water. You determine the weight of the sample plus the water plus the bottle to be 206.2 Gm. The tare weight of the bottle is 100 Gm.

   206.2 Gm. weight of bottle, water, sample
 − 100.0 Gm. weight of bottle
   106.2 Gm. weight of water and sample
    10.5 Gm. weight of sample in air
   100.0 Gm. weight of water held by bottle
   110.5 Gm. weight of water plus sample
 − 106.2 Gm. weight of water and immersed sample
     4.3 Gm. loss of weight in water

Sp. Gr. = $\frac{10.5}{4.3}$ = 2.442, the specific gravity

NOTE
The specific gravity of insoluble powders can also be determined by this method. Care should be taken to shake the powder with a quantity of water before filling the pycnometer to eliminate air bubbles and the error they can cause.

b. Solids insoluble in and lighter than water. The problem here is to make the solid sink into the water so that you can find out how much water it displaces. A weight or sinker, insoluble in water and heavy enough to cause the lighter sample to sink beneath the surface, can be attached. Since the loss of weight in water of the sample and sinker combined equals their total individual losses, it will be easy then to determine the loss of weight of the sample.

Example: A block of wax weighs 21.5 Gm. in the air. To this you attach a lead sinker which you have predetermined to lose 1.1 Gm. when immersed in water. Together they lose 25.8 grams when immersed in water. What is the specific gravity of the wax?

● *Step 1.*
Loss of weight of wax + sinker = 25.8 Gm.
Loss of weight of sinker   −   1.1 Gm.
Loss of weight of wax   = 24.7 Gm.
Weight of wax in air   = 21.5 Gm.

● *Step 2.* Apply the formula.

$$Sp.\ Gr. = \frac{21.5}{24.7}$$

$$Sp.\ Gr. = 0.87$$

c. Solids soluble in and heavier than water. The problem here is solubility. By substituting a liquid in which the sample is not soluble for the water, you can then determine by proportion what the loss of weight in water would be. The following proportion will apply:

$$\frac{Sp.\ Gr.\ of\ oil}{Sp.\ Gr.\ of\ water} :: \frac{loss\ of\ weight\ in\ oil}{loss\ of\ weight\ in\ water}$$

Example: 20.311 Gm. of Copper Sulfate immersed in an oil having a specific gravity of 0.865 filling a 100 Gm. pycnometer weighs 98.859 Gm. Find the specific gravity of copper sulfate.

● *Step 1.*
Weight of $CuSO_4$ in air   = 20.311 Gm.
Weight of oil in pycnom.   = 86.5   (100 × 0.865)
Weight of $CuSO_4$ + oil   106.811 Gm.

Weight of oil +
  immersed $CuSO_4$ = 98.859 Gm.
Weight of oil displaced   7.952 Gm.

● *Step 2.* Substitute in proportion.

$$\frac{Sp.\ Gr.\ of\ oil}{Sp.\ Gr.\ of\ water} :: \frac{loss\ of\ weight\ in\ oil}{loss\ of\ weight\ in\ water}$$

$$\frac{0.865}{1} :: \frac{7.952}{x}$$

$$865x = 7952$$

x = 9.193, the loss of weight in water

● *Step 3.* Substitute in Sp. Gr. formula.

$$Sp.\ Gr. = \frac{20.311}{9.193}$$

$$Sp.\ Gr. = 2.209$$

NOTE
If the copper sulfate were in one solid lump, you could measure the loss of weight in oil directly by suspending it from a balance into the oil.

d. Solids soluble in and lighter than water. Here, the problem, and not a slight one, is to find a liquid lighter than the solid and one in which it is not soluble. When this is accomplished, the procedure is the same for solids soluble in and heavier than water (*c* above).

38. Application of specific gravity to pharmaceutical problems. Specific gravity, when known, is of great assistance to us as pharmacists in reducing metric and apothecary volumes to weight and, conversely, in reducing weights to volumes.

a. *Metric.*
- 1 ml. of water weighs 1 Gm.
- Sp. Gr. of water is 1.000.
- 1 ml. of any liquid with Sp. Gr. of 1.000 weighs 1 Gm.
- 1 ml. of a liquid with Sp. Gr. of 2.000 weighs (1 x 2.000) 2 Gm.
- 1 ml. of a liquid with Sp. Gr. of 1.5 weighs 1 x 1.5 or 1.5 Gm.

Therefore, the volume in ml. times specific gravity = weight in Gm.

(1) Example: What is the weight in grams of 1 liter of glycerin (Sp. Gr. 1.25)?

- *Step 1.* 1 liter = 1000 ml.
- *Step 2.* 1000 ml. x 1.25 = 1250 Gm., the weight of 1 liter of glycerin.

(2) Example: How many ml. of chloroform are there in 1480 Gm.? (Sp. Gr. of chloroform = 1.48).

$$x \text{ ml.} \times 1.48 = 1480 \text{ Gm.}$$

$$x = \frac{1480}{1.48} = 1000 \text{ ml. or 1 liter of chloroform}$$

b. *Apothecary.* There is no convenient weight-to-volume comparison in the apothecary system. However, you may derive a working formula from the steps below.

- *Step 1.* In the metric system, 1 gram of water or any liquid with a specific gravity of 1.000, has a corresponding volume of 1 ml. In the apothecary system, a fluidounce of water or any fluid with a specific gravity of 1.000 does not weigh 1 ounce, nor does a fluidrachm weigh a drachm, nor a minim weigh a grain.

- *Step 2.* BUT, 1 fluidounce of water at 25° C. weighs 454.6 grains. Since there are 480 minims in 1 fluidounce, a minim of water weighs 454.6 ÷ 480 = 0.95 grain.

- *Step 3.* 1 fluidounce of any liquid having a specific gravity of 1.000 weighs 454.6 grain. 1 fluidounce of any liquid having a specific gravity of 2.000 weighs 454.6 x 2.

- *Step 4.* Conclusion. 1 fluidounce of any liquid weighs (in grains) 454.6 x specific gravity. Thus the following formula:
454.6 x Sp. Gr. x number of fluidounces = weight in grains.

(1) Example: How much does f ℥ii, ℥iv of glycerin weigh? Sp. Gr. of glycerin is 1.25.

- *Step 1.* f ℥ii, ℥iv = 2.5 fluidounces.

- *Step 2.* Substitute in formula:
454.6 x 1.25 x 2.5 = weight in grains

```
   454.6         568.25
 x  1.25       x   2.5
 ------        -------
  22730         284125
   9092         113650
   4546        1420.625, weight of glycerin
 ------
 568.250
```

- *Step 3.* Convert to highest terms.
1420.625 rounded off (.625 → .63 grains)
20 gr./℈, so 1420 ÷ 20 = 71℈
3 ℈/ʒ, so 71 ÷ 3 = 23ʒ + 2℈ remainder
8 ʒ/℥, so 23 ÷ 8 = 2℥ + 7ʒ remainder

- *Step 4.* Collect the amounts.
℥ii ʒvii ℈ii gr ss(.63)

(2) Example: What is the volume of 250 grains of a liquid with a specific gravity of 0.942?

- *Step 1.* Formula.
454.6 x 0.942 x y (No. fluidounces) = weight in grains
454.6 x 0.942 x y = 250

```
    0.942
  x 454.6
  -------
    5652
    3768
    4710
    3768
  -------
  428.2332
```

y(428.233) = 250

$$y = \frac{250}{428.233}$$

y = .583 fluidounce

- *Step 2.* Reduce to correct terms.
8 fʒ = 1 f℥
therefore, .583 x 8 = 4.664 fluidrachms
60 minims = 1 fʒ
therefore, .664 x 60 = 40 minims

- *Step 3.* Combine the quantities:
f ʒ iv ♏ x l

39. Specific volume

a. Identification. Specific volume is much like specific gravity, except the comparison is between volumes rather than weights. Specific volume can be described as the ratio of the volume of one substance to the volume of an equal weight of a standard substance. As in specific gravity, the standard is water and the standard temperature is 25° C.

Since Sp. Gr. = $\dfrac{\text{weight of substance in air}}{\text{weight of equal volume of water}}$

Sp. Vol. = $\dfrac{\text{volume of substance}}{\text{volume of equal weight of water}}$

Then, Specific Gravity = $\dfrac{1}{\text{Sp. Vol.}}$ and

Sp. Vol. = $\dfrac{1}{\text{Sp. Gr.}}$; they are reciprocals

b. Sample problems.
(1) *Problem:* What is the specific volume of 750 Gm. of chloroform measuring 510.2 ml.?

- *Step 1.* Volume of chloroform = 510.2 ml.
  Volume of equal weight water = 750.0 ml.

- *Step 2.* Substitute in formula

  Sp. Vol. = $\dfrac{\text{volume of substance}}{\text{volume of equal weight water}}$

  Sp. Vol. = $\dfrac{510.2}{750}$

  Sp. Vol = 0.68

(2) *Problem:* Using the information in the previous problem, what is the specific gravity of chloroform?
Using the reciprocal formula:

Sp. Gr. = $\dfrac{1}{\text{Sp. Vol.}}$

Sp. Gr. = $\dfrac{1}{0.68}$

Sp. Gr. = 1.47, answer

```
      1.47
68/100.00
   68
   32 0
   27 2
    4 80
    4 76
```

40. Density

a. Identification. Density is the ratio between weight and volume of a substance; or, density = weight divided by volume, and is expressed not as a relative number, as specific gravity was, but with specific units as Gm./ml., lb/cu.ft., or gr./fl.oz.

From the formula:
$D = \dfrac{w}{v}$, we see that if we know density and volume we can determine weight; knowing density and weight, we can find volume; and knowing weight and volume, we can find density.

b. Sample problems.
(1) *Problem:* What is the density of alcohol if 250 ml. weigh 200 Gm.?

Density = $\dfrac{\text{weight}}{\text{volume}}$

$D = \dfrac{200}{250}$

D = 0.80 Gm./ml.

(2) *Problem:* How many ml. of mercury (density 13.6) would there be in a sample weighing 2000 Gm.?

$D = \dfrac{w}{v}$

$13.6 = \dfrac{2000}{v}$

$13.6\,v = 2000$

$v = \dfrac{2000}{13.6}$

v = 147.06 ml.

41. Temperature

a. Definition. What exactly is temperature? Temperature can be stated as being the degree of hotness or lack of hotness, or the *intensity of heat.* Relative temperatures can be sensed by touch in some cases, but the sense of touch can be very misleading. A piece of cloth and a piece of metal, although exactly the same temperature will feel differently to the touch. The cloth will not seem as warm or as cold as the metal. This is due to the rate at which the substance dissipates heat.

b. Measurement of temperature. Temperature, therefore, must be measured by a device which gives accurate degrees of heat. Such instruments are called thermometers. The thermometer is based on the principle of expansion and contraction of substances with change in temperature. The most common thermometers utilize alcohol or mercury. In order for readings obtained from expansion and contraction to be valid, the expansion and contraction must be uniform.

c. Liquid thermometer. The liquid thermometer consists of a fine capillary tube, hermetically sealed, with a bulb at one end. The tube is filled to a point on the capillary, the bulb serving as a reservoir. Upon elevating the temperature, the liquid expands and rises in the tube to a new level. Thus, calibrating the tube with known constant temperatures and dividing the space between with equal degrees, we have an instrument that will measure temperature. Figure 2-9 shows two liquid thermometers discussed below.

42. Temperature calculation. There are two different scales by which liquid thermometers can be calibrated—the Centigrade scale and the Fahrenheit scale.

a. Centigrade. The Centigrade thermometer is so calibrated that the melting point of ice is 0° C. and the boiling point of water is 100° C. By this scale, there is a difference of 100 degrees between the freezing and boiling points of water. The Centigrade scale has been adopted by the USP and NF as the official temperature standard. In fact, it is the standard temperature measuring device the world over.

b. Fahrenheit. The Fahrenheit thermometer is calibrated so that 32° F. is the melting point of ice and 212° F. is the boiling point of water. The difference between freezing and boiling on this scale is 180°. The Fahrenheit scale is used mainly for household purposes.

c. Importance of stating the scale. Because of the great difference between these two scales, you can see the importance of always stating which scale you are using when referring to a temperature. By itself, 40° means nothing; 40° Fahrenheit is approximately 4.4° Centigrade; 40° Centigrade is 104° Fahrenheit, a considerable difference.

d. Absolute temperature. We, as pharmacists, will not deal with the absolute temperature scale; however, you should be familiar with what it is. Remember only that *absolute* degree equals Centigrade degrees plus 273°. Expressed as a formula this becomes—

$$A° = C° + 273°.$$

43. Temperature conversion. Knowing that the range in degrees between the freezing and boiling points of water is 100° in the Centigrade scale and 180° in the Fahrenheit scale, it is obvious that one Centigrade degree is equal to 1.8 (9/5), the size of a Fahrenheit degree. Therefore, a 5-degree change in Centigrade temperature is a 9-degree change in the Fahrenheit scale. Since 0° C. equals 32° F., 1° C. must equal 32° plus 9/5° or 1.8°, or 33.8° F. Thus, we can derive several formulas. However, the basic formula is: 9C = 5F − 160, or 5F = 9C + 160.

a. Example: Convert −5° Centigrade to Fahrenheit.

- *Step 1.* Formula: 5F = 9C + 160

- *Step 2.* Substitute: 5F = 9 (−5) + 160
  5F = −45 + 160
  5F = 115
  F = 115 ÷ 5
  F = 23° F

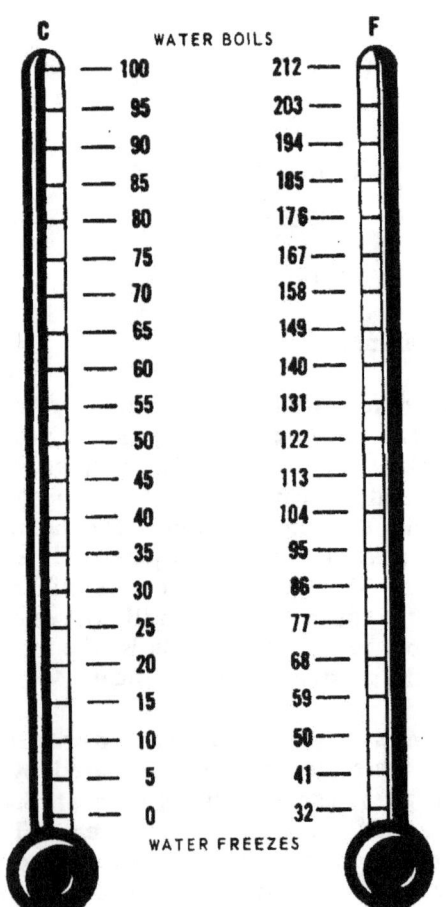

Figure 9. Thermometer comparison.

b. *Example:* Convert −40° Fahrenheit to Centigrade.

- *Step 1.* Formula: 9C = 5F − 160
- *Step 2.* Substitute: 9C = 5(−40) − 160
  9C = −200 − 160
  9C = −360
  C = −360 ÷ 9
  C = −40° C

c. *Example:* Convert 80° Fahrenheit to Centigrade.

- *Step 1.* Formula: 9C = 5F − 160
- *Step 2.* Substitute: 9C = 5(80) − 160
  9C = 400 − 160
  9C = 240
  C = 240 ÷ 9
  C = 26.6° C

44. Dosage

a. Importance of dosage calculation to the pharmacist. When a prescription reaches the pharmacist from the desk of a prescriber, the ingredients are specified, the quantities listed (perhaps in specific amounts, perhaps as ratio, perhaps as percentages), and the instructions to the patient are written in Latin, in pharmaceutical or medical terminology. The pharmacist must (1) fill the prescription, (2) check the prescriber for possible error of amounts and dosage, and (3) write the directions upon the label in terms which can be easily understood by the patient. For these reasons, an accurate knowledge of dosage is mandatory for the pharmacist. Imagine the consequences of the following:

(1) Error in converting a percent ingredient to the specific amount.

(2) Prescriber's inadvertent error in amount of ingredient to be used in preparation of a medicinal (with the accompanying error of the pharmacist not observing the error).

(3) Prescriber's error in calculation of dosage (again combined with the pharmacist's missing the error). Although errors are the exception rather than the rule, the pharmacist must be forever on his guard against them. It is not his privilege to look for errors, but his *duty*. The pharmacist is held responsible equally with the erring physician. Overdose, even though it may originate at the prescriber, if not corrected by the pharmacy technician may constitute negligence.

b. Approximate household equivalents. The approximate household equivalents shown in table 2-8 are useful in making calculations for number of doses in a medication and for translating directions into terms understandable to the patient. These approximate equivalents are in obvious discrepancy due to approximating equivalency between three different measures. In table 2-8, one teasp, 1 f ℥ (approx 4 ml.) and 5 ml. are not equal at all. However, the directions to the patient cannot read "Take 1 drachm" or "4 ml." or "5 ml." They must be written in some language that all literate persons can understand—thus, "one teaspoonful."

c. Medicine glass. Because of inaccuracy in household equivalents and because household spoons, cups, and glasses vary considerably in size, the patient should be strongly advised to purchase a medicine glass (fig. 2-10) for accurate dosage.

d. Calculation of dosage. Some of the dosage calculations you will be making most frequently are listed below. The following proportion can be established which will aid in solving dosage problems:

$$\text{Total doses} = \frac{\text{total amount}}{\text{size of each dose}}$$

(1) Calculating the size of an individual dose. When given the total amount of medication and the number of doses to be made, the size of each can be calculated by dividing. *Example:* A

Table 8. Approximate Household Equivalents

Metric measure	Apothecary equivalent (approximate)	Household measure
2 ml	f ℥ss	½ teaspoonful
5 ml	f ℥i	1 teaspoonful
8 ml	f ℥ii	1 dessertspoonful
15 ml	f ℥iv	1 tablespoonful
30 ml	f ℥viii (f ℥i)	2 tablespoonfuls
60 m	f ℥ii	1 wineglassful
120 ml	f ℥iv	1 teacupful
240 ml	f ℥viii	1 tumblerful

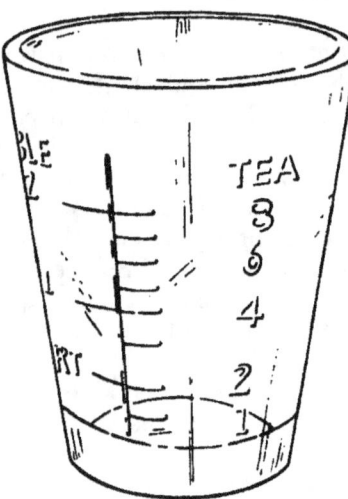

Figure 10. A medicine glass.

particular medication is to be taken 4 times daily for 1 week, and a total of 280 grains is being dispensed. What is the amount of this medication in a single dose?

- *Step 1.* What is the total number of doses?
  4 doses daily x 7 days = 28 doses, total

- *Step 2.* Formula.
$$\text{Total doses} = \frac{\text{total amount}}{\text{size of each dose}}$$

- *Step 3.* Substitute—
$$28 = \frac{280 \text{ gr.}}{x}$$
$$28x = 280$$
$$x = 10 \text{ grains in each dose.}$$

NOTE
The answer will always be in the same denomination as the total amount, or if the total amount is the unknown, in the same denomination as the individual dose.

(2) *Calculating number of doses.* The number of doses in a specific amount can be calculated if you are given the total amount and the size of the dose.

(a) *Example:* How many doses of 5 grains each will result from a total of 75 grains of total medication?

- *Step 1.* Formula.
$$\text{Total doses} = \frac{\text{total amount}}{\text{size of each dose}}$$

- *Step 2.* Substitute.
$$x = \frac{75 \text{ gr.}}{5}$$
$$x = 15 \text{ doses}$$

(b) *Example:* If the dose of a medication is to be one-half fluidrachm, how many doses will a patient receive, given an 8-ounce bottle of medication?

- *Step 1.* Since there are 8 fluidrachms to the fluidounce, 8 fluidounces would contain 8 x 8 = 64 fluidrachms.

- *Step 2.* Formula.
$$\text{Total doses} = \frac{\text{total amount}}{\text{size of each dose}}$$

- *Step 3.* Substitute.
$$x = \frac{64 \text{ fluidrachms}}{.5}$$
$$x = 128 \text{ doses, answer}$$

(3) *Calculating total amount of medication.* If you know the size of the dose and the number of doses prescribed, you can determine the total medication to be dispensed.

Example: A patient is to receive 1 fluidounce of whisky morning, noon, and night for an indefinite period of time. What quantity would be dispensed for 1 week's medication?

- *Step 1.* 1 ounce dose x 3 doses per day x 7 days per week equals 21 ounces. The formula may also be used as shown in step 2 below.

- *Step 2.* Formula.
$$\text{Total doses} = \frac{\text{total amount}}{\text{size of each dose}}$$
$$21 = \frac{x}{1}$$
$$x = 21 \text{ ounces, answer}$$

(4) *Calculating amount of a single ingredient.* The amount of a single ingredient present in a dose of a mixture of several medicinal agents can be determined by dividing the amount of that ingredient by the total doses.

(a) Example: Calculate the amount of *each* ingredient in a single dose of the following prescription.

```
Rx  Acetylsalicylic acid    ʒii  Ͻi  gr vii
    Acetophenetidin         ʒi   Ͻii gr v
    Caffeine                gr xss
    M. Ft. M.
    Div in caps, no. xxi
    Sig: Cap i q 4 h, prn.
```

- *Step 1.* Reduce all ingredients to *grains*.
  Acetylsalicylic acid equals
2 x 60 grains (per drachm)	= 120	gr.
1 x 20 grains (per scruple)	= 20	gr.
7 grains	= 7	gr.
	147	gr.

  Acetophenetidin equals
1 x 60 grains (per drachm)	= 60	gr.
2 x 20 grains (per scruple)	= 40	gr.
5 grains	= 5	gr.
	105	gr.

  Caffeine equals
10 1/2 grains	= 10.5	gr.

- *Step 2.* You know that the total amount is for 21 capsules; therefore, the amount in a single capsule would be—

$$\text{Total doses} = \frac{\text{total amount}}{\text{size of each dose}}$$

$$21 = \frac{147}{x} = 7 \text{ grains acetylsalicylic acid per capsule}$$

$$21 = \frac{105}{x} = 5 \text{ grains acetophenetidin per capsule}$$

$$21 = \frac{10.5}{x} = 1/2 \text{ grain caffeine per capsule}$$

NOTE

To check this prescription for possible errors, consult the USP or Remington for the dose of each of the ingredients and compare the dose with the amounts you have calculated to be in each capsule.

(b) Example: A solution contains 4/5 grain of a potent drug in 4 ounces. What dose must be given to provide 1/120 grain of the drug?

- *Step 1.* Formula.

$$\text{Total doses} = \frac{\text{total amount}}{\text{size of each dose}}$$

- *Step 2* Substitute.

$$x \text{ doses} = \frac{\frac{4}{15}}{\frac{1}{120}}$$

- *Step 3.* Remember that you can divide fractions by inverting the divisor and multiplying. Thus,

$$x \text{ doses} = \frac{4}{15} \times \frac{120}{1}$$

$$x = \frac{480}{15} = 32 \text{ doses}$$

- *Step 4.* Since you are to get 32 doses from 4 ounces, each dose must be one fluidrachm (8 fluidrachms = 1 ounce).

  e. Children's doses. Enough emphasis cannot be placed upon the calculation of dosage for children. Because of their size, weight, and incomplete development, they are not able to tolerate as much medication as adults. Although many factors besides weight and age play an important part in dosage, only these two will be discussed here. (Chapter 9 explains dosage factors in more detail.)

  (1) Formulas for calculating children's doses. Several formulas can be employed for calculating doses for children and infants; however, because of different degrees of response by children to different medications (e.g., children are extremely susceptible to morphine), it is best to become familiar with the correct doses through experience and to memorize doses as they present themselves. If at all in doubt about the size of a dose, ALWAYS check with the pharmacy officer or the prescriber. The most generally used formulas for calculation of doses for children are—

  (a) Young's rule (most widely used).

$$\frac{\text{child's age}}{\text{child's age} + 12} \times \text{adult dose} = \text{child's dose}$$

  (b) Clark's rule.

$$\frac{\text{weight of child (lb)}}{150} \times \text{adult dose} = \text{child's dose}$$

  (2) Example problems. Study the following examples carefully to see the application of the above rules.

  (a) Example: What would be the dose of elixir of phenobarbital for a child 3 years old? (Elixir phenobarbital contains 400 mg. of phenobarbital per 100 ml. Adult dose of

phenobarbital is 30 mg., up to 4 times a day.) Use Young's rule.

- *Step 1.* Rule.

$$\frac{\text{child's age}}{\text{child's age} + 12} \times \text{adult dose} = \text{child's dose}$$

- *Step 2.* Substitute.

$$\frac{3}{3 + 12} \times 30 \text{ mg.} = \text{child's dose}$$

$$\frac{90}{15} = 6 \text{ mg., the child's dose}$$

- *Step 3.* Since 100 ml. of phenobarbital elixir contains 400 mg., 1 ml. would contain 4 mg. Therefore; 1:x :: 4:6.

$$4x = 6$$
$$x = 1.5 \text{ ml., the dose for 3-year-old child.}$$

(b) Example: What would be the dose of tetracycline hydrochloride for a 3-year-old girl weighing 30 pounds? Usual adult dose is 500 mg. Use Clark's rule.

- *Step 1.* Formula.

$$\frac{\text{weight of child (lb)}}{150} \times \text{adult dose} = \text{child's dose}$$

- *Step 2.* Substitute.

$$\frac{30}{150} \times 500 \text{ mg.} = \text{child's dose}$$

$$\frac{15,000}{150} = 100 \text{ mg., the child's dose}$$

45. Concentration and dilution. Many times in pharmacy it is necessary to dilute or concentrate a substance in order to dispense the right dosage; the dilution of nose drops is one of the most frequently seen examples. Phenylephrine hydrochloride solution is a standard nose drop preparation. Its strength as it comes to us is 1 percent. Most of the prescriptions for phenylephrine solution will call for 1/4 percent. You can see, then, that it will have to be diluted before dispensing.

a. Mechanics of dilution. If 1 ounce of a 1 percent-solution of phenylephrine hydrochloride solution was diluted to a new volume of 2 ounces, the percent of the new solution would be 1/2 of the original 1 percent, that is, 1/2 percent. Perhaps it will be more apparent if you consider that 1 ounce of a 1-percent solution contains approximately 4.5 grains of active ingredient. By diluting the solution to a volume of 2 ounces, you still have only 4.5 grains of active ingredient in a volume of 2 ounces. Thus, you have halved the percentage. If the active ingredient remains constant and the volume of the solution increases, the percentage decreases. And if the active ingredient remains constant and the volume of the solution decreases, the percentage increases. The percentage strength and the volume of a solution are inversely proportional to each other.

b. Concentration–dilution proportion. Since volume and percentage strength of solutions are inversely proportional, the following formula or proportion applies.

$$\frac{\text{\% concentration of original solution}}{\text{\% concentration of new solution}} :: \frac{\text{new volume}}{\text{original volume}}$$

This proportion can be used to solve any concentration or dilution problem arising in the pharmacy.

(1) Example: You have 30 ml. of a 10-percent solution and want to make a 1-percent solution. To what volume must you dilute the original solution? Substituting in the proportion you have—

$$\frac{10 \text{ (original \%)}}{1 \text{ (new \%)}} :: \frac{x \text{ (unknown new volume)}}{30 \text{ (original new volume)}}$$

$$x = 300 \text{ ml., the new volume}$$

In a practical situation, then, you would dilute the original 30 ml. of 10-percent solution to a total volume of 300 ml. to prepare the desired 1-percent solution.

(2) Example: Make a 4-percent solution from 60 ml. of a 2-percent solution by concentrating the volume. Again, substituting in the proportion, you have—

$$\frac{2\%}{4\%} :: \frac{x}{60}$$
$$4x = 120$$
$$x = 30 \text{ ml.}$$

You must concentrate the 60 ml. of 2-percent solution to a new volume of 30 ml. in order to obtain the 4-percent solution.

46. Alligation. Alligation is a process for finding the value of a combination containing known quantities of known strengths; *for example,* to determine the strength of a solution resulting from the mixture of 100 ml. of 20-percent alcohol and

20 ml. of 10-percent alcohol. Actually, alligation is two different processes, alligation medial and alligation alternate. Alligation medial is used for determining percentage strength and alligation alternate for proportional number of parts.

   a. *Alligation medial.* Alligation medial is used in determining the percentage strength of a mixture of two or more ingredients of different strengths. Alligation medial can also be used to determine the resulting specific gravity of a mixture of two or more substances with different specific gravities.

   (1) *Example:* What percentage of codeine sulfate is contained in a mixture of 60 grams of a 15-percent codeine powder and 15 grams of a 40-percent codeine powder?

• *Step 1.* Find the amount of codeine sulfate in the total mixture.

   60 x .15 = 9.0 Gm. of codeine sulfate
   15 x .40 = 6.0 Gm. of codeine sulfate
              15.0 Gm. total codeine in mixture

• *Step 2.* Find the weight of the total mixture.
   60 Gm. + 15 Gm. = 75 Gm. total weight of mixture

• *Step 3.* Divide the amount of codeine by the total weight to find the percent of codeine in the mixture.

   $\frac{15.0}{75.0}$ = .20 or 20% codeine sulfate

   (2) *Example:* You prepare a mixture of 3 ounces of liquid A and 13 ounces of liquid B. What is the cost per ounce of the resulting mixture if liquid A costs $4.00 per pint and liquid B costs $1.44 per pint?

• *Step 1.* Find the cost per ounce of each ingredient.
   A = $4.00/pint ÷ 16 = $ .25/ounce
   B = $1.44/pint ÷ 16 = $ .09/ounce

• *Step 2.* Find the number of ounces in the total mixture.
   3 ounces of A + 13 ounces of B = 16 ounces

• *Step 3.* Find the total cost of these two ingredients.
   3 ounces at $0.25 = $ .75
   13 ounces at $0.09 = $1.17
                       $1.92 total cost of mixture

• *Step 4.* Find the cost per ounce of the mixture.
   $1.92 ÷ 16 = $0.12, cost per ounce

   (3) *Example:* What is the specific gravity of a mixture of 250 ml. of Glycerin (Sp. Gr. 1.25) and 500 ml. of chloroform (Sp. Gr. 1.48)?

• *Step 1.* Find the number of grams in each of the volumes.
   250 ml. x 1.25 = 312.5 Gm. of glycerin
   500 ml. x 1.48 = 740.00 Gm. of chloroform

• *Step 2.* Find the total volume and total weight of the mixture.
   250 ml. + 500 ml. = 750 ml., total volume
   312.5 Gm. + 740 Gm. = 1052.5 Gm., total weight

• *Step 3.* Divide weight by volume to find Sp. Gr.
   $\frac{1052.5}{750}$ = 1.403, the Sp. Gr. of mixture

   b. *Alligation alternate.* Alligation alternate is a method of determining the proportionate number of parts of two or more ingredients of known strength when they are to be mixed to form a desired strength. The parts can then be changed to represent volume or weight. A substance of greater strength is mixed with one of lesser strength to form a mixture of a strength somewhere between that of the two ingredients. For example, 50-percent alcohol can be mixed with 25-percent alcohol to produce 30-percent alcohol. It is not possible to mix 50-percent alcohol with 25-percent alcohol to get less than 25-percent or more than 50-percent alcohol. The increase in percentage from the smaller ingredient to the percentage desired, equals the parts of the higher percent ingredient, and the decrease in percentage of the higher to the desired equals the parts of the lower percent ingredient.

   (1) *Example:* What must be the proportion of 50-percent alcohol and 25-percent alcohol, mixed to obtain 30-percent alcohol?

• *Step 1.* Examine the situation. We desire a 30-percent alcohol solution from a 50-percent and a 25-percent solution. The 50-percent solution is 20 percent too strong and the 25-percent solution is 5 percent too weak. In other words, the 50-percent solution must decrease 20 percent and the 25-percent increase 5 percent.

● *Step 2.* Prepare a diagram and place the percentage you desire at completion in the center block. Place the highest percent ingredient (50 percent) on the left and the lowest percent ingredient (25 percent) on the right.

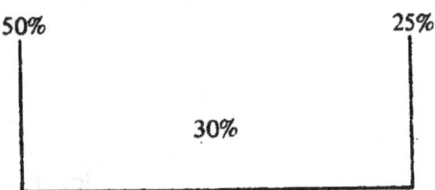

● *Step 3.* Subtract the percent you desire (center block) from the high percent and place your answer below the low percent. This answer represents the parts of the LOW percent you will need to make the desired strength solution.

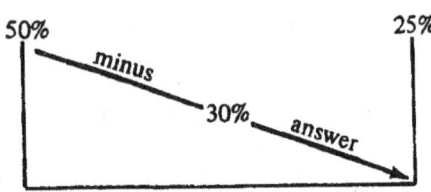

● *Step 4.* Subtract the low percent from the desired percent (center block) and place your answer below the high percent. This answer represents the parts of the HIGH percent you will need to make the desired strength solution.

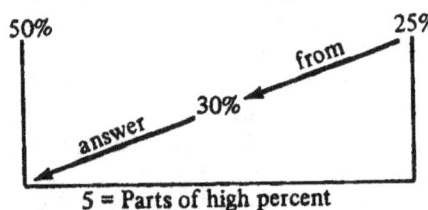

The paperwork from your completed problem, then, should look like this. It indicates that to make a 30-percent solution from 50-percent and 25-percent alcohol, you will need 5 parts of the 50 percent and 20 parts of the 25 percent.

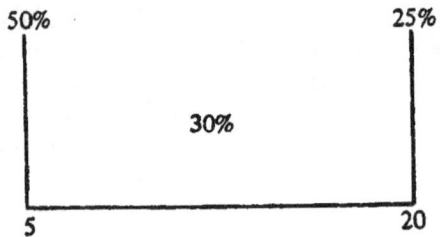

● *Step 5.* Express the number of parts in the denomination most suitable, such as ml., grains, grams, or ounces. Thus, 20 ml. of the 25 percent + 5 ml. of the 50 percent will make a 30-percent mixture; 20 ounces of the 25 percent + 5 ounces of the 50 percent will also make a 30-percent mixture.

(2) Example: In what proportion must you mix 95-percent, 10-percent, 50-percent, and 30-percent alcohol to make 40-percent alcohol?

● *Step 1.* Examine the situation. You desire a 40-percent solution by combining so many parts each of 95 percent, 50 percent, 30 percent, and 10 percent.

● *Step 2.* Although the setup looks a little different because there are 4 ingredients in this problem, use the same procedure, that is, to subtract the lesser percents from the desired to get the number of parts, and to subtract the desired percent from the higher percents to get the number of parts. This problem has been broken down into four diagrams to show each segment of subtraction. However, the problem should be worked from one diagram.

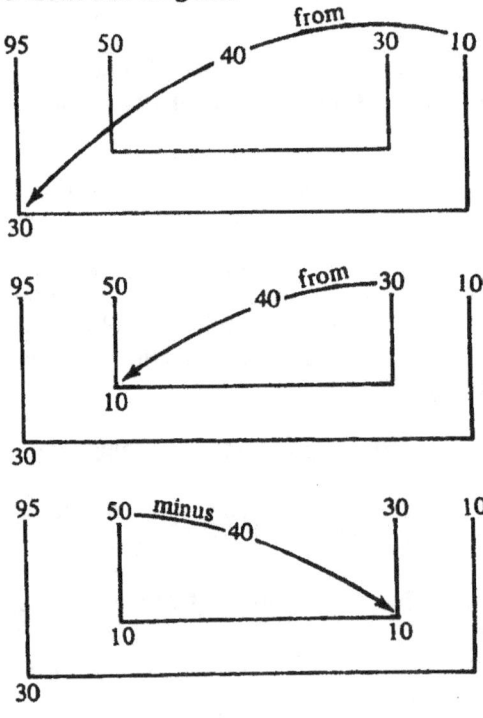

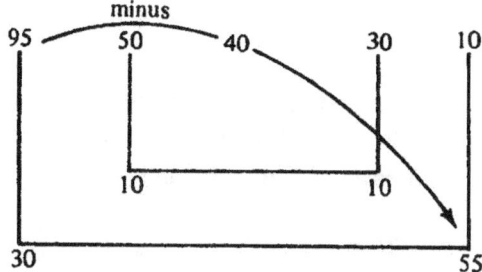

You therefore need—

    30 parts of 95% alcohol
    55 parts of 10% alcohol
    10 parts of 50% alcohol
    10 parts of 30% alcohol
    105 parts of 40% alcohol

● *Step 3.* By expressing the parts as ounces, you mix 30 ounces of 95 percent, 55 ounces of 10 percent, 10 ounces of 50 percent, and 10 ounces of 30 percent to produce 105 ounces of 40-percent alcohol.

    (3) *Example:* How many ml. of 10-percent, 20-percent, and 30-percent sodium hydroxide solution must be mixed to make a quart of 25-percent solution?

● *Step 1.* Examine the situation. You desire a 25-percent solution from the combination of 10-percent, 20-percent, and 30-percent solutions of sodium hydroxide.

● *Step 2.* Set up.

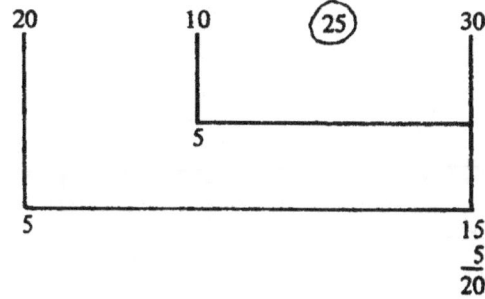

● *Step 3.* Thus you need—

    5 parts of 20%
    5 parts of 10%
    20 parts of 30%
    30 parts of 25% will result

● *Step 4.* Find what one part would equal. You know that there are 473 ml. in 1 pint, and therefore 946 ml. in 1 quart. The total number of ml. to be made is 946. You have a total of 30 parts of the solutions which are to equal 946 ml.; 1 part, then, would equal 946 ÷ 30 = 31.53 ml. per part.

● *Step 5.* Multiply the numbers of parts by the 31.53 ml. to find the number of ml. of each to be used.

    31.53 × 5 = 157.65 ml. of 20%
    31.53 × 5 = 157.65 ml. of 10%
    31.53 × 20 = 630.60 ml. of 30%

    (4) *Example:* How much water must be added to a pint of 95-percent ethyl alcohol to make 70-percent alcohol?

● *Step 1.* Examine the situation. You desire to make a 70-percent solution of alcohol from a 95-percent solution and a 0-percent solution (water).

● *Step 2.* Set up.

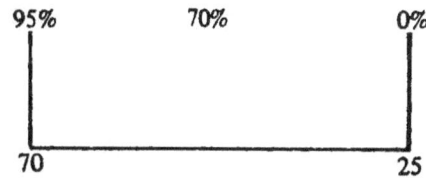

● *Step 3.* Thus you need—

    70 parts of 95% alcohol
    25 parts of 0% alcohol (water)
    95 parts of 70% alcohol

● *Step 4.* Solve. One pint contains 473 ml.

$$70 : 473 :: 25 : x$$
$$70x = 473 \times 25$$
$$70x = 11,825$$
$$x = 168.93 \text{ ml. of water required.}$$

    (5) *Example:* How many ml. of a 60-percent sulfuric acid by volume solution must be added to 344 ml. of 30-percent sulfuric acid and 172 ml. of 15-percent sulfuric acid to make 50-percent sulfuric acid?

● *Step 1.* Examine the situation. You desire to make a 50-percent solution of sulfuric acid by combining 344 ml. of 30-percent sulfuric acid, 172

40

ml. of 15-percent sulfuric acid, and x number of ml. of 60-percent sulfuric acid.

● *Step 2.* Find the percent strength of the mixture formed by combining the acids of known strength and volume.

$$344 \times 0.30 = 103.2 \text{ Gm.}$$
$$\underline{172 \times 0.15} = \underline{25.8 \text{ Gm.}}$$
$$516 \text{ ml.} \qquad 129.0 \text{ Gm.}$$

$129.0 \div 516 = .25$, or 25%, the strength of the mixture of the two acids.

● *Step 3.* Set up for a mixture of the 25 percent and the 60 percent to be added.

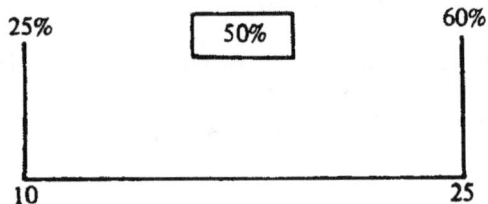

● *Step 4.* Thus you need—

25 parts of 60% sulfuric acid
<u>10</u> parts of 25% sulfuric acid
35 parts of 50% sulfuric acid

● *Step 5.* Since you have 516 ml. of the 25-percent strength solution, which represents 10 parts, find how many ml. will represent 25 parts.

$$10 : 25 :: 516 : x$$
$$10x = 516 \times 25$$
$$10x = 12,900$$
$x = 1,290$ ml. of the 60% sulfuric acid required.

INTRODUCTION TO PHARMACY

Section I. GENERAL

Purpose and scope. This manual provides guidance and information for pharmacy specialists. It will supplement instructions given in pharmacy classes and in organized on-the-job training programs and will serve as a reference for basic procedures performed by pharmacy personnel.

Section II. HISTORY, ETHICS, AND REFERENCES OF PHARMACY

History of Pharmacy
a. Derivation of names.

(1) The word "pharmacy" is derived from the Greek pharmakon, which originally meant "a charm," later "a poison," and finally "a drug." Pharmacy and medicine were professions of great mystery in early times. Disease was at first believed to be a manifestation of the presence of evil spirits in the body. To drive away these evil spirits, the physicians of ancient times employed a series of rituals consisting of chants, noises, ceremonies, and odors.

(2) Aesculapius, son of Apollo, was the Roman and Greek god of healing. The staff of Aesculapius, represented by a staff branched at the top with a snake entwined around it, is used as a symbol of medicine and as the official insignia of the American Medical Association. (It should not be confused with the caduceus, the "Herald's Wand," used by Hermes, or Mercury, which shows two serpents on a staff mounted by wings.)

b. Papyrus Ebers. Among early documents dealing with pharmacy and medicine is the Papyrus Ebers, dating from about the 16th century BC, or shortly before the time of Moses. (This scroll is named for Georg Moritz Ebers, 1837-1898, German Egyptologist, who edited the medical papyrus which he had discovered in Thebes.) This manuscript is a continuous roll more than 250 feet long and about a foot wide. It contains information about 700 remedies for afflictions, methods of compounding, and ways of conjuring away diseases. It indicates that diagnosis had been highly developed as an art for some time at this early period; some of the drugs it mentions are still in common use.

c. Hippocrates. Hippocrates, a Greek physician who was born on the Island of Cos in 460 BC, is called the "Father of Medicine." His fame is based largely on his assumed authorship of the Hippocratic Oath, which he exacted from his students. Some authorities, however, believe the oath was written after Hippocrates' death. This oath, still taken by modem physicians, is a code of conduct for the medical profession. Hippocrates taught the "humoral theory" of disease, which proposed that improper balance of the four humors of medieval physiology-blood, phlegm, yellow bile, and black bile-caused disease.

d. Galen. At the beginning of the Christian era, several Greeks and Romans were noted in medicine. Galen (131-201 AD), a Greek who became a Roman citizen, originated so many vegetable drugs by mixing and melting individual ingredients that these preparations are still called "galenical preparations" or "galenicals." Galen's Cerate is still synonymous for the term "cold cream," a preparation which he originated nearly 2000 years ago.

e. Pharmacy as a science. The beginning of the Crusades in the 11th century had a stimulating effect upon all areas of scientific and professional knowledge. Pharmacy was taught as part of the curricula of medicine in schools of this period.

(1) A decree of the German Emperor Frederick II in 1240 contains the first undoubted record of the separation of medicine and pharmacy. This edict regulated the practice of pharmacy in his kingdom of the two Sicilies. Under this regulation, physicians were neither allowed to operate pharmacies nor to realize any profit from selling medicine by clandestine arrangements with apothecaries. The management and responsibilities of these pharmacies were restricted and they were allowed only in principal cities.

(2) Toward the end of the 12th century, one of the first organized bodies of pharmacists came into existence in Florence as part of the guild of physicians and apothecaries.

(3) In the 16th century, Philippus Aureolus Theophrastus Bombastus von Hohenheim, Swiss physician and alchemist (1493-1541), advanced ideas about the internal use of chemicals in treating diseases, and was instrumental in the development of pharmaceutical chemistry. He is best known by the name "Paracelsus." His work greatly changed the train of thought in the medical field.

f. Pharmacopeias. A pharmacopeia is an official book of standards for drugs. Pharmacopeias are very valuable to physicians and pharmacists. The first official book of standards listing drugs for chemical use was issued in 1613. It was the sixth edition of the Pharmacopoeia of Augsburg, known as the Pharmacopoeia Augustana. Soon after this came the fust London Pharmacopoeia of 1618, the frrst pharmaceutical book of standards which was mandatory for an entire nation. Later, Scotland, Ireland, Germany, and the United States published similar works.

g. Modern pharmacy practice. Since these historic periods, the practice of pharmacy – insofar as its external appearances are concerned – has changed considerably, but it is still chiefly involved in the compounding, dispensing, and selling of remedial agents.

h. History of pharmacy in America.

(1) Even before Europeans arrived on the soil which now makes up the United States, scores of herbs were used as therapeutic agents by the Indians in this country. Some are still recognized in The United States Pharmacopeia and The National Formulary. Among the herbs that the Indians used were blackberry, cascara sagrada, dandelion, dogwood, elderberry, juniper, podophyllum, raspberry, senega, slippery elm, tobacco, white pine, wild cherry, wintergreen, and witch hazel.

(2) During the 17th century, pharmacy and medicine in America were closely identified with members of sectarian movements arriving in this country. Each group exerted its influence upon the nation's pharmacy and medicine by introducing the scientific knowledge and remedies its members had brought from their homeland. Throughout this century, the American housewife took over most of the medical care of her family and was often the only source of medical information available; this medical information was handed down from generation to generation.

(3) In the 18th century, the filling of prescriptions written by medical practitioners flourished into a specialized art. This prepared the way for the recognition of the profession of pharmacy as distinct from the profession of medicine. In 1775, the Continental Congress established the first Army hospital; the first military apothecary, Andrew Craigie, was on its staff.

(4) A definite trend toward the development of scientific and professional pharmacy was evident during the 19th century. Many pharmaceutical associations came into being. In 1817, South Carolina enacted the first legislation making an examination and a license prerequisites to the practice of pharmacy. Organized professional pharmacy began with the founding of the Philadelphia College of Pharmacy in 1822. In rapid sequence, several other colleges of

pharmacy were formed. During the 1800's, many notable figures of modem pharmacy exerted their influence. Some of the best-known men in this category were Joseph P. Remington, Eli Lilly, E. R. Squibb, Charles Dohme, and Frederick Steams. The American Pharmaceutical Association (A.Ph.A.), founded in 1852, set down a code of ethics similar to that of the Philadelphia College of Pharmacy.

(5) In the present century, the Federal Food and Drugs Act of 1906 recognized The United States Pharmacopeia and The National Formulary as the basis for drug standards. A revised Federal Food, Drug, and Cosmetic Act, enacted in 1938, established many new regulations. The Harrison Narcotic Act was passed into law in 1914 and limited the sale of opium and its derivatives. It required registration of all individuals and firms engaged in the purchasing, processing, compounding, and sale of narcotic drugs.

(6) Pharmacy in the Armed Forces is not new. Before World War II, enlisted men were responsible, under the supervision of physicians, for the pharmacy function. In 1943, legislation provided for the formation of a Pharmacy Corps, and licensed pharmacists of the Regular Army Medical Administration Corps automatically became members. The Pharmacy Corps was designated by insignia of a caduceus with a superimposed letter "P." In 1947, the Medical Service Corps of the Regular Army was established which absorbed the Pharmacy Corps. In today's Army, pharmacies are under the control of a pharmacy officer, who is a graduate, licensed pharmacist, except in rare cases where no commissioned officer who is a pharmacist is on duty. (This can occur when the unit's TOE does not contain a slot for such an officer. In this case, the duties of the pharmacy officer are assigned to a Medical Corps officer.) The pharmacies and dispensaries in the Army are further manned by additional pharmacy officers, plus enlisted personnel who are registered pharmacists or military trained pharmacy specialists. They all work under the control and supervision of the Chief, Pharmacy Service.

Pharmacy ethics. The term "ethics" is defined as the standards of conduct for a profession. It is a moral code by which the members of a profession must abide. Below are excerpts from the accepted Code of Ethics of the American Pharmaceutical Association:

a. *Obligation.* "The primary obligation of pharmacy is the service it can render to the public in safeguarding the preparation, compounding, and dispensing of drugs, and the storage and handling of drugs and medicinal supplies."

b. *Knowledge, skill, and integrity.* "The practice of pharmacy requires knowledge, skill, and integrity; therefore, the state laws restrict the practice of pharmacy to persons with special training."

and qualifications and license to them privileges which are denied to others. Accordingly, the pharmacist recognizes his responsibility to the state and to the community for their well-being, and fulfills his professional obligations honorably."

c. *The pharmacist and his relations to the public.*

(1) "The pharmacist upholds the approved legal standards of The United States Pharmacopeia and The National Formulary, and encourages the use of official drugs and preparations. He purchases, compounds, and dispenses only drugs of good quality."

(2) "The pharmacist uses every precaution to safeguard the public when dispensing any drugs or preparations. Being legally entrusted with the dispensing and sale of these products, he assumes this responsibility by upholding and conforming to the laws and regulations governing the distribution of these substances."

(3) "The pharmacist seeks to enlist and to merit the confidence of his patrons. He zealously guards this confidence. He considers the knowledge and confidence which he gains of the ailments of his patrons as entrusted to his honor, and does not divulge such facts."

(4) "The pharmacist keeps his pharmacy clean, neat, and sanitary, and well-equipped with accurate measuring and weighing devices and other apparatus suitable for the proper performance of his professional duties."

(5) "The pharmacist holds the health and safety of his patrons to be of first consideration; he makes no attempt to prescribe for or to treat disease or to offer for sale any drug or medical device merely for profit."

(6) "The pharmacist is a good citizen and upholds and defends the laws of the states and nation; he keeps informed concerning pharmacy and drug laws, and other laws pertaining to health and sanitation, and cooperates with the enforcement authorities."

(7) "The pharmacist supports constructive efforts in behalf of the public health and welfare. He seeks representation on public health committees and projects and offers to them his full cooperation."

d. *The pharmacist in his relations to other health professions.*

(1) "The pharmacist willingly makes available his expert knowledge of drugs to the other health professions."

(2) "The pharmacist refuses to prescribe or to diagnose; he refers those needing such service to a properly licensed practitioner. In an emergency and pending the arrival of a qualified practitioner, he applies such first aid treatment as is dictated by humanitarian impulses, scientific knowledge, and good judgment."

(3) "The pharmacist compounds and dispenses prescriptions carefully and accurately, using correct pharmaceutical skill and procedure. If there is any question in the pharmacist's mind regarding the ingredients of a prescription, a possible error, or the safety of the direction, he privately and tactfully consults the practitioner before making any changes. He exercises his best professional judgment and follows, under the laws and existing regulations, the prescriber's directions in the matter of refilling prescriptions, copying the formula upon the label, or giving a copy of the prescription to the patient. He adds any extra directions or caution or poison labels only with proper regard for the wishes of the prescriber, and the safety of the patient

(4) "The pharmacist does not discuss the therapeutic effects or composition of a prescription with a patient. When such questions are asked, he suggests that the qualified practitioner is the proper person with whom such matters should be discussed."

e. *The pharmacist and his relations to fellow pharmacists.*

(1) "The pharmacist strives to perfect and enlarge his professional knowledge. He contributes his share toward the scientific progress of his profession and encourages and participates in research, investigation, and study. He keeps himself informed regarding professional matters by reading current pharmaceutical, scientific, and medical literature, attending seminars, and other means."

(2) "The pharmacist seeks to attract to his profession youth of good character and intellectual capacity and aids in their instruction."

(3) "The pharmacist associates himself with organizations having for their objective the betterment of the pharmaceutical profession and contributes his share of time, energy, and funds to carry out the work of these organizations."

(4) "The pharmacist keeps his reputation in public esteem by continuously giving the kind of professional service that earns its own reward. He does not engage in any activity or transaction that will bring discredit or criticism to himself or to his profession."

(5) "The pharmacist will expose any corrupt or dishonest conduct of any member of his profession which comes to his certain knowledge, through those accredited processes provided by the civil laws or the rules and regulations of pharmaceutical organizations, and he will aid in driving the unworthy out of the calling."

(6) "The pharmacist does not lend his support or his name to the promotion of objectionable or unworthy products."

(7) "The pharmacist courteously aids a fellow pharmacist who may request advice or professional information."

(8) "The pharmacist is proud to display in his establishment his own name and the names of other pharmacists employed by him."

NOTE

Although this code of ethics was written for the graduate, registered pharmacist, it contains basic doctrine and moral guidelines for all who deal with pharmacy. Stand by this code at all times and your career will be a pleasant one for you, for the men serving with you, and for the patients you assist.

Compendia, references, and reference library. Pharmacy and its allied fields are so complex that one cannot hope to learn and retain all the data necessary for all situations. For this reason, every pharmacy must have a reference library of well-selected books such as those mentioned below. Having or acquiring the reference library is the first step; the second step is using it.

a. Official pharmacy references. There are two official books used by the pharmacist. They are The Pharmacopeia of the United States of America (commonly known as The United States Pharmacopeia or USP) and The National Formulary (NF). These are the pharmaceutical standards made official by the Food and Drugs Act of 1906 which was rewritten and re-enacted by Congress in 1938. It was amended in 1951 and 1962 and is now entitled the Food, Drug, and Cosmetic Act.

(1) The United States Pharmacopeia (USP). The USP is an authoritative book on drugs and their preparation. In it is a list of accepted medical drugs and chemicals, with descriptions of each; tests; purities; formulas; and average doses. The USP first appeared in 1820 and is now revised and published every 5 years by the United States Pharmacopeial Convention. This convention is made up of delegates from the professions of medicine, dentistry, pharmacy, and chemistry. The USP is restricted to drugs and preparations which have stood the test of modem research and continued use. Since agents are accepted by the USP only after continued

successful use, the newest ones are often excluded. The monographs, that is, the explanations of the individual preparations, contain the following information:

(a) *Official English titles.* Example: calcium hydroxide.

(b) *Botanical names* (for plant drugs). Example: Atropa belladonna.

(c) *Symbolic formulas* (in the case of chemicals). Example: Ca (OH)2.

(d) *Structural formulas* (in the case of organic chemicals whenever the formula is generally accepted by chemists). Example: aspirin.

$$\text{benzene ring with substituents: } -CO\,CH \text{ and } -O-CO-CH_3$$

(e) *Official definitions.* In order that no question shall arise as to the exact meaning of an official title, the USP states exactly what kind or variety of the substance should be used. Example: Acacia. "Acacia is the dried gummy exudate from the stems and branches of Acacia senegal (Linne) Willdenow or of other related African species of Acacia (Fam. Leguminosae)."

(f) *Purity rubric.* This term indicates the paragraph limiting the quantity of impurity allowed by giving the percentage of pure substance that must be present. Example: Aspirin. "Dry it over silica gel for 5 hours: It loses not more than 0.5 percent of its weight."

(g) *Official description.* This description usually consists of a concise statement of the drug's physical properties and appearance. Example: Aspirin occurs as "White crystals, commonly tabular or needle-like, or white, crystalline powder. Is odorless or has a faint odor. Is stable in dry air; in moist air it gradually hydrolyzes to salicylic and acetic acids."

(h) *Tests for purity and identity.* In the USP, the tests which establish the identity of a drug and those which insure the pharmacopeial minimum degree of purity are grouped under appropriate headings.

(i) *Assays.* Chemicals, preparations, and certain crude drugs have assays included in their monographs which are intended to insure their contents to be in accord with the "purity rubric."

(j) *Packaging and storage.* Certain official drugs and preparations have packaging and storage directions listed under the title of the same name. These specifications are intended to maintain the activity and potency of the drug or preparation for a maximum period. Example: Alcohol. "Preserve in tight containers, remote from fire."

(k) *Preparations available.* When the pharmacopeial substance is used in the manufacture of other pharmacopeial preparations, these preparations are usually listed. *Example:* Aminophylline."Suppositories usually available contain the following amounts of aminophylline: 100, 125,250, and 500 mg."

(l) Labels. If special labels are required, notations will generally be made in italicized print, but these may be made under the speciftc title of labels.

(m) Category. The drug is classified into groups according to its therapeutic use and action. Example: Aspirin. "Category: Analgesic; antipyretic; antirheumatic."

(n) Dose. The dose is given in the metric system. It is listed as the usual dose, the range of dosage possible without harmful effects, and the method or route of administration. Example: Aspirin.

"Usual Dose: Oral or rectal, 600 mg. 4 to 6 times a day as necessary.

Usual Dose Range: Oral, 300 mg. to 8 grams daily. Rectal, 300 mg. to 2 grams daily."

(2) The National Formulary (NF). The purpose of *The National Formulary* is to supply legal standards for drugs and formulations commonly used in medical practice which may not have been recognized for medical efficiency by the USP, but which have had long and customary use. The NF is much the same as the USP in arrangement. It, too, is revised and issued at S-year intervals to coincide with the USP schedule. It is pu blished by the American Pharmaceutical Association through its committee on the National Formulary.

b. Important nonofficial references. Besides the two official books already described, there are many other texts which are of great assistance to the pharmacist. The following books are not official, but are recognized as being standard references.

(1) United States Dispensatory (USD). The *United States Dispensatory* expands broadly on the USP and NF, adding information such as unofficial synonyms, pharmacology, toxicology, and dosage schedules.

(2) Pharmaceutical Recipe Book. The Pharmaceutical Recipe Book provides formulas for preparations not found in the official books which are frequently required in hospitals and pharmacies.

(3) Merck Index. The Merck Index contains listings of over 8000 chemicals and drugs, and information about each.

(4) New Drugs (ND). The ND is published by the Council on Pharmacy and Chemistry of the American Medical Association. It lists and describes the drugs that have been accepted by the council. The descriptions of the accepted drugs are based, in part, on evidence of information supplied by the manufacturer. Statements made by those commercially interested are critically examined and the drug is admitted only when such statements are supported by other evidence or when they conform to known facts. Drugs in the ND often have not been used in practice long enough to be admitted to The United States Pharmacopeia.

(5) Merck Manual. The Merck Manual essentially provides condensed medical information. It lists diseases, causes, prevention, treatment, prescriptions, prognoses, diagnoses, etc.

(6) Modern Drug Encyclopedia and Therapeutic Index. The book contains information on proprietary drugs (patented, trademarked medicinals) supplied by their manufacturer.

(7) Remington's Pharmaceutical Sciences. The "Remington," as it is most frequently called, is an excellent and most complete reference to the overall picture of pharmacy.

www.ingramcontent.com/pod-product-compliance
Lightning Source LLC
Chambersburg PA
CBHW082045300426
44117CB00015B/2621